The Ultimate
Productivity Book

Tina Konstant,
Robert Ashton,
Martin Manser and
Stephen Evans-Howe

Martin Manser is an expert communicator with a unique combination of skills and experience. He has compiled or edited over 200 reference books on the English language, Bible reference and business skills in a 35-year professional career. He is an English-language specialist and teaches English to business colleagues. Participants in his courses find them to be a safe place to ask questions and for their confidence to grow. Since 2002, he has also been a Language Consultant and Trainer, leading training courses in business communications for national and international companies and organizations on communications, project management and time management. www.martinmanser.co.uk

Robert Ashton is a successful business author, social entrepreneur and campaigner. He has worked in large corporations, small family firms and has started, built and sold his own businesses. He's also campaigned for and helped grow a community foundation that now distributes more than £1 million in grants every year. He currently works independently, helping organizations and individuals become more entrepreneurial. For more information about Robert, go to www.robertashton.co.uk
Follow Robert on Twitter: @robertashton1.

While an undergraduate at the University of Aberdeen, **Tina Konstant** was invited to deliver a series of practical speed-reading workshops to students and the local business community. She continued to refine and develop the material, which led to speed-reading and information management seminars delivered to businesses in the private and public sectors. She now consults in the oil and gas sector and writes on a range of subjects from Effective Reading and Information Management to Copywriting and Change Management.

Stephen Evans-Howe is a Chartered Safety Practitioner and has held a number of senior management and executive roles in a variety of engineering and service environments: petrochemical, aviation, theme parks and defence. He continues to work in industry, leading the implementation of people-based programmes, supporting safety and organizational culture change.

Teach Yourself®

The Ultimate Productivity Book

Manage your Time, Increase your Efficiency, Get Things Done

Tina Konstant,
Robert Ashton,
Martin Manser and
Stephen Evans-Howe

First published in Great Britain by Teach Yourself in 2023
An imprint of John Murray Press
A division of Hodder & Stoughton Ltd,
An Hachette UK company

1

Based on original material from *Managing Yourself In A Week*,
Time Management In A Week, *Speed Reading In A Week*,
Managing Stress At Work In A Week

A CIP catalogue record for this title is available from the British Library

Paperback ISBN 978 1 473 68944 2
eBook ISBN 978 1 473 68945 9

Typeset by KnowledgeWorks Global Ltd.

Printed and bound in Great Britain by Clays Ltd, Elcograf S.p.A.

John Murray Press policy is to use papers that are natural, renewable and recyclable
products and made from wood grown in sustainable forests. The logging and
manufacturing processes are expected to conform to the environmental regulations of
the country of origin.

John Murray Press
Carmelite House
50 Victoria Embankment
London EC4Y 0DZ

www.teachyourself.com

Contents

PART 1

Your Managing Yourself Masterclass

Introduction

Congratulations! You've been promoted to manager. However, after all the excitement has lessened, you begin to question yourself: ...can you achieve ... are you really equipped? This masterclass considers one important aspect of being a manager: being able to manage yourself.

The first step in managing yourself effectively is to become aware of yourself and evaluate your strengths and weaknesses. Maintaining focus on the tasks in hand is vital, alongside allowing opportunities for you to 'catch up' and process what is going on in your life. Asking what the next step is moves you on from inertia.

Good time management is an essential skill in being an effective manager, and a chapter is devoted to becoming more organized. This explains better planning and setting priorities, shows how to deal with time wasters, and gives practical steps on maintaining a diary and to-do lists. Further chapters consider techniques such as managing your mind, discussing thinking positively in developing strategies and making good decisions, managing emotions, not by ignoring them but allowing them to be expressed appropriately, and explaining how to increase confidence, deal with nerves and motivate yourself.

The final chapters consider developing trust and respect. This can be done through building strong relationships by applying good listening skills, as seen in working with your boss and colleagues. They also consider the importance of having good relationships outside work. The final chapter, on managing stress, invites you to look at what produces stress in you and discusses ways of dealing with its consequences. This masterclass offers handy guidelines that will enable you to take a grip on yourself and re-evaluate your way of working and your priorities in life. It is a quick and reliable guide to the basics of self-management in the world of work.

CHAPTER 1

Know yourself well

In this chapter we will consider what you are like as a person. We will look at:

- Your goals and values
- Your skills and abilities
- Your achievements, successes and failures
- Your preferred style of working

We will consider these with a view to thinking which areas are your strengths and which areas you may need to develop further.

We will also consider:

- The difference between managing and leading
- The difference between being efficient and being effective

My aim is to help you to:

- Understand the issues facing you and prepare the ground
- Develop your skills, techniques and knowledge
- Motivate yourself

Let's begin with a story ...

Another day had gone badly. Michael had had two rushed meetings that he was supposed to have led, but hadn't really had time to gather his thoughts for, and an appraisal that he hadn't prepared for at all. Finally, he'd been asked to come up with some strategic, long-term thinking. He hadn't even begun to tackle the main task that he had been assigned to that day (although at least he had tried to do some planning for it!).

Mike had been promoted to manager of a new department, and he knew he wasn't coping. He seemed to spend all his time – and energy – lurching from one crisis to another. His nerves were constantly on edge, his stress levels were high, and his self-confidence (such as it was) seemed to be draining away by the day. He had started off with high hopes of changing things – changing lots of things: structures, priorities... Maybe he had begun too strongly and hadn't spent time building good relationships with his colleagues, somehow expecting that they would agree with all his plans immediately. And now everything seemed to be failing. Even at home, his relationships were strained and uneasy. He was spending too much time at the office, so he hardly saw his children during the week. Even on weekends, something urgent often seemed to come up unexpectedly. As for his relationship with his wife, well...

Deep within himself, when he had a few moments to stop and think, Mike knew something was wrong. He couldn't keep on blaming the people around him. He knew he had to sort himself out.

Do you identify with Mike? Maybe he hadn't had enough training for his present position; maybe he'd been promoted to the level of his incompetence.[1] Certainly he hadn't learnt to

---

[1] The so-called Peter Principle: 'In a hierarchy, every employee tends to rise to the level of his incompetence.' This semi-scientific statement was formulated by the Canadian educator Dr Laurence J Peter (1919–90) who with Raymond Hull (1919–85) wrote the book *The Peter Principle – Why Things Always Go Wrong*, published in 1969. The Principle holds that so long as the managers are competent, they will continue to be promoted. Eventually they will reach a position which is beyond them and they will not progress any further.

manage his time, nor how to delegate tasks to others. In brief, he hadn't learnt to manage himself.

Being able to manage yourself begins with being aware of yourself, what kind of person you are.

Self-awareness

Your goals

In this chapter I want to encourage you to think more deeply about your life and the kind of person you are.

The US leadership expert, John Maxwell (in *The 21 Indispensable Qualities of a Leader*; Thomas Nelson, 1999), asks three questions to help you work out a personal vision for your life:

- What makes you cry?
- What makes you dream?
- What gives you energy?

It can be useful to spend some time responding to these questions. Then ask yourself whether the main part of your life actually matches your answers. If it doesn't, then think what you could do to change your life.

You might be in a job in which you feel fulfilled: that is good! Or you might be in a job that you cannot change and is in conflict with, for example, a deep desire you have to help needy people. Because you cannot discern a way out of that job in the foreseeable future (and you've responsibilities with family, bills to pay...), you might consider volunteering with a local charity one evening a week or at weekends to channel that desire to help others.

Your values

What motivates you? What drives you? What underlying values and beliefs do you hold?

- Do you have integrity?
- Are you honest and firm in having strong moral principles that you follow? Or are you pretending to be someone you're not?

- Do you work too hastily to try to save time or money but, in doing so, are you less thorough than you know you should be?
- Do you guard what enters your mind and take control of your thoughts?

Other aspects you need to consider are:

- Do you enjoy your position of power and authority as a manager?
- Do you have many grand ideas, but do they remain only as ideas that do not become real?
- How important is money to you?
- Are you ambitious?
- How important are your family relationships to you?
- Are you trustworthy? You will only inspire trust in others if you yourself are reliable and responsible. If you say you will do something by a certain time, do you do so? (Colleagues will notice if you are constantly late in meeting deadlines, and so will take that as permission that they can act similarly.)
- Are you straightforward and avoid acting unfairly or dishonestly?
- Do you start projects with good ideas and enthusiasm, but fail to follow them through? Or do you continue with projects until they are successfully completed?
- Do you want to learn and grow as a person, or have you reached a plateau?
- What is your prevailing attitude in life and work?
  - Positive? Confident? Committed? Enthusiastic? Affirming? Caring?
  - Unmotivated? Disengaged? Negative? Cynical? Unappreciated? Frustrated? Pessimistic? Rude?

Your skills and abilities

As a manager, you need various core qualities of skills and behaviour. Mark yourself on a scale of 1 to 5 of how you think you perform on the following (1 = poor, 5 = excellent). Then ask a trusted colleague to mark you, and check to see if your scores agree.

		You	Colleague
1	Good with people: approachable and able to get on with others, to motivate others and respect colleagues	❏	❏
2	Good team leader: respecting others, recognizing colleagues' skills and focusing on their strengths	❏	❏
3	Good negotiation skills: able to secure win–win situations	❏	❏
4	Good skills of delegation to trusted colleagues: empowering them, to avoid becoming stressed by taking too much on yourself	❏	❏
5	Good at resolving conflict	❏	❏
6	Good listener: showing empathy towards others	❏	❏
7	Good computer skills, e.g. on spreadsheets	❏	❏
8	Good manager of your time: good at planning	❏	❏
9	Committed to your work: having an active, positive belief in it; believing in your company, products/services and staff (on the basis that enthusiasm is contagious)	❏	❏
10	Good general management skills: able to think strategically, chair meetings well, take the initiative and make decisions	❏	❏
11	Organized: someone who is careless or sloppy in their professional life will not be a good manager	❏	❏
12	Good numeracy skills: being proficient with figures; able to manage budgets	❏	❏
13	Good business sense: take advantage of opportunities, keep an eye on costs	❏	❏
14	Having an eye for detail: someone who is thorough and meticulous is needed (however, also see the next quality)	❏	❏
15	Able to see the big picture: someone who only sees details will quickly become overwhelmed and unable to see things in perspective and move forward	❏	❏
16	Able to keep track of different processes ('keep several balls in the air') at the same time, able to document progress clearly	❏	❏

17 Proactive: staying in control and thinking
   ahead ❑ ❑
18 Able to analyse matters and discern what is
   significant ❑ ❑
19 Creative and flexible in finding solutions to
   difficulties: what worked three years ago might
   not work now ❑ ❑
20 Able to stay focused on the goal: patient and
   determined ❑ ❑
21 Able to focus on the needs of your clients/
   customers ❑ ❑
22 Able to recruit and maintain (and retain!)
   good staff: develop, train or coach other
   colleagues well ❑ ❑
23 Results-orientated ❑ ❑
24 Considerate of the environment, workplace and
   staff well-being ❑ ❑

(We will consider many of these in more detail throughout this masterclass.)
Looking at these results:

● Consider which skills are most important in your role at the present time
● What are your three greatest strengths (the ones you got the highest scores for)? You should concentrate on ('play to') your strengths as far as you can
● Which are your three greatest weaknesses (the ones you got the lowest scores for)? Consider these points carefully:
   – Some of your weaknesses are a necessary part of your job and you need to recognize them as areas to develop and work at
   – Others may not be an integral part of your job, so try to match your weaknesses with the strengths of colleagues

For example, I am good with words: writing books has been my livelihood for three decades, which I have always done on the computer in Word. But I also have to be reasonably good with numbers to ensure that the books I write are not too short or too long, and also that they are profitable as far as I can control.

I also lead training courses as part of my work. So while the skills in Word come relatively easily, I have had to teach myself skills in Excel and PowerPoint to reach a more than basic level in those. However, areas that are not central to my job – for example, designing book covers for digital versions of my books – I delegate to a colleague who is much more skilled than me.

Your achievements in life

- What have you achieved in your life so far? Think of things related to work and also those not related to work. Ask friends and colleagues. Also, look back at the past few years and consider where you have been successful
- What weaknesses are you aware of in your life? They may be to do with certain business skills, e.g. that you only see the detail and do not see the wider situation as a whole. Or if the weaknesses are more personal, it can be helpful to share those with a trusted colleague or friend
- People often say you need to learn from your failures, and that is true. But you also need to learn from your successes. Why were these achievements successful? Can you repeat some of the elements that led to that success?
- Accept responsibility for your life. You cannot always blame your circumstances on other people. Sometimes we are the ones at fault and we need to be humble enough to admit our mistakes, focus on the future, and move on to the next step

Your style of living ... and working

Think through the following:

- Which energizes you more: being with other people or being by yourself?
- When responding to new ideas, do you react spontaneously ('thinking on your feet') or do you prefer to take your time to reply?
- Do you work best in normal, regular and highly structured patterns of work or does an immediate deadline or crisis bring out the best in you?

- Do you have interests outside work that are important to you?
- Do you work best as a leader or as a second-in-command?
- Do you work best alone or as a member of a team?
- Do you work best in a large company/organization or in a small one?
- How open are you about sharing your life with other people?

A change of lifestyle

Jack enjoyed his work, but gradually it took over his whole life. Eventually he became ill. He consulted a doctor, who advised a complete change of lifestyle. He needed to leave work punctually, eat a healthier diet and have more sleep. He also realized he needed to spend much more time with his family (and switch his mobile off over mealtimes and when reading his young children their bedtime story) and pursue ordinary leisure activities. So he took up badminton and played one evening a week. Over time, Jack's life improved considerably: he achieved more and became a much more rounded person.

Sharing yourself

When you are new to a job, how much do you share of yourself to your colleagues? What you are good at, what you are not so good at, personal matters such as your birthday?

As you get to know colleagues more, you gradually disclose more of yourself.[2]

Accept yourself

For years, I was introverted, and no number of people telling me to become less so helped at all. Gradually, over the years, I relaxed and found my own identity. Accept yourself.

[2] The framework of the 'Johari window' is helpful here. It is based on a window divided into four panes representing the four types of personal awareness: open, hidden, blind and unknown. The Johari window is named after *Jo*seph Luft and *Harry* Ingham, the American psychologists who developed it in 1955. It is widely used to promote improved understanding in corporate environments and in self-help groups.

We have all had difficult experiences in life up to this point; the key thing is to how we respond to them. Some may have been particularly difficult and we may need to seek professional help to deal with them. People who are brave enough to pluck up the courage to seek help often find that it helps them enormously, and enables them to go on to do things they previously found difficult or even impossible. Stop thinking so much about how other people perceive you. Don't let their opinions stifle your own personality, style and view of the world. Be yourself – and be kind to yourself too.

Managing and leading

What are the differences between managing and leading? Here is a rough definition: *managing is turning leadership into action*. Let me explain that in more detail: leaders set a particular course: we're going to expand into the Latin American market. Managers put that into action: we're going to understand the culture, build a base, recruit staff there and implement a whole range of other activities to make the basic idea of 'expanding into the Latin American market' a reality.

So leaders set the overall direction, guide, influence, and give vision; managers implement that vision, working out the detail in terms of organizing people, planning and budgeting. You will probably have agreed with this last sentence. However, are you aware that there is another aspect of leadership: that of emotions? Leaders appeal to the emotions to set a course of change, wanting to inspire people to follow a vision. Managers, in contrast it seems, have the less exciting task of ensuring that the work, in all its detail, is completed.

In practice, however, the distinction between 'leader' and 'manager' may not be so clear cut. Your role may be 'team leader', and your duties will concentrate on the detailed tasks, systems and processes needed to ensure the work is completed. However, you will also need leadership skills to motivate your team to achieve these goals.

Working efficiently and effectively

Note there is a difference between working efficiently and effectively: *efficient* means 'well organized, achieving results with minimal waste of resources such as time and money. *Effective* is more than that: it means also achieving the right results. You can do the wrong thing efficiently, but as managers you want to be *effective*.

For example, I was discussing auditing procedures with a colleague in the banking industry. She said they were *efficient* – it was relatively easy to define tasks that satisfied all the requirements ('ticked all the boxes'). When I asked if such tasks would be *effective* in moving the bank forward, however, she was uncertain.

Remember: As a manager, you will want to be more than merely *efficient*: you will also want to be *effective*.

Measuring your success

It is important to note specific actions throughout this masterclass. Where possible, action points should be SMART:

S   **S**pecific: defining the desired results
M   **M**easurable: quantifiable so that you know whether the objectives have been reached
A   **A**chievable: realistic objectives that are not too easy, but will develop and challenge ('stretch') your resources and skills
R   **R**elevant: are concerned with your life and work
T   **T**imed: giving a date for completion

Some commentators add:
E   **E**valuated: progress on achieving SMART actions is reviewed at a future meeting
R   **R**eported: evaluated progress is reported and recorded

Summary

In this chapter we have begun to lay the foundation for managing yourself more effectively by looking at your life. Important factors include:

- self awareness
- efficient and effective working

Exercise

Answer the following questions, taking into account what we have considered in this chapter.

1 Are you content where you currently are as a person or have you reached a plateau and would like to learn more to grow?
2 Do you have a clear sense of purpose in life and at work?
3 What are your strengths? Choose one and consider how you can develop it to become even more proficient.
4 Which one quality do you need to cultivate more? What are the next steps you need to take to do this? Make sure your action points are SMART.
5 What interests outside work could you develop more?

Fact-check (answers at the back)

1. In order to manage yourself better, you need to:
   - a) ignore your life ❏
   - b) consider your life ❏
   - c) remain the same ❏
   - d) check social media websites constantly ❏

2. Considering your goals and values is:
   - a) useful if you have the time ❏
   - b) a waste of time ❏
   - c) an important first step to managing yourself ❏
   - d) helpful just to discuss with others ❏

3. 'I am prepared to change my life in order to manage myself better':
   - a) true ❏
   - b) false ❏
   - c) I'm not sure ❏
   - d) I don't care ❏

4. To reflect on your attitude at work is:
   - a) too serious ❏
   - b) useful if you have the time ❏
   - c) a waste of time ❏
   - d) important ❏

5. When you consider areas that are your strengths, you should:
   - a) deny you ever have them ❏
   - b) delegate them to others to increase their competence ❏
   - c) identify and then forget them ❏
   - d) make sure you use them in your job ❏

6. When you consider areas that are your weaknesses, you should:
   - a) have training in each area to increase your competences significantly ❏
   - b) ignore them and deal only with your strengths ❏
   - c) distinguish between areas that are important in your job and areas that you can delegate to others ❏
   - d) delegate each one to someone else ❏

7. You should learn from your successes as well as your failures:
   - a) false ❏
   - b) true ❏
   - c) 'I have had no failures' ❏
   - d) 'I have had no successes' ❏

8. In your work, you want to:
   - a) be efficient ❏
   - b) be effective ❏
   - c) be efficient and effective ❏
   - d) go home early every day ❏

9. S and T in SMART actions stand for:
   - a) sensible and timed ❏
   - b) strategic and technological ❏
   - c) specific and trusted ❏
   - d) specific and timed ❏

10. Now that you have completed this chapter, you are going to:
    - a) choose one area of your life to work on ❏
    - b) try to find ten things you can change this week ❏
    - c) do nothing ❏
    - d) read it again ten more times ❏

CHAPTER 2

Manage your focus clearly

Introduction

In this chapter, we move on from knowing yourself to beginning to tackle how you can make progress and develop as an effective manager.

We will look at:

- staying focused in your work, working when you can concentrate best and undertaking your main task(s) with few distractions
- making time to think creatively about future goals, evaluating your present position and then beginning to make changes happen
- giving your mind some 'breathing space', allowing you to digest all that is happening to you and coming up with fresh thoughts and ideas
- growing personally

Stay focused

Today, my main task is to write a third of this chapter: I know from past experience that it takes about three good mornings' work to write each chapter for a book.

However, there are so many other things I could do: I have already taken my wife to work, and a car surprised me by its speed on a roundabout, so I could dwell on that. I also have many other items on my to-do list: check my accounts online; prepare for a meeting tomorrow (I started my preparation for that yesterday, but other thoughts have occurred to me since then); send out a marketing email; expect a colleague to phone to discuss future collaboration; check some material on a reference book; and respond to or initiate several other minor emails for personal arrangements for a family party.

I am now faced with a basic choice:

1 I could first deal with all the relatively minor things that need to be done (ideally most of them today) and then pursue my main task – writing this text – or:
2 I could pursue writing my main text first of all, and then try to fit in as many of the other things as possible, as time permits during the rest of the day.

I have chosen 2: my intention is to work on this chapter for a good two hours and then take a break. During my break, I will order most of my other remaining tasks, including any others that have since come in from my emails, and tackle them in order.

The criteria I work by are as follows:

1 Know when – which time of day and which day of the week – you work best.
2 I know that I work best first thing in the morning and also early in the week (for me, Monday and Tuesday). I therefore protect that time as far as possible in order to complete my main task(s). So my Monday and Tuesday mornings are special times that I guard as I am very unwilling to see them wasted.

Pursue the main task first.

The main task may be the one that will take the longest, or it could also be the most difficult, the most important or the one that I least want to tackle. I consider this last aspect especially important. Each day brings work that I don't particularly want to do, so I make myself undertake that as soon as I can. In this way, I feel psychologically better as I have a sense of achievement after I have completed it, or at least dealt with its most difficult or most significant part. (I know that – for me – the longer I postpone tackling tasks I don't want to do, the more difficult they seem.)

I was once teaching this principle to a colleague who gave talks at weekends, so Monday is her rest day and Tuesday the first day of her working week. Knowing that she worked best in the mornings, I asked how she had spent the previous Tuesday morning, expecting her to say she prepared her talks then. However, she replied that that was when she went for travel inoculations for her next foreign trip. I suggested that that was not the best use of her Tuesday mornings and that should be done on, for example, a Thursday afternoon. I spoke to her three months later and she was now using Tuesday to prepare her talks.

Pursue the other, less important, tasks later.

In other words, keep the main thing the 'main thing'. The main thing for me today is to complete about one third of this chapter in order to maintain the schedule that I have set myself, which is in keeping with the publisher's deadline and the deadlines I have set myself for my other work.

If I had pursued my tasks the other way and undertaken the less important items first, I know what would have happened. (I have done this extremely occasionally, just to see the results ... I and don't recommend it at all.) If I had pursued all the other relatively minor tasks first:

I would have become side-tracked from my main task of writing this chapter. I would then have had only a small amount of time left at the end of the day, so I would not have actually completed my main work.

I would have become further side-tracked. I would answer an email and then another email could come in, and I would say to myself, 'While I am answering this one, I might as well just do that one too.'

I would not have built up any momentum in my work. It is true that I would have ticked off many (relatively minor) tasks, but because each one is comparatively short, I would never have picked up the pace and speed I need to get through a significant amount of work as easily as I would have done if I had started my major task first.

So, the guideline here is: concentrate on – pursue – your main task vigorously. Don't get side-tracked or distracted from your main task. Of course, this is only a guideline: there will be times when a crisis occurs and plans have to be abandoned or modified. It is also worth scheduling time to work on your minor tasks at a later date so that you can be certain they get done and don't become crises themselves.

Note that while completing your major task, switch off your mobile phone and emails. You don't want to be distracted.

See also Chapter 3 on priorities.

 Know when you work best, and use that time for the task that is the most difficult or the one you least want to do.

Make time to think

I am convinced that we spend too little time thinking. We are so busy with the present that we don't spend enough time thinking whether we are spending our time productively. To put it in terms of Chapter 1, we may just about be efficient but we don't take time to see whether we are being effective.

So what are you to think about? Here are some guidelines:

- Set long-term goals. What are your company's or organization's long-term aims? If you don't have any then you are sure to fulfil them, because they are non-existent! If you do have such goals, are your present policies likely to achieve them?
- Dream dreams. It's amazing how random thoughts or wishes can turn into big things. If you want to do something, do it. I did this once with dictionaries. I remember it now.

Our daughter was still a baby. I was thinking about words beginning with the letter 'G' ... a few were interesting, *galore* ('plenty') is an example of an adjective that follows the noun it refers to (*whisky galore!*); *galvanize* ('stir into action') is an example of a word named after a person, Luigi *Galvani*. I suddenly had a brainwave – what if on every page of a dictionary we could highlight a few words that were remarkable in a distinctive way? And so the idea came about for a book that I later worked on with my friend and colleague Nigel Turton. It was originally published by Penguin as the *Wordmaster Dictionary* and sold well. It is an 'ordinary' dictionary, but on nearly every page alongside main dictionary entries we highlighted in a boxed panel a particular word with an interesting history, idiom, grammatical feature, point of usage, etc. My creativity paid off!

'What is the hardest task in the world? To think'

Ralph Waldo Emerson, 1803–82, US poet, essayist and philosopher

● Undertake a SWOT analysis: This is a technique to help you develop creative thinking in a business context. In it, you analyse where your business/project/department is going, and it helps you make sure you've got a strong strategy

Strengths	What are you better at than your competitors? What is your USP (unique selling proposition)?
Weaknesses	What do your competitors perceive as your weaknesses? Is morale low? Is your leadership committed? Are there gaps in the skills of your colleagues?
Opportunities	What changes in the market or changes in lifestyle can you exploit to maximize your profits?
Threats	Is the market for your product declining? Are key colleagues on the verge of leaving? Is your financial backing stable?

Conducting a SWOT analysis to analyse where your company/organization currently stands will help you think creatively.

This may lead to your adopting a new strategy that your competitors have not thought of. For example, in 2004 Amazon set up a covert team to unsettle its own business; the outcome of that team's work was the Kindle.

Other things you may need to be aware of:

- Realize that your role as manager is more than just making sure things run smoothly. You also need to initiate change. This may mean challenging the current way of doing things
- Evaluate what you are doing; question it. You are not being awkward for the sake of it, you are checking to see if you could work more effectively. Allow creative ideas, which may then generate other more realistic options
- Always conclude your thinking time by asking, 'What are the next steps? What practical thing do I/we need to do to begin to put our plans into action?' You might need to discuss your ideas with senior managers, or write an email to a colleague with your thoughts. In other words, do something. Focus on the next thing you need to do in order to achieve your goal, to make your goal a reality

My son Ben wanted to go to Japan so he realized he needed to learn Japanese. He therefore arranged lessons with a friend of my wife's every Thursday evening for two years. His desire to go to Japan would have remained a dream if he hadn't taken the initiative and done something about it

Give your mind some 'breathing space'

As well as blocking out time to think, give yourself time to unwind and relax – time to recover from the stresses of work. Plan in 'down' time, time when you are not concentrating. Commuting by train can provide an opportunity to do this. For example, yesterday I had meetings in London. On my hour-long journey into London by train, I was engaged in background reading for writing this masterclass. However, on my return trip, I deliberately decided not to read anything. I chatted to the man sitting next to me for a while and, after he got off the train at a station earlier than mine, I had some ideas, which I wrote down, following up on ways to tackle the project we had discussed at my earlier business meeting.

Your subconscious needs time to process all that is going on. We are inundated with so much – too much – information that we don't take time to digest properly what we are taking in. I think it is often more a matter of the *quality* of information, not the *quantity*. There is sometimes no shortage of information (although, on occasions, I realize that we are missing vital pieces of information), but what we lack is the breathing space for our minds, to allow our brain the freedom to think creatively. We need to give ourselves the opportunity to reflect, allowing our subconscious to explore fresh possibilities and solve problems.

I expect you are familiar with this: you wake up in the morning and think of the answer to a problem that you had failed to solve the previous day, despite giving it a lot of thought then. Or you go for a walk, or are on holiday, and suddenly and unexpectedly you think of an original idea or a fresh insight that is just what you need.

You can get a lot achieved if you give your brain time to think.

Are you growing as a person?

Confession time: about fifteen years ago, I felt I had stopped growing inwardly as a person. It wasn't that I thought I knew it all, I knew I didn't. But I had lost that fresh motivation in my work. It was then that I noticed friends and colleagues around me were saying things like, 'When you retire, what will happen to all the knowledge you have built up?' and, 'Martin, I've learnt a lot from you.' I then began to realize that maybe I had accumulated certain competences and knowledge, so I started to think in different directions: that as well as writing, maybe I could pursue training and teaching in some of the skills I had learnt.

That experience also taught me the need to reflect regularly (for example, at least once a month) on the nature of my work and whether what I was doing was stretching me. Ideally, discuss with colleagues the trends in your industry. Pursue training, read books, consult websites, discuss with colleagues the trends in your industry, question assumptions in an effort to find fresh approaches.

If you have had a failure or a great disappointment, then try to return quickly to your normal activities or your previous level of enthusiasm. Don't let one negative experience affect the whole of your life. In golf, if you have a bad score at one hole, you still need to keep playing the rest of the game. Bring that theory into your day-to-day life. The ability to recover from difficulties in life wins admiration from others: people greatly respect those who have learnt to come back from an unpleasant experience.

Discuss things with a coach or mentor

Discuss all these matters with your coach or mentor, if you have one. If you don't, encourage your company or organization to set up coaching or mentoring or, if that is not possible, find someone you can discuss your thoughts with. Listen to their comments and observations. (We will discuss listening in greater depth in Chapter 6.) Be open to constructive criticism to help you grow as a person. All the time, do what you can to work well and grow as a person. Life will never be perfect. Work from where you are now. And remember, you may need to adjust your expectations.

Discussions with a mentor

Sarah met regularly with Janet, her mentor. Janet wasn't Sarah's line manager, so Sarah felt able to discuss her work freely and confidentially with Janet. In particular, Sarah was able to talk through not only her short- and mid-term training needs, but also her long-term career aspirations.

Janet was a good listener: she noted what Sarah was saying, and also what she was not saying. She could 'read (and listen) between the lines' and ask good questions. Janet could discern things that Sarah was not aware of.

Janet brought an objective perspective and helped Sarah see herself as a whole person, as well as offering guidance on the development of her future career.

Summary

In this chapter we have emphasized the need to:

● Think when – what time of day and which day(s) of the week – you work best
● Focus your mind on one particular task
● Complete that task as far as possible, and only then undertake other less important tasks
● Think: give yourself the opportunity to think creatively about your life
● Act: at the end of any significant time of thinking, ask yourself, 'What is the next step I must undertake to advance this thought to turn it into reality?'

Exercise

1 Look at your to-do list. Think which task is the longest/most important/the most difficult/the one you least want to tackle.

2 Write down when – what time of day and which day(s) of the week – you work best.

3 Revise your diary such that you deliberately try to deal with the task you answered in question 1 during the period you answered in question 2.

Fact-check (answers at the back)

1. Knowing when – what time of day and which day(s) of the week – you work best is:
   a) very helpful ❑
   b) futile and unproductive ❑
   c) useful if you have the time to think about it ❑
   d) so useful that it will be forgotten immediately ❑

2. During the time when you work best, you should:
   a) complete the small routine tasks to get them out of the way first ❑
   b) make sure it is always full of meetings ❑
   c) check your emails constantly ❑
   d) deal with the most difficult task or the one you least want to do ❑

3. At work, you should aim to:
   a) check your social media websites constantly ❑
   b) complete the small routine tasks to get them out of the way first ❑
   c) tackle the most difficult task or the one that you least want to do before dealing with less important tasks ❑
   d) spend you whole day filling in your time sheet ❑

4. When you are working on your one main task, you should:
   a) allow yourself to be distracted ❑
   b) switch off your emails and your mobile phone so that you can concentrate ❑
   c) ask your colleagues to interrupt you every ten minutes ❑
   d) check your text messages and emails every two minutes ❑

5. Building up momentum by tackling one task at a time is:
   a) helpful, as you achieve more ❑
   b) a waste of time ❑
   c) completely unrealistic ❑
   d) helpful if you have the time ❑

6. At the end of a time of creative thinking, you should:
   a) forget all your discussions as if they never happened ❑
   b) move on to the next task ❑
   c) reward yourself ❑
   d) plan the next step you need to make to put your thoughts into action ❑

7. At work, you need more time to:
   a) eat ❑
   b) think ❑
   c) socialize with colleagues ❑
   d) have business meetings ❑

8. In a SWOT analysis, SWOT stands for:
   a) storms, welcome, offices, trouble ❏
   b) study, work, opportunities, time ❏
   c) strengths, weaknesses, opportunities, threats ❏
   d) steps, wisdom, output, thinking ❏

9. Giving your mind more 'breathing space':
   a) is a great idea in theory, but impractical ❏
   b) makes you fall sleep very quickly ❏
   c) allows time for you to come up with fresh ideas ❏
   d) is a great idea for when on holiday ❏

10. Coaching or mentoring can help you:
    a) avoid the real work ❏
    b) think about your skills and future career ❏
    c) complain about everyone and everything ❏
    d) become arrogant ❏

CHAPTER 3

Manage your time effectively

Introduction

In this chapter we move on to practicalities and consider:

- Clarifying your job in terms of priorities
- Distinguishing between what is urgent and what is important
- Making the most effective use of your time
- Things to do while commuting
- Keys to successful meetings
- Planning and allowing for contingencies
- Dealing with interruptions
- Delegating tasks
- Working out how much you cost your organization
- Using a diary and to-do list
- Dealing with things that waste your time
- Dealing with procrastination
- Using office technology effectively

Clarify your job

Set priorities

> ### 'No amount of "tricks of the trade" will avoid the need to set some sort of priority when allocating one's time.'
>
> Sir John Harvey-Jones (1924–2008), former chairman of ICI

1 Take a piece of paper or open up a new document on your computer and write in the middle of the page what your job role is in six words. Around that role, list the tasks – the various parts of your job (what you actually do) – under different headings. Now look at that paper.

2 Write A, B, C, or D alongside each task that you do:
   A: for tasks that are important and urgent, e.g. dealing with crises
   B: for tasks that are important but not urgent, e.g. undertaking forward planning and building relationships
   C: for tasks that are not important but urgent, e.g. dealing with interruptions to your work
   D: for tasks that are neither important nor urgent, e.g. checking social media websites

A Important and urgent	B Important but not urgent
C Not important but urgent	D Not important and not urgent

3 Count up how many As, Bs, Cs and Ds you have:
   As:
   Bs:
   Cs:
   Ds:

Which category of your work has the highest rating: A, B, C or D? Now think which category most of your work should be in. The answer is B: tasks that are important but not urgent should occupy as much of your time at work as possible.

4 Now go through your tasks again. Look at the As: what practical steps can you take to turn the As into Bs? You may need to work with colleagues on this.

For example, John's colleagues in the finance department expect him to complete a task during week 2 of each month – the busiest time every month for him – but to do it, he needs information from another department that only arrives that week. John asks his colleagues in that department to supply him with information earlier, in week 1, so that he is less stressed.

5 Set up a planning diary, either on hard copy (paper) or as a computer table or spreadsheet for each day of the week (Figure 1). If you are working on hard copy, write in pencil so that you can erase certain tasks and reassign them to other times. Put your tasks as outlined in 3 at particular times each week.

Begin with Bs, making sure that you put the difficult jobs and the jobs that you don't want to do in the time (day of the week and time of day) when you are most alert. (Look back at Chapter 2 for more information on this.) For example, if you work best in the mornings, try to undertake your core work then, e.g. from 9 am to 12 noon (as in Figure 1).

Next, look at each A. Consider if you can turn any of these into Bs (see step 4 above).

Fill in any remaining As and then Cs and lastly any relevant Ds.

6 Question whether you need to do any of the Ds at all. Are any of the Ds rather like junk mail or spam that you should not be considering at all? If so, don't waste time even thinking about them.

7 What aspects of your job recur (e.g. weekly or monthly)? Insert in the relevant cells the tasks you regularly do on those days/weeks, e.g. a regular meeting on Thursday afternoons, or John's finance work in week 2 of every month. Question whether these are the best times for you.

8 Assign some thinking time to a particular day, e.g. Friday morning (after your Thursday meeting).

9 You may discover that there is too much to fit into one week. If so, could you aim to fit in all your work over a two-week cycle rather than in one week? For example, could you hold your regular Thursday meetings only twice a month, in weeks 1 and 3 rather than every week?

10 Make sure you include preparation time in your plan. For example, if your regular meeting is on Thursdays, start your preparation on Tuesdays. (Don't start on Wednesday: a crisis might arise then and, if you become involved with that, you will not be able to do your preparation. Furthermore, beginning your preparation on Tuesday allows time for your subconscious to work to produce other thoughts – as we discussed in Chapter 2.

What we have done here is to try to stand back and manage better the time that you can control. (There will always be some time that you cannot control, e.g. if you are stuck in a traffic jam on your way to work.)

These plans can then form the basis of your diary and to-do list. Even if you don't achieve this completely every day and only for three days a week instead of five, then that may be better than you are achieving at the moment and is still a useful foundation to work from.

Use a diary and to-do list

Now we've created our diary and to-do list, here are some guidelines on how to use them:

● It doesn't matter whether you have an electronic or paper diary/to-do list, as long as you have one

Figure 1 Weekly plan

	Monday	Tuesday	Wednesday	Thursday	Friday
8 am					
9 am	Core work	Core work	Core work	Core work	Thinking time
10 am	Core work	Core work	Core work	Core work	Core work
11 am	Core work	Core work	Core work	Core work	Core work
12 noon					
1 pm					
2 pm				Team meeting	
3 pm		Prepare for Thurs Team meeting			
4 pm					
5 pm					
6 pm					

● Work out your own preference: have one that you can carry with you everywhere
● Put all your key activities in your diary
● List all regular activities, e.g. any meetings that recur, for example 'first Tuesday of the month'. Do not rely on your memory for these. If you have not entered them in your diary, when a colleague phones to ask if you are free at that time, you may say yes, having forgotten you have a regular meeting. I personally have an A4-week-to-view hard copy book, in which I list all my key activities
● Use your diary as a basis for planning your to-do list. Compile your to-do list at the end of the previous day (if you leave it to the start of a new day, you will waste precious time). Tick off, cross out or delete items as you complete them
● At the end of the week, list the key activities you want to complete the following week
● If you don't complete items on one day, move them to the next

- Regularly check your to-do list during the day to make sure you are on track. (For some time, I didn't bother to do this, and found that I didn't complete tasks on the list, so it is worth doing)
- Order your items to ensure you tackle the hardest/most difficult/the ones you least want to do sooner rather than later

Make the most effective use of your time

Dealing with a few major issues has greater value than dealing with lots of minor ones. For example, 80% of the difficulties you face at work may come from three major issues and 20% from ten minor issues. This ratio is known as the *Pareto Principle*, or the 80:20 rule.[3] It is a more effective use of your time if you concentrate on the few major issues that lead to 80% of the difficulties than become preoccupied with the many issues caused by the 20%.

Work well

Here are some tips to work well and become more efficient:
- Get something right first time. Having to redo work you did not do well first time around takes more time: not only do you have to take time to find the parts that have been done poorly and then correct them, you also have to deal with any effects the bad work caused, e.g. loss of credibility or damaged reputation

> *'The best preparation for good work tomorrow is to do good work today.'*
> Elbert (Green) Hubbard (1856–1915), American businessman, writer, and printer

---

[3] The *Pareto Principle is* named after the Italian economist and sociologist, Vilfredo Frederico Pareto (1842–1923).

- Before you take a break, write down the next two or three things to do after the break. Also, if thoughts occur to you at times of day when you are not working, note them on your phone or write them down physically (I keep a notepad by the side of my bed to jot down such thoughts)
- If you can, say no to more non-relevant work, (see Chapter 7)

Things to do while commuting

One way to make better use of time is to use your commute effectively. Here are some suggestions of what you can do. Some of these ideas are clearly more suitable for travelling by train, others for driving.

Reading

- Reading the newspaper or a magazine
- Catching up on emails
- Reading background material
- Reading something completely unrelated to your work

Listening

- Listening to music
- Listening to the radio
- Listening to an audio book
- Listening to, and learning, a new language

Playing

- Playing games and puzzles

Sleeping

- Catching up on sleep

Watching

- Watching a video

Thinking

- Preparing for the day ahead or reviewing how the day has gone
- Thinking how to tackle difficulties

- Preparing for a presentation or difficult conversation
- Working out what to eat at home

Of course, there are many other things that you can do whilst commuting to work. How about being mindful of the drive/train ride in and enjoying the 'now'. This is a good technique to give the brain time to think.

Keys to successful meetings

For meetings to be effective, you need to:

- Know the purpose of the meeting
- Prepare for the meeting
- Keep meetings as short and as focused as possible
- Make sure that actions are well written up so that individuals know clearly what actions to take and by when

Plan a task

Planning is essential to working effectively and making good use of your time. The key elements of planning are:

- Breaking down a large task into its constituent parts
- Knowing your outcomes: what you want to achieve
- Knowing your deadline
- Knowing your resources, e.g. in terms of personnel and finance

If you do not know how long a particular task will take, don't guess by plucking a figure out of the air, but work on a sample and use that as a basis. For example, I once thought that checking 100 items in a reference book would take me a maximum of three hours. However, when I undertook a sample for half an hour, I discovered that I only completed three, and each one had taken me an average of ten minutes. 100 x ten mins = 1,000 mins = 16.7 hours, which is considerably longer than the three I originally thought.

Note that you will come up with various reasons why you were slow, for example you were learning what you have to do and you were interrupted. These might be true, and you will probably increase momentum as you work on a task, so the overall time might come down to say 12 or 13 hours, but this is still considerably higher than the original estimate of three hours.

When planning, note that the time spent undertaking admin (e.g. commissioning, checking, preparation, participation, and follow up of meetings) is likely to be far more than you think.

 When planning, the time spent doing admin is likely to be far more than you think.

In planning schedules, remember to allow for:

- Holidays, both by individuals and public holidays
- Other work that individuals might undertake at the same time. For example, a colleague might be compiling a report for another department on the days you have allocated for him or her to be available for your project
- Unproductive time. You may sit at your desk from 9 am to 5 pm with a break for lunch, but how much of that time is actually productive? Maybe five hours
- Contingencies. Unplanned events that could significantly delay your projects. Allow 10–20% of the time as contingency

Deal with interruptions

Do all you can to minimize interruptions and build up momentum in your work. To illustrate this, consider two trains travelling along the same track to London, each covering 90 kilometres. One is non-stop and takes only 55 minutes; the other stops six times and takes 95 minutes. Ask yourself which train your work is more like: the fast or slow train? The more you can minimize interruptions, the more you will achieve. Furthermore, as you build up momentum, you will become increasingly absorbed in your task as you focus on it and your work will flow more easily.

- As far as possible, take control. Arrange meetings that fit best with your schedule, not other people's
- If someone phones you at an inconvenient time, ask them to call back at a certain time that is convenient to you. Don't say, 'I'll ring you back' – that means you will have to add them to your to-do list, which is probably too full already. Give your caller the responsibility to call you back
- Not all interruptions come from others: we sometimes interrupt ourselves by checking our emails constantly and responding to them immediately. (It may only take you a minute to answer an email but you will lose several minutes' concentration.) Schedule in regular times to check emails
- Delegate more, ensuring you give clear instructions. Train colleagues up so you can delegate more

Delegation

There are many reasons why managers don't delegate: you think you can do it better yourself; members of the team are too busy; the task is too urgent; your colleagues aren't quite ready to take on such demanding work... Most of these reasons are essentially about the fact that you don't trust members of your team to carry out the tasks. But when will they be fully ready? When will they have enough time?

You need to settle on three important ideas:

- **Plan ahead as much as you can**. Spend time doing this. You know when key tasks (e.g. the annual budget) are required. Schedule in sufficient planning time in your diary
- **Delegate work to those who are nearly ready** to receive it. No-one will ever be fully ready – were you? The delegated tasks will stretch those who are nearly ready for them. And that's what you want, isn't it?
- **Delegate more rather than less**. There are a few matters you cannot delegate (e.g. managing the overall team, allocating financial resources, dealing with confidential matters of performance management and promotion), but you can and should delegate many of your tasks and some routine administration

How to delegate

- Know your team. Who would be the best person to carry out the tasks you want to delegate? Remember what I just noted: choose colleagues who are nearly ready. If no-one is at that level, then provide some training so that at least some of them are. Share the load wherever possible, but don't delegate too much work to your best colleague
- Be clear about the tasks you want to delegate. This is the most important part of delegating. Don't give vague instructions (e.g. 'Could you just write a short report on failings in security?'), but be specific. Explain yourself well ('I'd like a 10-page report giving examples of major security breaches, together with possible reasons behind them and recommendations on how to avoid them in future.') Allow plenty of time to explain the task and give an opportunity for your colleague to ask you questions so they can clarify what you want them to do
- Check that they have understood the task you want them to undertake. Don't do this by just asking, 'Have you understood what I want you to do?' but phrase the question to be something like 'Could you summarize what you will be doing?' Their response will show how much they have understood your explanation
- Give sufficient significant background details so that your colleague knows why they are doing the task and where their task or activity fits into the overall scheme of things
- Where possible, follow up any spoken instructions in writing with a full brief, outlining the work
- Break the task or activity down into its constituent parts. Write briefing instructions, but don't just write in abstract terms: give examples of what needs to be done
- State the date and time you want your colleague to complete the work by. Remember that what may take you (with all your experience) only half a day will probably take the colleague you are delegating the task to much longer, e.g. two days
- Agree how often you want them to report back to you, particularly (but not only) when they have completed certain agreed targets

- If a colleague is slow at doing his or her work, ask them to give you an update on their progress by the end of each day
- Be clear about the authority and responsibility you are giving your colleague with this work. After all, you remain ultimately responsible as manager, even though you have delegated the work
- Provide the necessary equipment and other resources (and if necessary further training) that they need
- Let them decide the details of how they will undertake the work
- Where problems or difficulties arise, encourage your colleague to come to you about them, but also to bring their own thoughts on possible solutions, together with (for example) any figures on financial costings for such solutions and the time implementing them would take. This makes better use of your time: they are closer to the details of the task than you are. Your task is then to make a decision based on the suggestions. Getting your colleague to think things through for themselves also increases their skills
- When they have completed the task, thank your colleague, expressing your appreciation. Recognize them and their achievement

Working out how much you cost your organization

It isn't just you who needs to worry about your productivity and efficiency as a leader. Everything you do at work has an impact on your organization too. The less efficient an employee is, the more it costs.

If you have an annual salary of £30,000

÷ 48 (52 weeks – 4 weeks holiday) = £625 per week

÷ 5 (days per week) = £125 per day

÷ 5 (productive hours in that day; could be as low as 2!) = £25

× 2.7 per hour (to cover office overheads) = £67.50

So the cost of five managers attending a meeting lasting seven hours would be £2,363 (67.5 x 5 x 7), *which is probably higher than you thought.*

Note these figures are what you cost your company – not what you earn.

Twenty things that can waste your time ... and your response to them

1 Saying 'I'll just finish these small tasks first' but never starting your main task seriously. Response: start your major task first whether you feel like it or not.

2 Indecision by managers. Response: remember that making no decision is also a decision in itself. Be courageous and either make a decision, or encourage a decision to be made. Make sure that SMART actions are agreed.

3 Poor internal communications (e.g. with your boss). Response: discuss the issues with them (see also Chapter 6.

4 Your own perfectionism. Response: do less! You don't need to triple-check every cell in a spreadsheet in which the numbers have been computer generated.

5 Lack of concentration. Response: motivate yourself – promise yourself a reward upon completion within a certain time.

6 Fear of getting something wrong. Response: ask for help; go on a training course. Ask for feedback.

7 Surfing the Internet for social networking purposes. Response: be stricter with yourself. Avoid non-work internet until lunchtime.

8 Colleagues needing help. Response: ensure you help them in your less than prime time, if possible. Schedule them in so they know you will do it.

9 Someone who just wants to chat. Response: talk during lunch or after work.

10 Panicking colleagues. Response: tell them you will help them this time but not in future. Don't allow responding to others' crises become a regular occurance.

11 Other colleagues constantly interrupting. Response: schedule and make known the specific times when you are available.

12 Looking for things. Response: store or file items more sensibly; throw more things away.

13 Phone calls. Response: turn off your mobile during prime time; screen other calls. Ask the caller to call back at a specific time.

14 Having things you need far away from you. Response: move them closer; get organized.

15 A growing to-do list. Response: prioritize items:
   ● Put one star beside unimportant matters
   ● Put two stars beside important matters
   ● Put three stars beside important and urgent matters
   ● Do the three-star items first: now

16 Not knowing where to start in a task. Response: break a larger task down into smaller steps. If necessary, just start somewhere.

17 Constantly thinking of new ways of doing tasks that have been done many times before. Response: for tasks that recur, create templates and file them where you know where they are.

18 Hesitating about over what to write. Response: write something or draw a mind map Ask yourself the question words *who, why, what, when, how, where, which*? to set yourself thinking. You can always go back and edit it later.

19 Answering emails all the time. Response: set certain times when you will check and answer them.

20 Trying to do too many different things. Response: Constantly opening and closing computer files takes time in itself; you will build up momentum if you do fewer tasks well. Use your star list (see 15).

Five steps to deal with procrastination

Procrastination is postponing things you need to do until later (*cras* is Latin for 'tomorrow'). You can spend a lot of time being very busy, but not actually work on the jobs that need doing.

1 Focus on the result, not the activity. Set yourself a target of what you can achieve in ten minutes. Then, after that ten minutes, set yourself another target of what you can achieve in the next ten minutes and so on.

2 Make yourself plan better in future – use that diary and to-do list.
3 Break down a big task into smaller, manageable chunks. Take one step at a time, however small.
4 Ask for help from others, but don't use your fear of failure as an excuse for doing nothing. Do something: even write an outline, which can then be a basis for developing further ideas.
5 Don't wait until you feel motivated or you will wait forever. For more on motivating yourself, see Chapter 5. Do one small step now.

Five principles of effective time management

1 Know what time of day and day(s) of the week you work best and protect that time. Use it for thinking/hard tasks – e.g. no emails!
2 Tackle the hardest task – the thing you don't want to do – first.
3 Handle pieces of paper/complete a task at one sitting. Handle a piece of paper only once. To see if you are doing that, put a red dot at the top right-hand side of a piece of paper every time you handle it. When you have finished the task, you should only have one red dot on each piece of paper.
4 Use slack time well, e.g. for writing, reading, making a phone call, filing (electronic or manual), clearing your in-tray, reading a periodical.
5 If you have 30 minutes available for a task, aim to fit in a task that might take at least that amount rather than one that will only last 20 minutes, leaving you spare time.

Remember 3Ds: do – dump – delegate: .

Do -	deal with it. If you need to do it, think: • how long something will take. If it will take literally between 30 seconds and 2 minutes, then do it now • if it is urgent and important, start it now • if it is less urgent, or will take more than 2 minutes, then defer it by planning when you will do it, depending on how important it is
Dump -	If you don't need it, and it's not important, get rid of it – throw it away. You can recycle non-confidential paper, but you should make sure you shred papers that are confidential
Delegate -	pass it on to someone else.

'Work expands so as to fill the time available for its completion.'

– 'Parkinson's Law', named after the English historian and journalist Cyril Northolt Parkinson (1909–93).

To make good use of your time, use office technology effectively

- Use Outlook; share files online; arrange invitations to meetings automatically; flag emails to follow up so they don't get lost
- Synchronize electronic/digital devices; use Dropbox to share documents; cloud computing; coordinate calendar and contacts
- Create more templates and checklists so you don't have to repeat the same work each time
- Use speed-dial on the phone; list of contacts
- Use predictive text

Certain software packages offer other time-saving devices:

- Use 'track changes' to note changes that colleagues make to documents
- Use templates; create macros
- File material under names you can remember and would be intuitive to colleagues in your absence. Or better still, agree standard formats for filenames
- Use shortcuts, for example:
  - shift F3 to change capitals
  - shift F7 for a substantial thesaurus
- Use automatic reminders, e.g. for birthdays
- Use 'autocorrect' for words that you type often. This is the facility that is preloaded onto your computer and automatically changes, for example, 'freind' to 'friend'. So if you are often typing the name of your company 'Kramer Consultants', you can set up your computer so that every time you type 'KC1' (for example) it is automatically changed to 'Kramer Consultants'. Look up 'autocorrect' under 'Help' to find out how to set it up; it isn't difficult and it will save you a lot of time

Look under the 'Help' function of your computer programmes to learn how to use these shortcuts. A small amount of time invested now can save hours later on.

Summary

Someone who manages their time well will:

- Plan well
- Know when they work best
- Meet schedules and deadlines
- Concentrate on priorities
- Participate effectively in meetings
- Create 'blocks of time', e.g. to check emails or make routine phone calls.
- Handle interruptions well
- Be organized
- Delegate when possible
- Make good use of meetings
- Use slack time well

Exercise

1 List the tasks that you do at your work and try to move as many urgent and important ones ('As') to important but not urgent ones ('Bs').

2 Compile a weekly plan of the tasks you do, using the principles outlined in this chapter.

3 Think of a schedule that you are compiling: make sure you have included some contingency time.

Fact-check (answers at the back)

1. As regards priorities:
   a) I've no idea what the priorities of my job are ❏
   b) I know what my priorities are and stick to them most of the time ❏
   c) I set priorities but never stick to them ❏
   d) I'm so concerned with the urgent that I never consider priorities ❏

2. When thinking about my job, I need mostly to do:
   a) tasks that are not important but urgent ❏
   b) tasks that are neither important nor urgent ❏
   c) tasks that are important and urgent ❏
   d) tasks that are important but not urgent ❏

3. I get side-tracked by unimportant parts of my job:
   a) all the time ❏
   b) rarely ❏
   c) most days ❏
   d) never ❏

4. I plan my time:
   a) never ❏
   b) occasionally in my head ❏
   c) nearly always ❏
   d) I've no time to do that ❏

5. I have a work diary:
   a) but never use it ❏
   b) and am a slave to it ❏
   c) and use it nearly all the time to plan ❏
   d) I've no time to do that ❏

6. I write a to-do list:
   a) what's that? ❏
   b) and am a slave to it ❏
   c) and keep to it as far as I can ❏
   d) but never look at it during the day ❏

7. When I compile a schedule, I allow time for contingency:
   a) always ❏
   b) never ❏
   c) when I remember ❏
   d) what is 'contingency'? ❏

8. I check my emails:
   a) 24 hours a day ❏
   b) all the time during the working day ❏
   c) when I come back from holiday ❏
   d) at regular times through the working day ❏

9. I delegate:
   a) tasks to colleagues who I want to develop ❏
   b) badly ❏
   c) the tasks I don't want to do ❏
   d) never ❏

10. I wait until I feel motivated before I start work:
    a) always ❏
    b) never: I push myself to do something even if I don't feel like it ❏
    c) usually ❏
    d) occasionally ❏

CHAPTER 4

Manage your mind decisively

Introduction

So far, we've looked generally at becoming aware of what kind of person you are – your skills, values, motives, beliefs, attitudes – and then we looked at managing your focus: keeping the main thing the main thing and not being distracted. We also considered it important to have 'free' time so that you can have some 'breathing space', and then in the previous chapter we considered managing your time better.

We now turn to managing your mind and thoughts. In this chapter we will look at:

- Thinking positive thoughts
- Developing ways of thinking
- Looking at the example of different aspects of decision making: defining your aims, collecting relevant information, identifying different options, considering risks and consequences, and making and implementing the decision
- The role of intuition
- Solving problems
- Challenging assumptions and being imaginative
- Ways to remember things
- Reading more effectively

Think positive thoughts

'Nurture your mind with great thoughts, for you will never go any higher than you think.'

Benjamin Disraeli (1804–81), English statesman, prime minister and
novelist

Our mind is the base of our reason and decision making.
Just as we are encouraged to watch what we eat in order to
maintain a healthy lifestyle physically, so we also need to be
alert to what we take into our minds. That will strengthen us
and help us respond positively to negative things around us.

What we take into our minds affects what flows out of us.
Therefore, we need to guard what we take into our minds and
be careful what we look at and read. We need to keep up-to-
date with the news, and also with trends in our industry and
useful aspects of business thinking. We also need positive
input into our minds to counteract the negative things that we
constantly face.

It is also good to stretch our minds and discuss matters with
people we disagree with. They might be right, and even if they
are not we will have refined our own understanding.

Develop your thoughts

When I am faced with a task that needs thought, I draw
a pattern diagram (also known as a mind map). This is a
very useful way of opening up a subject. In a group setting,
'brainstorming' is a similar tool.

Take a blank piece of A4 paper. Arrange it in landscape
position and write the subject that you are considering in the
middle. (Write a word or few words, but not a whole sentence.)
You may find it helpful to work in pencil, as you can rub out
what you write if necessary.

Now, towards the edge of the paper, write around your
central word(s) the different key aspects that come to your
mind. You do not need to list ideas in order of importance;

simply write them down. To begin with, you do not need to join the ideas up with lines linking connected items.

If you get stuck at any point, ask yourself the questions *why, how, what, who, when, where, how much* and *how many*. These may well set you thinking.

When I do this, I am often amazed at: (1) how easy the task is: it doesn't feel like work! The ideas and concepts seem to flow naturally and spontaneously. (2) how valuable that piece of paper is. I have captured all (or at least some or many) of the key points. I don't want to lose that piece of paper!

An example of a pattern diagram for the subject of buying a new computer system is:

Users

- Which company departments will use the system?

Locations

- On company's two sites

Time available

- Should be ready for 1 Jan

Kinds of computers

- Laptops
- iPads
- Latest technology
- How long is it intended to last?

Cost

- Budget
- Check figures with Finance Director

New computer system

IT department

- Who will build the new system?
- Who will install the new system?

Old system

- Keeps crashing
- Secure?
- Software: Out of date
- Slow, constant problems

Accounts department

- Will they move over to new system?
- They introduced a new system only 6 months ago

Link to Intranet

Website maintenance

Security

Think creatively

Other ways to encourage you to think creatively

1 Turn the subject on its head: for example, rather than thinking of ways to improve customer service in a restaurant, think of the factors that would make the customer service in that restaurant the worst in the city – e.g. no-one greets you, you have to wait a long time before ordering, the food, when it eventually arrives, is tasteless, etc.

2 Imagine yourself in a successful situation: how would you feel?

3 Pick a concrete noun and see how the problem you are trying to define is different from that.

4 Do word association: e.g. if something has a high quality, ask yourself and others what associated words that raises in your mind? Best? Expensive? Prestigious?

5 Draw the problem that is facing you: what colour is it; what shape? Or act it out as a play.

6 Consider your problem as a metaphor: a journey as a ship's voyage; a company working together as a team; increasing sales as climbing a mountain; new life as blossom on a tree. What do these fresh ways of thinking suggest?

See also Chapter 2.

Decision making

Let's take an example of developing thoughts in terms of decision making. We can list the various steps in making a decision:

Define your aims clearly

You need to identify:

● What is the real issue that you need to make a decision about and what are secondary issues?

● The time when the decision has to be made by. Is that timescale realistic? If not, can you work out a strategy to find more time?

● What kind of person you are, especially as regards your values, what motivates you at work and what is the way in which you work?

● What your personality is as regards decision making: e.g. are you naturally decisive or indecisive, or are you cautious or rash?

● Who in your company or organization makes the decisions. Is it only you as manager, or do you involve others? When a decision is made that affects colleagues, the greater the

involvement of colleagues in the decision-making process, the stronger their motivation
● Who will implement the decision?

Collect relevant information

As regards the decision you need to make, you need to:

● Understand the context
● Gather relevant information, including consulting experts as necessary
● Work on your costs and schedules for implementing the decision

Identify different options

When you consider a range of techniques to help you identify different options in your decision making, you should:

● Consider imaginative alternatives: widen your thinking so that you don't stick with what you are used to and don't choose the first option that offers itself
● Challenge assumptions; see also later in this chapter
● Consider where you can concentrate your resources so that they are used most effectively
● Consider the timing: work out which tasks need to be done before others can be started
● Examine a situation carefully before 'jumping to conclusions'. If you are a negative person by temperament, don't give up but always look at the options and manage your way through them

Consider risks

Assessing risk means knowing how and when things could go wrong and working out ways to deal with them. It is important to manage risks so that the threats of possible risks are minimized. For example, if you are making decisions about managing a project, risks are the uncertain events that could happen which would prevent your project from being carried out successfully. Is the schedule realistic? Have sufficient financial resources been made available? Are roles and responsibilities clear? Are you measuring the quality of what you are producing objectively enough? Have you allowed for contingency in your schedule and costings?

Risks need to be identified, assessed and then dealt with. The one key point to remember is that you will not survive in business without encountering certain risks, so it is better to plan to deal with them rather than be surprised when they unexpectedly arise.

Consider the consequences

Every decision has consequences, but your task as manager is to:

- Be aware of the consequences of choosing different options
- Evaluate the consequences of choosing different options
- Minimize the risks of choosing different options

To do this, you need to do more than just imagine that you might choose a particular option. You need to actually think what would happen if you did choose it. Be both subjective (e.g. what would it feel like?) and objective (e.g. what would be the profit or loss?). Use criteria that are in line with the values you and/or your company or organization hold.

Here you deliberately think of:

- What would happen if you did nothing? Sometimes this is a valid option. Sometimes the response to a crisis (not always!) can be to continue as if nothing has happened and the crisis might exhaust itself and fade away
- What would happen if the decision was not made *now*? Can you delay it?
- What would happen if the decision was not made *by you*? Is it your decision to make – or is it the responsibility of you and others?
- What would happen if you adopted each of the options that emerge? You need to do this *before* you make your choice.

For example, when preparing for negotiations, consider whether agreeing to deliver the products within three months is a realistic schedule for you. If it is not, don't offer it in the first place
● What possible future situations could develop

Don't ignore your intuition
'I just know', 'I felt that was right', 'I had a hunch that ...', 'The thought just came to me'. How often do you use or hear such phrases? Intuition has a role to play in the decision-making process.

It can be defined as 'the power of knowing something without evident reasoning'. There may be no logical explanation for something; you discern the truth about a person or situation and you just know it is right.

For me, intuition is important, but it is only one factor in the decision-making process. If I am tired or stressed, my emotions can play havoc with my thinking processes, so I have to be careful.

Intuition is linked to your depth mind, your subconscious, as we discussed in Chapter 2. It seems that your depth mind digests a myriad of thoughts – analysing, synthesizing and evaluating them – resulting in an intuitive thought coming to your consciousness.

That is why it is useful to 'sleep on it': sleep for a night before making a significant decision. Sometimes this is plain common sense. I have an informal rule for myself that I do not send out a costing for a project without sleeping on it. A while back, I costed a project one day and, when I checked my figures the next day, I realized I had for some inexplicable reason calculated the figure to be only half the correct total. So there is ordinary wisdom as well as intuitive reason behind the need to 'sleep on it'. Don't ignore the thoughts that occur to you when you are taking a shower or driving home from work and are not thinking about a problem. Allow your subconscious mind the opportunity to do its work and let fresh ideas emerge when you are not thinking about making the decision.

Evaluate the different options

Having too many options can be overwhelming and lead to confusion, which can also add time to the decision making. To be more efficient, evaluate your options and see which ones can be eliminated. You should:

● Reduce the number of options available, to enable you to make a decision
● Establish certain objective criteria against which you can assess each of your different options
● Consider the consequences of each option and their advantages and disadvantages. You may need to make a compromise
● List the resources needed to fulfil each option, e.g. costing
● Assess risks: knowing how and when things could go wrong, and therefore being prepared for them

Make the decision

You will eventually arrive at the point of coming to a decision. Having defined the core issues, gathered information, identified and evaluated the various options, and weighed up each of the options in your mind, you now need to make the decision. Next, you need to implement it, communicate it to all the relevant colleagues and, if necessary, set in place good monitoring controls to help you track progress.

Solve problems

Here are some guidelines to help you find a satisfactory way of dealing with a problem or difficulty:

● Ask if it is your problem. Is it your responsibility to respond to it? Is it someone else's? Or is it just one of those things you have to live with? If the problem is yours:
  – how important is it? Will solving it have a significant effect on your work?

- how urgent is it? If the problem will become more serious if you do nothing about it, then act sooner rather than later
- *Occasionally, however, some problems can turn into positive opportunities, so don't always think you have to solve them all*
- Get to the root of the problem. Think; discuss with other colleagues; analyse the problem by separating it into its parts to help you define it more closely and understand it more fully
- In particular, concentrate on the causes – not the symptoms or effects – of the problem. So if someone's work is below standard, don't keep on moaning about it by giving examples but try to find out why and ask whether they need training, or whether they would be more suitable for other kinds of work
- Keep on asking questions, especially the question 'Why?' so that you gain a complete understanding of the real issue. Problem solving is often more about asking the right questions than giving the right answers
- Gather information as to the extent of the problem. If the quality of products is failing, does this affect 1 in 1,000 products or 900 in 1,000?
- Concentrate on the big issues. Don't get bogged down in detail
- Use your experience. As you progress as a manager, you will develop that sense of 'I've been here before – how did I solve the problem last time?' Use your colleagues' experience: how did they solve a similar problem?
- Consider different responses. Here are some techniques you could use to respond creatively to problems:
  - Brainstorm with colleagues: take a flipchart. Ask one person to state the problem and then get him or her to write down ideas as the problem is thought about and discussed from different angles, e.g. what would your customers' and your competitors' viewpoint be? Encourage the participants to build on one another's ideas; don't criticize or evaluate them. At the end, participants can agree how to take the best ideas to the next stage

- Draw up a flow chart that shows the series of steps
  of all the different stages that led to a problem, how
  the problem is expressed (i.e. its symptoms) and the
  connections between the problem's causes and effects
- Think 'outside the box'. Is the problem difficult to put into
  words? Then draw it or work out if you are better explaining
  it by a painting, in a piece of music or by role play
- Draw a pattern diagram (see earlier in this chapter)
- Conduct a SWOT analysis (see Chapter 2).

Challenge assumptions

When you are generating ideas and coming up with estimates,
challenge the assumptions you make.

● Be prepared to think differently, e.g. be explicit if your
  present strategy is failing. Face up to the 'elephant in the
  room', the subject everyone is aware of but is not discussed
  because it is too uncomfortable
● Are you keeping up with (if not acting in advance of) trends in
  your industry?
● Don't be overcautious

Develop your memory

Developing your memory is one of the skills that will help you
become a more effective manager. It will train your mind and
deepen your understanding.

When meeting someone for the first time, concentrate
particularly: think hard as the other person says their name. If
appropriate, write it down as soon as you can. If you are not sure
of the spelling, ask and or write down some phonetic version of
the name. Using their name when talking to them sometimes
will help reinforce the memory of their name in your mind.

Try to establish some association between what you are
trying to remember and something you already know, e.g. a
woman's name Daphne and the visual association of a daffodil:
maybe she is wearing a yellow ribbon or dress.

Develop a set of initial letters to remember a list of things:

I do this quite often if I am shopping, e.g. for toothpaste, milk and a newspaper: TMN. I may remember a sentence, ToMorrow's Newspaper, to remind me, or a picture of someone sitting in an armchair reading a newspaper with some toothpaste on the arm of the chair. The more unusual the picture, the more memorable it will be.

Read more effectively

As a manager you will have a lot of material to read – for example, emails, reports, websites, professional literature, contracts, technical manuals, etc.

Here are some guidelines to help you read more effectively:

● Decide on your aims in reading a particular text. Do you want to simply check a fact, gain an overall sense of a text, grasp a detailed knowledge of a subject (for example for a report or presentation you have to prepare) or evaluate the writer's arguments and views?
● Vary the speed at which you read a text, depending on the kind of text you are reading. Spend more time on important and/or difficult parts of the text and less time on less important and/or easier parts
● Try not to mouth words as you read them. Mouthing words in this way not only slows you down but also means that you focus on the words rather than their meaning
● Put your finger immediately to the right of the first word on the paper/screen and move your finger across the line of words at a speed that your eyes can keep up with. You will find that your finger gently 'pulls' you along at a faster rate than your normal reading speed. Alternatively, put your finger on the paper/screen and move your finger down the page at a speed that your eyes can keep up with, reading just above it
● For some important work, take notes of what you have read. Summarizing the author's argument in your own words can be a particularly useful tool
● If you want to undertake a more detailed read of part of a text:

  – Find out which sections of the text you want to read. Consult the contents/list of chapters or index. Or if you are reading on screen, use the 'find' facility to locate the words you are most interested in. Survey or scan the text to get a wider view of it. As you do that, you will begin to see the writer's key words and phrases

- Look out for the signposts: the introduction and conclusions; the words *firstly*, *secondly*; the beginning of paragraphs; such expressions as *on the one hand* and *on the other hand*, which guide you in seeing the structure of the text and can be helpful to your understanding

- Focus on the key words and, even more importantly, key phrases

- Reword the main points in your mind, on computer or on paper. Express the author's key points in your own way. Think about the author's argument: do you agree with him/her? Does the text make assumptions that you disagree with? Ask questions of the text and see if they are answered. Engage your mind

- At the end of reading, see if you can recall the main points, or even better, see if you can explain the main points to someone else. You could even review what you have read later to check that you still recall it

---

Effective reading ... and good time management

As a manager, Sarah was methodical about her reading. She only checked her emails a few times a day, dealing with essential matters as they arose. She didn't bother to check the many junk emails she received, but simply deleted them.

Sarah allocated Friday mornings, when she knew she generally received fewer emails, to important but not urgent reading material that enabled her to do her job more effectively.

As she was preparing to relax for the weekend on Friday afternoons, she read non-urgent but useful material that kept her up-to-date with other trends in the industry, which were not directly related to her job but developed her wider professional knowledge.

Of course, sometimes very urgent matters arose which meant that she could not always keep to this methodical time allocation, so in such cases she was flexible. Generally, however, Sarah was able to allot sufficient resources of time to reading what was useful and essential, and to manage her time well.

Summary

In this chapter we have considered your mind and thoughts in practical terms, especially in the context of decision making, creative thinking and problem solving. Things to be aware of include:

- how you think and feel
- how good your memory is
- effective reading
- what your time management is like

Exercise

1 Do you take time to think? Are your thoughts positive? How can you make them even more positive?

2 Draw a pattern diagram for a subject you are thinking about or have to write a report on.

3 Which step in decision making do you need to work more effectively at?
- Defining your aims
- Collecting relevant information
- Identifying different options
- Considering risks and consequences
- Making the decision
- Implementing and communicating the decision
- Tracking and monitoring progress

4 What method could you use to remember things, e.g. people's names, better?
5 Which point about reading was particularly new to you that you will put into practice? When is the next opportunity for you to do this?

Fact-check (answers at the back)

1. Thinking is:
a) a luxury these days ❏
b) a waste of time ❏
c) important, to be an effective manager ❏
d) useful if you have the time ❏

2. Thinking positively is:
a) useful if you have the time ❏
b) necessary to rise above the problems of life ❏
c) too idealistic ❏
d) a stupid idea ❏

3. A pattern diagram is a useful way:
a) to start to tackle different aspects of a subject ❏
b) just to draw lines on a page ❏
c) of spending ten minutes ❏
d) what is a pattern diagram anyway? ❏

4. When making a decision:
a) I just guess ❏
b) I think of a number and double it ❏
c) I look at all the different options but never actually make a decision ❏
c) I identify the issue, collect information and evaluate the different options ❏

5. Considering risks and consequences is:
a) important ❏
b) a luxury in this fast-paced world ❏
c) a waste of time ❏
d) useful, if you remember ❏

6. Your intuition is:
a) always an infallible guide ❏
b) one factor in the decision-making process ❏
c) unreal ❏
d) never something you should consider ❏

7. When solving a problem, it is necessary to:
a) blame the person whose fault it is ❏
b) get to the root of the problem ❏
c) spend all the time thinking about minor details ❏
d) pass the responsibility of solving it back to your boss ❏

8. Challenging assumptions:
a) is just part of your nature if you are an awkward kind of person ❏
b) always wrong ❏
c) essential to do on every occasion in life ❏
d) can sometimes be useful in leading to a fresh answer ❏

9. I have a bad memory:
a) so I can't do anything about it ❏
b) so I work to improve it ❏
c) and I've forgotten what I can do about it ❏
d) but I can still remember details of my childhood ❏

10. I read:

a) everything very slowly ❏

b) everything very quickly, not being able to recall anything I have read ❏

c) carefully and selectively, sometimes making notes or trying to express the content in my own words ❏

d) nothing, ever ❏

CHAPTER 5

Manage your emotions carefully

Introduction

I like trains. If I am leading a workshop or giving a presentation somewhere, I prefer travelling by train to driving my car as the train gives me time to think and read. But events do happen that are outside of our control. Twice I've been on trains that have been severely delayed because of suicides. It's interesting to see how we as passengers react. All too easily, the initial thoughts that I and my fellow passengers have are ones of anger at the inconvenience we have to suffer because of the delay. When I've found myself becoming angry, however, I have had to make myself think of the victim and their family: their experience must surely be far more intense than mine. We cannot always control what happens to us in life, but we can control our emotional response to such events.

In this chapter, we look at the area of managing our emotions:

- Don't ignore feelings
- Recognize your own emotional make-up
- Manage your thoughts
- Challenge assumptions
- Express feelings
- Don't blame, but reframe
- Be positive, and become more resilient and confident
- Motivate yourself

Don't ignore feelings

Think of an incident in your life when something bad happened to you. For example, in one job I discovered I was being paid less than a colleague who was doing the same work and who had a similar background, skills and experience to me. The issue itself was pay, but alongside that I felt angry, undervalued and unimportant.

In other words, there is the incident itself, then, underlying, there are the emotions surrounding the incident. Sometimes, after we have dealt with the facts, the unpleasant effects from the incident remain, or as we say, 'we are left with a bad taste in our mouth'; we still have to cope with our feelings, which should not be ignored. In this case, my sense of identity was affected.

Recognize your own emotional make-up

Different cultures express emotions differently. I have some African friends and they tend to be exuberant and show their emotions quite regularly. I'm more British and I'm not very emotional. I'm normally fairly even-tempered and I rarely cry. Generally, life is a steady course but I do have emotions and these surface from time to time. I feel great sadness and anger at the many injustices in the world. I become angry when I see resources of time and money being wasted.

Looking back, my parents did not often express their feelings towards each other. We didn't generally discuss emotions as a family – what counted were events. So I am having to learn to handle that part of my life: to accept feelings as part of a natural and healthy life.

It is here that we sometimes go wrong. It is wrong to ignore our emotions. We are surrounded by the claims that 'Real men don't cry', that it is wrong to feel anger or express fears, but we cannot always have strong feelings of happiness.

So it can be helpful to think: what is your emotional make-up? What is your attitude to your emotions? Which emotions do you find easy to express? Which more difficult?

I find it helpful to write down my feelings and also explore them with my wife and some trusted friends. In that way, I can accept them, usually see their significance and can be helped to move on.

Sometimes our feelings spill over into judgments about others. For example, we may help someone a lot over many years but they never thank us. Our anger may burst out into a judgment: 'You only think about yourself all the time, never anyone else.' Note that this is different from a statement about our feelings, which might be, 'I feel hurt. I thought we were friends.'

Manage your thoughts

The way in which we can manage our feelings is to manage our thoughts. Remember that emotions are not thoughts. However, they can affect how we act.

Dealing with fear

Fear can be a stumbling block in making progress in life: fear of failure, of what might happen, of what others think of us. Fear can make us feel weak, draining our energy.

Positive ways of dealing with fear include:

- Ask yourself, 'What's the worst that can happen?' If the worst really did happen, think what you would do
- Take small steps – if you are fearful of giving a 30-minute presentation, try a three-minute one to start with, then a five-minute one, and gradually build up to 30 minutes. Begin by setting small goals. Fulfilling those will develop your confidence. Set yourself realistic expectations. When I go on a long-haul flight, I keep an eye on our progress. For example, I work out when on a 13-hour flight what percentage of the journey I have covered after say 45 minutes (6%), 1.5 hours (12%) and so on. Focusing on the end goal, dividing up the overall journey time and measuring progress in a concrete way helps me feel I am on my way to reaching the goal

- Sometimes, the fear doesn't go away: Don't wait for courage; *be* courageous. I used to think that courage is the opposite of fear, but it isn't: courage is an inner strength to *decide* to do something difficult or dangerous, even if the fears are present
- Don't be too cautious, if that is your natural tendency. I am naturally quite cautious. I remember leaving my house many years ago to go to a publishing meeting. A little voice inside me said, 'Why are you going? You know that nothing will happen.' I made myself go, however, and at the meeting we agreed to compile a book that later sold well over 80,000 copies. What if I had listened to my naturally cautious self and had not been adventurous? You can be so cautious that you never do anything. Ask yourself what have you always wanted to try? Is now the time to do it? If not now, then when?

Challenge assumptions

We have feelings, which are based on certain thoughts. These thoughts are in turn based on certain assumptions. So we may need to challenge such assumptions to see if they are really true. If they turn out to be false, we can change our thoughts.

For example, if you are having a difficult conversation with a colleague, you may make assumptions about the intentions of the other party. However, you see and hear only what a person is doing and saying, not the intentions behind what they have done or said.

In order to challenge assumptions about others' intentions, you need to uncover what their intentions are. A clear, neutral, moderate statement such as 'I realize that I don't really know how you see this matter' can be a way to open up a conversation to its next stage. By acknowledging that you do not understand someone else's intentions – and that you are committed to understanding them and their views – can be a significant step forward in encouraging a colleague to express and articulate their intentions.

Sheila was jealous

Sheila was jealous of Rosey. It seemed Rosey was always chosen to be project leader. Sheila was angry: she felt she was always being ignored when it came to being chosen to lead projects and she thought she had skills that were not being recognized. She talked things over with a close colleague, Jinju, who helped her see that she was responsible for her own feelings. Sheila's feelings were real enough, but she needed to realize she could choose how she responded to them. Sheila also came to see that the feelings she was bottling up inside her were better expressed in a safe context rather than in personal anger towards Rosey.

Over time, Sheila took responsibility for herself. She learnt to face up to her own insecurities and to become more patient with both herself and Rosey. Gradually, Sheila even began to respect Rosey's qualities as a leader, even though her style was different from Sheila's. In due course Sheila's manager felt she had grown in personal maturity so much that she was chosen to lead projects.

Express emotions

Earlier in this chapter, we discussed the need not to ignore emotions. But we need to do more than that: we need to express them. Here, I think it is helpful to see expressing feelings as one stage and solving a problem as a separate, later stage. So if someone loses their temper and is allowed to express themselves freely for a few minutes, that clears the air and then they will probably feel better. We must resist the temptation to try to stop someone in the middle of expressing their anger, but allow them to release their feelings and then move on from that.

As we allow people to air their own opinions and express deep emotions, the result can – if managed well – be that some long-standing issues can be resolved, leading to stronger, more trusting working relationships.

If you have some long-bottled up emotions within you, consider finding a trusted colleague and asking them if you could have a chat about them with the goal of releasing those feelings in the first instance, rather than trying to find solutions for them immediately.

Acknowledge the emotions
of your colleagues

After feelings have been expressed, it is important to acknowledge them, perhaps by saying, 'I didn't know you felt that way.' Acknowledging the expression of feelings is an important step because in so doing you are affirming your appreciation of the other person's feelings. For more on affirming others, see Chapter 6.

Our sense of identity

When we criticize someone, for example for the poor quality of their work, they may feel threatened and become defensive. They may start to justify themselves, reminding us of all the good aspects of their work. Moreover, when our work is criticized, it is not just our work that is affected; deep within us we feel threatened and our sense of identify may be damaged.

After giving a brief presentation a few years ago, a colleague told me my work was 'not professional'. I was surprised, hurt and confused. My self-image was challenged and my sense of self-worth was attacked.

If our identity is attacked, we feel insecure and may begin to believe what is being said about our character, skills or knowledge: 'Maybe I am no good, after all.' Here we need to think realistically about ourselves – we are neither perfect in every way nor extremely incompetent. We need to manage our thoughts (see earlier in this chapter and Chapter 4) and let the facts influence our thoughts.

Don't blame; reframe

During a difficult conversation with someone, it can become relatively easy to blame the other person: 'It's all your fault that the report is three days late. You should have finished it earlier.' A better way is to see what each side has contributed to the difficulty. Maybe you were slightly late in giving your colleague the figures they needed for the report. Here, it is important to be professional and assert that your aim is not to blame anyone. Instead, you want to discover what went wrong, the reasons for that and what each colleague, including yourself, can learn from it.

Reframing is changing the way someone thinks about something they perceive as difficult and negative into seeing it in a more positive manner.

I first encountered reframing when I was coaching a colleague who hated interviews. She said she did not cope at all well with one-to-ones. But she also told me she enjoyed negotiating. She relished the challenge of preparing for a negotiation, listening for clues as to the other party's intentions, discussing alternatives and reaching an agreement. So my suggestion that she should adapt and reframe her thinking and see interviews positively and as a means of negotiation was a moment of sudden enlightenment for her.

TIP *Don't blame; reframe.*

Think positively

Eddy felt frustrated. He began the job well, but soon became frustrated by the endless meetings and office politics. He started to feel trapped and could not change his situation. He could see no way out. He sat down with a friend, Ravi, and they chatted. Ravi told him to take a long look at his situation: having a job and being paid for it was better than having no job, like some of his friends from school. Eddy and Ravi discussed how there were a few positive things about his job, like the opportunities it gave him to travel to various cities and meet new people. As he thought about them he realized he was not so badly off after all.

Build up your confidence

Ways in which you can increase your confidence include:

- Prepare better. If you lack confidence at giving presentations, then work harder at your preparation. The more prepared you are, the more you will feel in control and the greater confidence you will have. You will then feel less nervous. Your preparation could include relatively simple things like dealing with practical arrangements or taking a copy of your PowerPoint presentation (saved in an earlier version of PowerPoint to be on the safe side) on a memory stick so that if your laptop fails you can use a colleague's
- Remind yourself that you have been asked to take on your present role. Believe in yourself more. Other colleagues have believed in you enough, so have some confidence in yourself!
- Be confident in your own style. Your way of dealing with your job is just that: your own, and it is as valid as anyone else's. You don't have to follow the style of your predecessor exactly

Deal with nerves

Almost everyone is nervous in some aspects of their job. For example, I admit that I am nervous before nearly every presentation I give and every time I have to speak in public. I have found the following helpful:

- If you're giving a presentation, practise what you will say in advance (especially the beginning and end). Practising beforehand helps you realize you need to work hard at choosing the right words and also lets you know how long the presentation will last
- Focus on other people, not yourself. If you are giving a presentation, as soon as the participants begin to arrive, start talking to them. As you do this, often your own nervousness will decrease
- Accept your nervousness
- Watch out for warning signs that affect you personally: e.g. stomach rumbling (or worse), dry throat, shallow breathing, tension in your body, fast heartbeat

- Learn what works for you to reduce tension: e.g. sipping water, taking deep breaths, eating and drinking sensibly, having a plan
- Practise the relaxation techniques that work for you, e.g. walking, deep breathing
- Have adequate sleep
- Wear comfortable clothing that you feel at ease in
- Have a support group of close friends who you can text: they can offer help and support
- Visualize how you will feel at the end of a difficulty
- Reward yourself with a treat: I find the thought of eating a bar of chocolate at the end of the presentation sometimes helps me through the day

(For further ways of dealing with stress, see Chapter 7.)

Motivate yourself

Ways in which you can motivate yourself include the following:

- Accept yourself and the difficult situation you are in: you cannot do anything to change the past or present, but you can do something about *your response to* your present situation
- Look back at past successes, however small: remind yourself of past achievements and think about how you achieved them
- Learn from others; take advice – have a coach / mentor (look back at Chapter 2)
- Do something, however small, even if you don't feel like it. Don't just sit there feeling sorry for yourself. Focus on the next thing you need to do in order to achieve your goal in order to make your goal a reality. Remember the saying: the journey of a thousand miles begins with one step. It might be researching an online course of study or emailing someone or calling someone by phone. Do something!
- Focus on results, not activity. Set yourself a target to see how much you can achieve in ten minutes, then repeat that ten minutes later
- Have close friends who can support and encourage you

- Try to remain positive. Even in the face of difficulty, there is always hope
- Don't allow yourself to become irritated by minor things: think of far greater injustices in the world
- Don't take someone's comments about your work personally. Become more resilient. The intention behind their remarks is for you to work better. Look to see how you can rise above your emotions, humbly accept your errors, take responsibility and do your best to improve
- Think what your family, e.g. your parents, went through to help you reach where you are today

 Don't wait until you feel motivated – sometimes you just have to push yourself.

See also dealing with procrastination in Chapter 3.

Not giving up hope

Tara had had a difficult life. Her dad had just died and she looked after her mother, brother and sister. She didn't give up hope, however. She asked friends to help her and she studied hard. Eventually she was able to get a job abroad and send money back to her family. By not feeling sorry for herself and by constantly taking the initiative, she did not give up hope but remained positive. Through hard work, she became successful.

Summary

In this chapter we've seen that we cannot ignore emotions. You may need to explore your own emotional make-up and consider how emotional you are.

Positively, we have seen that you need to:

- Realize you cannot change what has happened, but you can change your response to it
- Take responsibility for your own actions
- Move beyond blaming others: reframe
- Have courage
- Become more resilient
- Work on your own character to overcome difficulties
- Be positive: think what can you do and begin to do that
- Do something, however small. Every step is a step forward
- Don't be self-centred; consider others

Exercise

1 How would you describe your own emotional make-up?

2 Do you allow your thoughts to control your emotions or vice versa? Think of times when

you have allowed your emotions to control your thoughts. How would you act differently now with hindsight?

3 Think of one emotion – e.g. fear, jealousy or insecurity – that affects you strongly. What positive steps can you take to deal with it?

Fact-check (answers at the back)

1. I have strong feelings, so I:
a) need to pretend they don't exist and ignore them ❏
b) spend all my time thinking only about them ❏
c) need to express them in a safe context ❏
d) need to express them constantly. ❏

2. Knowing your own emotional make-up is:
a) a waste of time ❏
b) 'Shut up!' ❏
c) the only thing that counts. ❏
d) useful ❏

3. The way to manage your feelings is to:
a) emphasize them ❏
b) drink more juice ❏
c) manage your thoughts ❏
d) ignore them. ❏

4. Discussing feelings:
a) is a waste of time ❏
b) can be important ❏
c) could become unpleasant so I avoid it ❏
d) is the most important thing in the world ❏

5. I challenge assumptions:
a) where appropriate ❏
b) never ❏
c) always, so that's all that I do ❏
d) what's an assumption? ❏

6. If someone is expressing their feelings, you should:
a) interrupt them ❏
b) tell them to stop and calm down ❏
c) avoid them ❏
d) let them do so. ❏

7. Reframing is:
a) seeing something positive from a negative perspective ❏
b) seeing something negative from a positive perspective ❏
c) what you do to old photographs ❏
d) introducing change management. ❏

8. When I am in a difficult situation:
a) I blame other people ❏
b) I don't do anything ❏
c) I take responsibility and choose how to respond ❏
d) I think only about my difficulty constantly. ❏

9. I'm not a confident person, so:
a) I buy more and more books on increasing my self-confidence ❏
b) I need to work at changing myself more ❏
c) I cannot do anything about it ❏
d) I will become increasingly insecure as I get older. ❏

10. When I don't feel motivated:
a) I think only about my past failures ❏
b) I eat more ❏
c) I pity myself for a whole week ❏
d) I make myself do something ❏

CHAPTER 6

Manage your relationships successfully

Introduction

*'The simple act of paying positive attention
to people has a great deal to do with
productivity.'*

Tom Peters (1942–), American writer on business management.

You are called upon to manage yourself, but a significant part of your working life will be with colleagues. How can you manage your relationships with them?

In this chapter we will look at the importance of:

- Building good rapport and trust
- Listening more carefully
- Asserting yourself
- Managing conflict
- Managing your boss so you can work well with them
- Motivating your staff: a significant part of your work is to focus on others, to develop their skills
- Not neglecting family and friends

Build good rapport

For me, the key to establishing good rapport with people – a sense of mutual respect, trust and understanding – is to listen to them.

As a manager, you will need to do a lot of listening: to your boss as they direct your work, to colleagues as you talk about your work, in meetings as you discuss a range of subjects and make decisions, as you interview staff, solve problems and use the phone.

There are many reasons why listening is difficult:

● We tend to focus on what we want to say; by contrast, listening demands that our concentration is on someone else as we follow the sequence of their thoughts
● The person we're listening to may speak unclearly, too fast or repeat themselves
● The person we're listening to may be a non-native speaker and so does not speak in standard English
● We were probably not taught to listen. I vaguely remember school lessons trying to teach us reading, writing and speaking but I don't think I was ever taught to listen (or maybe I wasn't listening during those lessons!)

But listening is a really valuable skill. Have you ever felt really burdened by something and opened your heart to someone else? At the end you feel relieved and can say, 'Thank you for listening.'

The importance of listening

Listening:

● Focuses on the other person. Often when someone else is talking, we're focusing on thinking about what we are going to say as a reply
● Values the person you are listening to as an individual in their own right. This will help you understand why they are working or speaking as they are
● Helps you understand the point at which a person is. For example, if you are trying to sell something to customers,

you want to build a good relationship with them. By listening, you will discern who is interested and who is not, so you can use your time more valuably and concentrate on the more likely potential clients

- Encourages you to ask the right questions. As you focus on the other person, you will want to know more. We can distinguish:
  - Closed questions: ones that can be answered by a straight 'Yes' or 'No': 'Was the project late?' 'Yes.' 'Will you be able to give me the figures by 5 pm?' 'No.'
  - Open questions: ones that get people talking. Open questions begin with *why, how, who, when, where, what*. 'Why do you think the project is running late?' 'Because we didn't plan enough time for the extra work the customer now wants.'
- Means that you do not listen only to the words a colleague is speaking: you can perceive their response to what you are saying by being sensitive to their body language and tone of voice
- Allows you to 'listen between the lines', to become aware of any underlying messages that the speaker isn't able to verbalize
- Allows you to distinguish between facts and opinions. You will hear both, and you can discern what is objective information and what are the subjective thoughts on such information. You are then in a position to evaluate what has been said
- Enables you to gather information so that you can solve problems and make decisions more effectively
- Builds trust between people: you show that you are genuinely interested in them. This forms the basis to help you work well with them. Listening often improves relationships
- Offers an opportunity to develop more all-round relationships. For example. if a colleague says, 'I'm off on holiday tomorrow,' you can either ignore that signal (but ignoring it is possibly slightly rude), or you can use that as a hint that he or she wants to tell you more about themselves: 'Great, where are you going to?' 'Hong Kong'. You can then

remember to ask them, 'How was Hong Kong?' when you next see them

● Can resolve disagreements. If colleagues are in conflict with one another, listening to and understanding the opinions of either, or both, sides – whilst not necessarily agreeing with them – is an important first step in settling a disagreement

● Helps you understand people better. As you listen carefully to someone, you will discover more about that person: what is important to him or her, how they think and what they are feeling. Having such knowledge helps you work better with them, even if you don't like them or agree with their opinions

---

Susie was angry

Susie was angry. She worked late every evening to complete her tasks in the project but she felt her work was not appreciated or valued. It was only when a new colleague, Jan, started to work alongside her that something happened. Jan was concerned less about herself and her own work (which she did well) and more about her colleague – she cared enough to stop and listen to Susie. Susie was in tears as she poured out her heart to Jan, telling her about the real pressures she was working under. At the end of their conversation Susie told Jan, 'Thanks for listening. You're the first person I've been able to talk to about these things.' Having someone to talk to who truly listened to Susie really helped her, and she started to feel better.

Tips on better listening

Here are some ways to help you improve your listening skills:

● Be responsible. Realize that listening is an active skill and as such is hard work. Concentrate. For example, when I meet someone for the first time, I listen particularly attentively to catch their name. If I think I've heard it accurately, I'll say it back to them, e.g. 'Great to meet you, Nick!' If I didn't hear their name properly, I'll say, 'I'm sorry I didn't quite catch your name' or ask (if it is unusual to me and seems difficult to spell), 'Could you spell that for me please?'

- Focus on the other person, not yourself. Don't be tempted to interrupt the other person while he or she is talking. Stop and really listen to what the other person is saying. Make eye contact with them. Notice their body language. Be interested in them. Rephrase what they've said in your own way to help you clarify the meaning in your own mind. For example, 'So what you're really saying is that we should have put in place more effective monitoring controls.' Such a rephrasing process is called 'reflective listening'
- Be willing to accept the reasoning and opinions of others as valid. Be willing to acknowledge that you may make false assumptions and may have prejudices
- Be flexible in your response. If you are truly focused on the other person rather than on yourself, you will have a variety of responses available to you
- Discern the main points of what is being said. Speakers may or may not structure their argument well. Often, in informal talks or meetings it can be difficult to distinguish between, for example, facts, opinions, examples and ideas. It is important to try to work out the speaker's main point(s)
- Do your best to remain attentive, even if the other person is not; do not become distracted
- Write down in note form if you need to remember what a speaker is saying and you might otherwise forget it. Making notes can help you concentrate and avoid the sense that 'things go in one ear and out of the other'
- Don't be afraid of silence. Silence is part of a conversation. It can be:
  - A junction: which way will a conversation turn?
  - A time to catch up and digest what has been said
  - An opportunity for the other person to express their thoughts further
  - An opportunity to reflect on what has been said

At his interview, Harry was asked about which management style he adopted. Wisely he responded that he had several, to suit different occasions, the people he is managing and the tasks they are doing, rather than having a 'one-size-fits-all' approach.

So at times he said his style is democratic, involving the whole team in the decision-making process. He uses this especially in change-management situations when he wants the team to feel and be committed to change. At other times, particularly when dealing with very urgent matters, he is directional and simply has to tell people what to do ('The customer has changed his mind and wants new figures by 3 pm today'). He added that that wasn't his preferred style, however, preferring to give responsibility to his team members, together with training, support and clear instructions and trusting them to get on with the tasks using their own good judgment.

Assert yourself

Respect is two-way in a relationship and so it is important that colleagues show respect towards you as well as you showing respect to them.

Assertive communication is different from:

- Being passive: letting other people treat you badly
- Being aggressive: forcefully insisting on your own rights and treating others badly

Being assertive means that you will:

- Respect others' rights as well as your own and be fair to yourself as well as other people
- Be proactive rather than reactive; prepare well and be flexible. Sometimes you will need to be firm; at other times you need to be more restrained
- Focus on people's behaviour, not criticizing them or ignoring their identity
- Set boundaries
- Communicate firmly and confidently. At times you will need to be courageous and stand up for what you believe is right

We can consider assertiveness in two areas: saying no to further commitments – see Chapter 7 – and managing conflict.

Manage conflict

At times you are bound to meet conflict. Trust breaks down. Personalities clash. Each department wants to avoid the most cutbacks or wants a bigger slice of the budget.

Deal with conflict quickly; tackle the issues. Don't be cautious and fearful about speaking directly and clearly about difficulties.

I've found the books *Difficult Conversations: How to Discuss What Matters Most* (by Douglas Stone, Sheila Heen and Bruce Patton; Michael Joseph, 1999) and *The Peacemaker: A Biblical Guide to Resolving Personal Conflict* (by Ken Sande; Baker Books, 1991) very useful. The following is based on what those authors helpfully suggest:

- Distinguish the incident – what's happening/happened – from feelings about the incident. Consider separately: ·
- The incident – someone said something; someone is to blame. Try to focus on the real issue. Remain calm. Listen closely. Ask open questions. Understand other people's interests as well as your own
- Feelings about the incident, e.g. anger, hurt
- The identity of the person. Sometimes a person's identity, including their own self-worth, will feel threatened. Calmly affirm your respect for them
- Intervene sooner rather than later, i.e. don't let the situation become out of control
- Listen until the other person feels heard and you discover the core issue
- Discern and respect your colleague's point of view and intentions, even though you may disagree with them
- Look at the issue in a positive way; it can be helpful to refer to the values of your company or organization
- Treat your colleague with respect
- Do what you can to resolve the issue and maintain the relationship if possible: prepare and evaluate possible creative solutions to agree on the way forward

Manage your boss

The way you handle your boss is crucial. You need to understand what kind of person they are (e.g. what is important to them and their strengths and weaknesses) and how they work. Then you can adapt your style of working to suit them. Some bosses want a clear written statement of the facts of the case before a meeting; others may want you to give them the facts at the meeting. Some prefer a one-page summary; others a long, detailed report. Some prefer to communicate by phone, others by email.

TIP *How you handle your boss is crucial: you need to know what kind of person they are and how they work and then adapt your style to suit them.*

- Discuss priorities with your boss and make decisions with them. Discuss what they want you to do, especially if they continue to give you task after task. Agree on your goals and then, when they give you an additional task, discuss with them whether that achieves the agreed goal or not. If necessary, give them the responsibility of making the decision: 'Actually, I'm working on [this project] now: what do you want me to do?' Learn to say no where necessary
- If you can see a problem that is likely to happen, alert your boss sooner rather than later, so that he/she is aware of it and can act accordingly before the matter becomes serious
- Discuss expectations with your boss. Don't assume you know what they want and that they know what you want
- Fill in the gaps in a supportive way. One boss I had was a poor communicator but I knew what he was trying to say, so in meetings I was able to express it more clearly than he could. In a meeting, if your boss cannot remember the details, then supply them. At the end of a meeting, summarize what you have to do. If your boss is not decisive

and you know what the right decision is, help them along: 'We should do this, because ...'
- Focus on what you can do to move things forward: 'We can deliver the order to China on time if Kate helps us. Shall I ask her?' [rather than: 'We'll miss the deadline to deliver the order to China unless you ask Kate to help us']
- Don't come to your boss only with a problem; come with the problem and one or two possible solutions. You are closer to the issues; it is a better use of your time and your boss's if you do so: 'This is the problem ... and I think we could do either ... or ...'
- Prove that you are trustworthy in small things and your boss will delegate more to you. If you make a promise to complete something by a certain time, make sure you keep that promise

Dealing with an incompetent boss

Some bosses see themselves as important and perfect and they don't like to think their authority is being undermined. But the reality is that some bosses do not have the knowledge or skills to fulfil their jobs well. In fact, none of us is perfect and no-one knows all the answers. So realize that your boss has strengths and weaknesses. Here are some suggested tactics:

- Point out errors indirectly and tactfully. At times it may be appropriate to say, 'You may not have realized, but ...' or 'I'm sure it was an inadvertent error'
- Check your facts are accurate before criticizing your boss
- Discuss the difficulty and possible ways forward with a trusted colleague or friend who will keep the matter confidential
- Try all you can to avoid being disloyal to your boss when you are with colleagues
- As a last resort, go to your boss's boss

Motivate your staff

It's Thursday afternoon and members of your team have, it seems, stopped working and are discussing tonight's football match. You try to get them back to work, but fail. And it's like that all too often. How can you motivate your staff?

Someone who is well motivated is positive, does their job well and enthusiastically and wants more responsibility. Such a person can boost the morale of colleagues and help them work well. On the other hand, someone who is poorly motivated will not seem to care about their work. They may turn up late for work and complain about small details. Such a person can have a negative effect on other colleagues.

Here are some tips to motivate staff:

- Show your trust in your team members by giving them greater responsibility and delegating more of your own work to them (see Chapter 3)
- Allow them to become experts in an area. Early in my career of dictionary writing, my boss saw my interest and skill at checking long verb entries in a dictionary (e.g. *do, go, get, make, set*), gave me the responsibility of editing these and so I became an expert in explaining English idioms (e.g. *do up*, 'renovate', *get out of*, 'evade a duty')
- Delegate whole tasks where possible. I once delegated three different aspects of the same task to three different people, who all felt frustrated and unfulfilled at the thirds they were given
- Delegate work clearly. Do colleagues know exactly what is expected of them? Vague and unclear instructions not only demotivate colleagues but also waste time
- Show that you value them. Listen to them. Be available for them to bring their concerns to you. Understand them. Try to find out 'what makes them tick'. Talk *to* them (not *at* them). Find out what interests them outside work
- Show that you value their work. Affirm them and recognize their achievements:
  - In public by praising them in front of their colleagues and/or
  - In private, affirming they are a valuable member of the team. Even saying, 'Thank you, you did that well' is an acknowledgement of gratitude

- Bring in food or buy each of them little treats, e.g. chocolate.
- Issue certificates for achievements: it's amazing how competitive colleagues can be for a certificate
- Don't criticize individuals in public or in front of colleagues
- Don't remain aloof. At one organization I worked at, I didn't mix socially with colleagues and therefore had difficulties later. I learnt from my mistake and altered my behaviour in later jobs
- Work generally at good communications. Communicate with colleagues, both formally in meetings and informally as you walk down the corridor for a coffee break. By 'communicating' I mean *speaking*, not emailing or texting! Spend time informally talking to people (and remember their names). Don't look down on people. I recall a comment on a teacher friend years ago: 'He even talks to the cleaners.' If you need something in a hurry, you will already hopefully have built up a store of goodwill
- In group meetings, focus on building a team, constantly affirming the team's commitment to reach the goal and recognize their progress on the way
- Encourage uncooperative colleagues to try a new system if they are reluctant to follow it. Or even ask them if they could suggest new ways of solving a problem
- Know their strengths and weaknesses. Try as far as possible to make sure they are 'round pegs in round holes' rather than 'square pegs in round holes'. This may be difficult as there will always be aspects of work (perhaps unexciting administrative tasks) that it seems no-one wants to do
- Focus on specific, measurable and achievable (SMART) actions, not on vague ideas: look back at Chapter 1
- Try to remain positive, even when doing a structured task. That structured task is a significant part of a bigger picture
- Offer coaching and opportunities for development to all colleagues in areas they need further help in
- If you have come to the end of a project, celebrate that fact by all going out for a meal

- Involve colleagues in decision making and setting budgets. If your company or organization is undergoing a period of change, then involve your colleagues at an earlier, rather than a later, stage, explaining the issues to them. They will then feel valued
- Encourage them to make positive suggestions as to how to work more effectively
- Ask a trusted colleague to come with you to a meeting of other managers. Let them accompany you for a few meetings and then gradually delegate some of the responsibilities to them
- Be aware of colleagues who moan constantly, who find minor fault in everything. Keep focused on what you want to achieve and avoid becoming distracted and dragged down by the moaners
- Do all you can to ensure their work is interesting and challenging. No-one likes boring repetitive tasks. Make sure your colleagues' work contains at least some interesting tasks that will stretch them

Earning respect

Colin was promoted. He stood out among all the other colleagues as the most competent member of the team, so it was natural that he was chosen to be the team leader.

However, when Colin was promoted to that role, things did not go well. In his inexperience in leading, he thought that if he just told his team members to do something then they would do it immediately. He also tried to introduce too many changes too quickly. Talking it through with his mentor, he was told that first he had to earn respect from the individuals under him. He learnt the hard way that he had to demonstrate his leadership skills and introduce changes more gradually (his mentor had said, 'Go for "Evolution" not "Revolution"'), and then the team would be ready to commit themselves to his vision.

Don't neglect other relationships in your life

It is important not to neglect other relationships in your life such as family and friends. If you have children, make time for them. The story is told of a successful top executive who felt he had 'wasted' a day fishing with his son. The son, however, saw that as one of the best days of his life: his dad had spent a whole day with him. For more on other relationships outside work, see Chapter 7.

> *'No-one was ever heard to say on their death-bed, "I wish I had spent more time at the office".'*
>
> Rob Parsons, *The Sixty Minute Father*

Summary

In this chapter we have considered practical ways of managing the relationships in your life. Keys include:

- Respecting and valuing people
- Listening to colleagues better
- Building trust
- Managing conflict professionally
- Asserting yourself: knowing when to be firm and when to be more restrained
- Communicating well
- Knowing your boss's emphases, strengths and weaknesses, and style of working, and adapting your style and work accordingly
- Making time for family and friends

Exercise

1 How good a listener do friends and colleagues say you are? Choose one aspect of better listening, e.g. making better eye contact or stopping interrupting someone, and practice it until it becomes automatic.

2 Think about your boss. What are their emphases, strengths and weaknesses? Their style of working? How can you better adapt your style to work more productively with them?

3 Think about an area of conflict at work. What can you do more to listen to people's different viewpoints and distinguish the incident from feelings about the incident? What questions of identity are at stake? What are the next steps for you to undertake?

Fact-check (answers at the back)

1. Relationships at work are:
   a) very annoying ❏
   b) non-existent: I just shout at my colleagues all the time ❏
   c) all very easy ❏
   d) difficult at times, so I need to work at them ❏

2. As an aspect of communicating, listening is:
   a) essential ❏
   b) nice to have, if you have the time ❏
   c) a waste of time ❏
   d) a luxury ❏

3. Listening:
   a) makes colleagues proud ❏
   b) destroys people ❏
   c) builds trust ❏
   d) increases self-confidence ❏

4. Listening helps you:
   a) focus on yourself ❏
   b) understand people better ❏
   c) gossip more easily ❏
   d) disagree more knowledgeably ❏

5. Asserting yourself means:
   a) being forceful and aggressive ❏
   b) being firm and fair to yourself and others ❏
   c) letting others treat you badly ❏
   d) becoming more confident towards others ❏

6. The way to handle conflict is:
   a) shout more loudly ❏
   b) solve the problem as quickly as possible ❏
   c) listen so that you understand the issues ❏
   d) what? we don't have any conflict here ❏

7. The key to managing your boss well is to:
   a) know what is important to them, their strengths and weaknesses and their style of working ❏
   b) work without paying any attention to them ❏
   c) criticize them disloyally in front of others ❏
   d) praise them constantly ❏

8. A key to motivating staff is:
   a) never delegate any work to them ❏
   b) shout more loudly at them ❏
   c) let them go home early ❏
   d) give them greater responsibility. ❏

9. A further key to motivating staff is:
   a) recognize their achievements ❏
   b) constantly point out their mistakes ❏
   c) give work only to colleagues you like ❏
   d) never involve them in decision making. ❏

10. As regards my family:
    a) I think about them all the time when I am supposed to be concentrating on my work ❏
    b) they see me at weekends and on holiday: isn't that enough? ❏
    c) I don't know who they are ❏
    d) I make time for them ❏

CHAPTER 7

Manage stress thoroughly

Introduction

Stress can affect not only our work but also our whole life. Stress occurs where our body is called upon to do more than it can usually cope with.

Just as stress reveals itself in different ways in different people, so each one of us also needs to develop our own personal strategies for dealing with stress.

At times we all feel a little overwhelmed: answering emails, managing people, teams, policies and procedures, projects ... How can you avoid getting stressed out by everything?

In this chapter we will look at:

- What stress is
- How stress shows itself
- How to deal with stress practically, e.g. by being more assertive and saying no
- Ways of adjusting your lifestyle to cope with stress

Acknowledge stress will come

Acknowledge that stress will come. In fact, a little stress may be good for you – some people work best with the pressure of an immediate deadline. However, if stress becomes out of control it can become a problem. Be alert to signs of stress in yourself.

Recognize stress

Times when stress may come:

● Difficult relationships	● Giving a presentation
● Financial problems	● Examinations
● Health issues	● Unrealistic deadlines
● Moving home	● Feeling undervalued
● Bereavement	● Traumatic events
● Starting a new job	● The threat of redundancy

Signs of stress include:

● Physical symptoms:	● Loss of appetite
● Inability to sleep properly	● Repetitive nervous actions such
● Aches, pains, tightness of	as nail-biting
muscles, headaches	● Using alcohol, tobacco, caffeine,
● Upset stomach, nausea	etc.
● Difficulty swallowing	● Putting on weight

Other symptoms:

● Becoming annoyed easily	● Constant feelings of
● Feeling like screaming	disappointment
● Finding yourself in tears	● Constant worry and anxiety
● Feeling helpless as things get out	Constant frustration with
of control	colleagues and work
● Isolating yourself from others and	● Not thinking straight; distracted,
becoming absorbed with yourself,	confused
not wanting to discuss matters	● Putting off making decisions
with others	● Unable to concentrate
● Constant low energy levels	● Unable to relax
● Deep, cynical attitude to work	● Loss of perspective: little
● Feeling overwhelmed as if things	problems become large
are completely beyond your	● Micromanaging: exercising too
control	much control
● Feeling bad about yourself,	● Focusing on unimportant details
questioning your abilities	● Making mistakes

How to deal with stress

Recognize that for certain periods in your life you may need not to do certain things at all. For example, a few years ago I spent six weeks solidly writing a significant part of a dictionary and reduced all personal commitments to an absolute minimum. At the end of that six-week period, I began to take on other commitments again.

If it all gets too much, visit your doctor. In the meantime, here are some ways of dealing with stress.

Communicate with colleagues more personally

Communicate more face to face with people. Getting to know people more deeply means more all-round relationships; you can defuse stress by talking to people, not by emailing them. Before the age of email, colleagues would get up from their desks and talk to a colleague. Of course, I'm aware of the benefits of email, but sometimes old-fashioned methods work well too. Speak to colleagues on the phone, too. Telephoning someone is a better way of building a relationship with someone than email or text messaging.

Sixteen practical ways of dealing with stress

1 Build in regular patterns of exercise and breaks
2 If you are looking at a computer screen for a long time, take a short break (e.g. five to ten minutes) every hour
   ● Physical exercise helps, however brief. Try to get some fresh air during the working day
   ● Join a gym; play sport. During the first few years of my working life I pushed myself too hard and became ill. I had to learn to take regular exercise. So I made myself take regular walks around the block of houses where I live: I have been walking round the block normally twice a day for 25 years. I have variations: I find the occasional walk in a nearby park at lunch particularly helpful

- Build in regular times off. Don't overfill every moment of your 24 hours. For example, if you're busy for two weeks, make sure in week three you have some personal slack time. Look forward to regular time off. One colleague deliberately sets himself something special to look forward to every six weeks

3 Talk problems over with friends. Plan in times to meet with people you like, rather than these who will drain you and reduce your energy reserves. You can share good things in your life as well as difficulties. As the proverb says: 'A trouble shared is a trouble halved': it often helps to discuss your problems with someone else. As someone who has been self-employed for most of my working life, I have had to deliberately make regular times (for me, mostly over lunch) for appointments with friends and colleagues to discuss life and work issues. At times, I have made myself open up and express myself on personal issues with friends to seek their advice, awkward though such experiences are. Some accountability is good for us

4 Take yourself less seriously. Another proverb states that 'Laughter is the best medicine'. Laughing is an excellent remedy to restore good health and keep well

5 Eat and drink sensibly. You know the rules – apply them! You can't remain healthy in the long term on a diet of junk food, and drinking and smoking excessively

6 Switch the TV/computer off earlier and get more sleep: if you can wake up without an alarm clock, then you are getting enough sleep

7 Have a life outside work. Bring some balance to your life. The proverb 'All work and no play makes Jack a dull boy' is a true one: people who do not make time for leisure activities risk damaging their health, the quality of their work and/ or their personal relationships. We all need to take a break from work. Spend time with your partner, family or friends. Join a club. Volunteer to help others

- Take up a hobby that is not related to your work. Volunteer to help others. Do something regularly that is not related to your work. A friend works in industry in a high-level job, but is always back home to spend Friday evenings at his model-railway club. Having an interest outside work helps you unwind and relax

- Take holidays without feeling guilty ... and without all your electronic gadgets! Take up other activities and be reminded what it is like to be human. These will give you fresh motivation, creativity and renewed energy. I know you will come back to hundreds of emails: a colleague sets her return to work on a Thursday for that reason, so that she can clear her emails ready for the following Monday, however the time off will do you more good than a clear inbox.

8 Don't overcommit yourself by making promises you know you cannot keep. Be realistic

9 Cut out aspects of your job that you do not need to do. I once met a colleague who was working on four projects that were far beyond the scope of his work, so I told him to stop work on all of them. He was so far immersed in one of them that he had to complete it, but he realized he could drop the other three

10 Discuss matters with your boss. Can you be relieved of some areas of work? Can some activities be delayed?

11 Focus on what you can do, and do that – a little is better than nothing

12 Talk things over with a coach or mentor. They can help you develop your career and work through the relevant issues (see Chapter 2)

13 Learn relaxation techniques for your body: many people find yoga helpful. Simple deep-breathing techniques can work wonders – focus on the positive in your mind.

14 Listen to music – whichever style helps you unwind and energizes you

15 Evoke the senses. When I am stressed, I try to think of one of two situations: the gentle lapping of water on a shore of a lake in Austria; sipping a cold cola in a restaurant in France. Both of these situations are memorable to me because they evoke the senses. What memories could you use?

16 Try not to let your work life affect your personal life. Do your best to leave work behind when you finish work. It is important to cultivate friendships with people outside work

Try to spend some time every day doing something you enjoy.

 TIP *Don't overcommit yourself by making promises you know you cannot keep. Be realistic.*

Under pressure

Elaine was under pressure. She was actually doing two jobs, each taking up three days a week. She was getting very stressed and knew she could not continue doing such work indefinitely. She told her manager Ron at both informal one-to-ones and at the formal half-yearly appraisal she expressed the frustration she felt in her work. Unfortunately, Ron said he would act to resolve the difficulty, but over a period of several months nothing happened. He awkwardly avoided eye contact with her whenever they passed in the corridor.

Things turned out better, however, when Ron moved on and he was replaced by Sheila. Her motto was 'under promise and over deliver' so, for example, when she said she would check the financial data for the previous month by the end of week three in the following month, invariably she had completed it by the end of week two. Within a few weeks of Sheila taking on Ron's role, she had sorted out Elaine's work patterns to everyone's satisfaction. Soon Elaine began to enjoy her work again.

Learn to say no

Do you find it difficult to say no? Perhaps it's because you want to avoid confrontation, or because you want to be liked and appreciated, or you enjoy the feeling of being needed. However, no-one can do everything, so you will be doing yourself (and your work) a favour if you only take on work you can cope with. Here are some tips to help you say no:

● Be aware that others may be trying to make you feel guilty if you were to say no

- Say no sooner rather than later. Generally speaking, the more you delay something, the more difficult it could become to say no. Be more assertive
- Work at good relationships (see also Chapter 6) generally so that you know people well enough that they will not feel offended if you say no
- Be clear about your own role and priorities. Have these constantly in mind. Is what you are being asked to do a significant distraction from that? If so, then say no
- Be aware of what you have been trained to do. You may need to refuse to participate in a task or project that you have not been trained for. Other people in the team may be more able to do certain projects
- Be aware of your own values. If you are being asked to go beyond these (e.g. if you are asked to lie for your boss), then say no clearly
- Consider the effects of taking on further tasks. Would undertaking them lead to delays in fulfilling your existing commitments?
- Be reasonable towards yourself: you have a right to say no
- Practise making such responses as: 'I'd love to help, but I'm already fully committed/stretched.' You could add: 'I hope you find someone else who can help you.' 'I'm fairly busy but if you want to send me a short email letting me know exactly what you want and how you feel I could help, I'll look at it.'
- Suggest an alternative: 'I'm not really sure I'm the right person to deal with this. Why don't you ask ...?'
- If your boss is asking you to take on further responsibilities, put the onus back on him or her by asking which activity he or she wants you to tackle
- Discuss what precisely needs to be done
- Compromise on what needs to be done; negotiate: 'I'll cover your shift if you do mine on Saturday', but make sure they do so
- Don't apologize; don't say, 'I'll come back to you later if I find I have time,' because that adds to your already committed to-do list. Ask your colleague to come back to you later (fortunately, they probably won't). Or you could say, 'You could see if I'm less busy next week'

Saying no to further commitments

Bob felt flattered to be asked to join a committee to look at succession planning, but he wasn't sure. He felt he was already fully stretched and that a further commitment might just be too much. Over lunch with Mike, the chairman, they discussed the responsibilities of the role, which confirmed Bob's concerns, so he said no at that time. However, he added that he thought it likely his other commitments would lessen six months later when he was due to have an assistant who could cover some of his responsibilities. Sure enough, six months later, Mike asked Bob again and then, with some fresh capacity because he then had his assistant, Bob accepted the offer.

Summary

In this chapter we have looked at stress and seen that it will affect us. We have considered how it might show itself and different ways of dealing with it. Key ways include:

- communicating with colleagues
- learning to say no
- living a healthy lifestyle
- having a life outside of work

Exercise

1 How does stress show itself in your life?
2 Think of a time when you have been stressed. How well did you cope with it?
3 How, on reflection, could you have coped with it better?
4 What can you do practically to reduce the stress you know you will face in the future?
5 Consider now, in advance, strategies for saying no to requests that you know will come in your work.
6 What three things have you learnt from reading this masterclass?

Fact-check

1. Stress affects:
   a) no-one: what is the problem? ❑
   b) everyone: that is why we need to consider it ❑
   c) a few weak people ❑
   d) people who have now left the company ❑

2. Everyone suffers stress:
   a) happily ❑
   b) in different ways ❑
   c) in the same way ❑
   d) 24 hours a day, 365 days a year ❑

3. One way of dealing with stress is:
   a) to shout more loudly all the time ❑
   b) quit my job ❑
   c) become even more introverted ❑
   d) use email less and speak to people more ❑

4. Regular exercise:
   a) is a waste of time ❑
   b) helps reduce stress ❑
   c) is all I think about all the time ❑
   d) makes me even angrier ❑

5. Talking over difficulties with friends is:
   a) impossible, as I haven't got any friends I can talk to ❑
   b) a silly idea ❑
   c) very helpful ❑
   d) all I do ❑

6. Having finished this masterclass, I will spend more time:
   a) compiling more to-do lists but never using them ❑
   b) planning my time more effectively ❑
   c) reading more books on being a manager ❑
   d) eating in the canteen ❑

7. Thinking time is:
   a) useful to help you become even more effective as a manager ❑
   b) wasted ❑
   c) all I do ❑
   d) nice if you have the time ❑

8. An important way to build better relationships is to:
   a) talk more ❑
   b) be silent more ❑
   c) listen more ❑
   d) eat more ❑

9. I realize I need to work harder at:
   a) only work relationships ❑
   b) only personal relationships ❑
   c) my own life ❑
   d) all relationships in life, both at work and outside work ❑

10. Since reading this masterclass, I feel:
    a) even more arrogant because I never really needed it ❑
    b) more equipped to manage myself better ❑
    c) overwhelmed by even more to do ❑
    d) nothing at all ❑

7 × 7

1 Seven key ideas

- Know when – what time of day and which day of the week – you work best. Protect that time as far as possible for your key work that requires most concentration; don't say to yourself that you will just get a few smaller things out of the way first.
- Listen better to build trust in relationships.
- When planning, remember that the time spent doing admin is likely to be far more than you think.
- Don't wait until you feel motivated or you will wait forever. Push yourself.
- How you handle your boss is crucial. You need to know what kind of person they are and how they work, and then adapt your style to suit them.
- Don't overcommit yourself or make promises you know you cannot keep. Be realistic in your expectations of yourself ... and others.
- Stay fresh: don't stagnate; keep changing and making progress. Continue to dream dreams.

2 Seven best resources

- Stephen Covey, *Seven Habits of Highly Effective People* (Simon & Schuster, 2004). First published in 1989, this is a highly influential management book.
- http://www.businessballs.com/ – Website offering fresh ideas on business training and organizational development.
- http://www.mindtools.com/ – Website helping users learn practical skills to become an effective manager and leader, e.g. on problem solving, decision making, time management and communication skills.

- http://www.businessknowhow.com/ – Website providing guidance on business ideas, marketing, leadership, etc.
- Brian Harris, *The Tortoise Usually Wins: Biblical Reflections on Quiet Leadership for Reluctant Leaders* (Paternoster, 2013). Written from a Christian perspective, exploring quiet leadership from the viewpoint of those who by temperament are quiet, reluctant leaders.
- http://www.peterfuda.com/ – Website of Dr Peter Fuda, a leading authority on business and leadership transformation.
- http://www.ted.com/ – TED talks: a non-profit organization with the aim of spreading ideas, especially in the form of short, powerful talks (18 minutes or less).

3 Seven things to avoid

- Poor time management: not delegating enough; having unrealistic expectations of yourself and others.
- Micromanaging: managing a task or people (including yourself) in a way that is too detailed. Concentrate on the big picture.
- Not being focused: doing too many things badly.
- Poor relationships: focusing on wanting people to like you rather than being an effective team leader.
- Being overcome by stress too often.
- Thinking that your job is to keep things running smoothly rather than initiating change.
- Not regularly reviewing what you do against clear priorities and objectives.

4 Seven inspiring people

- Tony Buzan, inventor of mind maps who has developed techniques to help people think more creatively. See http://www.thinkbuzan.com.
- Stephen Covey, for his influential book *Seven Habits of Highly Effective People*.

- Daniel Goleman, for his significant books *Emotional Intelligence* (Bantam Books, 1995; Bloomsbury, 1996) and *Focus: the hidden driver of excellence* (Harper Collins USA, 2013; Bloomsbury, 2013)
- John Kotter, for his work on leading change management, e.g. *Leading Change* (Harvard Business School, 1996). See also http://www.kotterinternational.com.
- Edward de Bono, for his work on creative and lateral thinking, e.g. *Six Thinking Hats* (Little Brown and Company, 1985). See also www.debonogroup.com.
- John Maxwell, writer and speaker on leadership. See http://www.johnmaxwell.com.
- Mike Bechtle, expert on practical communication. See http://www.mikebechtle.com/.

5 Seven great quotes

- 'The best preparation for good work tomorrow is to do good work today.' Elbert (Green) Hubbard (1856–1915), American businessman, writer, and printer.
- 'Remember that time is money.' Benjamin Franklin (1706–90), American statesman, scientist, and author.
- 'Any committee is only as good as the most knowledgeable, determined and vigorous person on it. There must be somebody who provides the flame.' Claudia (Lady Bird) Johnson (1912–2007), widow of former US President, Lyndon B Johnson.
- 'In an information-rich world, the wealth of information means a dearth of something else: a scarcity of whatever it is that information consumes. What information consumes is rather obvious: it consumes the attention of its recipients. Hence a wealth of information creates a poverty of attention and a need to allocate that attention efficiently among the overabundance of information sources that might consume it.' Herbert A. Simon (1916–2001), American psychologist and economist.

- 'The simple act of paying positive attention to people has a great deal to do with productivity.' Tom Peters (1942–), American writer on business management.
- 'Success is that old ABC – ability, breaks and courage.' Charles Luckman (1909–99), American architect.
- 'No-one was ever heard to say on their death-bed, "I wish I had spent more time at the office"' Rob Parsons, founder Care for the Family, *The Sixty Minute Father.*

6 Seven things to do today

- Check your progress through the day by looking at your to-do list.
- At the end of today, write tomorrow's to-do list; at the end of your working week, plan the major tasks you want to achieve each day of the following week.
- Put in your diary time to think, or better still put in your diary three times to think. Two may drop out, but make sure you keep one of them.
- Put in your diary every month a review to check your progress in your short-, medium- and long-term goals.
- Put in your diary time with family and friends and breaks (holidays).
- Begin to tackle a major task you have been putting off. The first task may be to list some of the things you need to do. If so, begin to do that, putting realistic dates by each step. In other words, do something, however small. Every step is a step forward.
- Try to plan in some time every day doing something you enjoy.

7 Seven trends for tomorrow

- Administration will constantly try to take over your life. Do what you need to do, but make sure you do at least the minimum.

- Technology will constantly produce innovations. Make sure technology saves you time.
- Thinking time will get squeezed out: *make* time to think.
- Increasingly large organizations will develop as companies merge and buy one another out: know your role; play to your strengths as far as you can.
- Unimportant things will try to take over your life: make sure you set priorities and manage well the time you can control.
- The number of meetings will go on increasing: know the purpose of every meeting you go to; make sure the actions are well written up so that you and your colleagues know clearly what actions to take and by when.
- More and more communications will be undertaken by email. Remember the more personal ways of communicating in person or by phone.

PART 2

Your Time Management Masterclass

Introduction

People have been writing about time management for at least 800 years. Yet most of us still find it virtually impossible to clear our desk by the end of each day. We all over-commit, struggle to prioritize and allow ourselves to be distracted. Of course, times change, but finding enough time in the day to get everything done has always been a challenge. When St Marher wrote in 1225 that 'Time and tide wait for no man', he did not have phones ringing or emails pinging. But he clearly recognized the problem we all have getting things done. After all, medieval monks, like the rest of us, enjoyed a chat. And, of course, household chores like shopping were far less simple than they are today!

Much more recently, Douglas Adams (author of *The Hitchhiker's Guide to the Galaxy*) wrote that he loved 'the whoosh deadlines made as they rushed by'. In other words, he found it almost impossible to start a task until it was almost too late to complete it on time. I bet you can relate to that phenomenon – I know I can.

CHAPTER 8

It all starts with you

In this chapter we're going to think about you. You are the most important person in the whole time management equation. Furthermore, you are different from me and everyone else because each of us is unique. No two people have the same mix of ability, aspiration, interests and experience.

We'll start by encouraging you to reflect on where you find yourself in the world today and where you plan to go tomorrow. Life is, as they say, a journey and in this chapter we're going to map the next stage of the trip. A simple principle we need to explore is that the more you want to do something, the faster and better you'll do it.

We also need to take a look at how you work best. Are you a lark or an owl? Does your boss give you the freedom to plan your time or does work seem an endless treadmill? You might feel in control, or you might feel completely overwhelmed, in which case we need to help you dig yourself out from your work pile.

In this chapter you're going to find answers to three questions:

- Where do I really want to go?
- How do I work best?
- What's holding me back?

Where are you going?

In one of the most famous speeches of the 20th century, civil rights activist Martin Luther King said, 'I have a dream.' He was a powerful speaker because he had such a clear vision of what he wanted to bring about: the end of racial discrimination in the USA. His speeches are still remembered, even though he died almost 50 years ago.

Political campaigners are often single-minded like Martin Luther King. They devote all their time and energy to a single cause, often regardless of the risk. You, on the other hand, may not have a cause you feel strongly enough to die for, but that doesn't mean you cannot be passionate, single-minded and determined. Only when you know what you want from life can you go out and get it.

> **'You never achieve success unless you like what you are doing.'**
>
> Dale Carnegie

Define your dream

Your dream is every bit as important to you as Martin Luther King's dream was to him. No one person's dream is better than another's. All dreams are equal. What you need to have, though, is a crystal-clear vision of your dream. It needs to be something that you can see, feel and know – deep down – you can achieve.

Although it's good to be ambitious, your dream also needs to be realistic. Very few people achieve immense wealth, global fame or rise through the ranks to lead a large organization. The truth is that few actually want to. In fact, some people simply want to stay as they are, but feel more in control of their lives.

Ask yourself these questions and start to define your dream.

- In five/ten years' time what do I want to spend most of my time doing?
- What appeals most to me about this?
- What path do I need to follow to realize my dream?

The length and difficulty of the journey to your dream will depend on its magnitude and complexity. As you can see from the case study, Wendy took her ambition one step at a time. She might eventually become a head teacher, but sensibly she started by training to work in the classroom. Working with youngsters was her dream.

TIP *The sooner you can spend more time doing what you enjoy at work, the more motivated you will be and the more you will achieve.*

How do you work best?

We all work in different ways, and function best when in tune with our body clock. For example, you might:

- prefer to be outside in all weathers or enjoy always being indoors in the warm
- be happier as a member of a large team or prefer to work on your own
- feel more productive at 8 a.m. or at your best at midnight
- enjoy the freedom to decide what needs doing or perform well only once you have been given a detailed task list each morning.

Few of us have the luxury of total choice over how we work. Even the best jobs have less enjoyable aspects. If you were a bus driver, for example, you may have chosen the job because you enjoy driving and meeting people. Cleaning the bus at the end of the day or checking the oil are less pleasurable, but no less important. We all have to accept aspects of our work that we don't really enjoy. Some tasks you just have to get on and do.

A flexible working day

You will already know how you work best, although you might not have thought about how you can flex your working day to accommodate your body clock. If you're lucky, your company gives you the flexibility to start early or finish late, depending on your preference. Even if this is not possible, you can adapt your working routine so that you undertake the most important tasks when you are at your most alert.

Let's start by dividing the day into quarters. Then look at how differently a morning or afternoon person might choose to spend their day.

Time of day	Morning person (lark)	Afternoon person (owl)
Early morning	• Priority task	• Priority list for the day • Routine tasks
Late morning	• Secondary task	• Secondary task
Lunchtime		
Early afternoon	• Admin or meetings	• Admin or meetings
Late afternoon	• Routine tasks • Priority list for tomorrow	• Priority task

You'll see from the table that morning people:

● start the day with the most important task
● end the day listing the next day's priorities.

Evening people, however:

● start the day listing the day's priorities
● end the day with the most important task.

TIP *If you work best in the morning, try going in to work an hour early so you're in full flow when your colleagues arrive. Then take a long lunch break.*

Schedule your time

The last section introduced a couple of concepts we'll explore in more detail in Chapter 11. These are prioritizing tasks and breaking the day down into chunks.

Priority tasks are those that are most important to you right now. This might be because they are crucial to your job, or because you have been putting them off and the deadline is fast approaching. These are the tasks you focus on when most alert and able to give them your best.

Breaking the day into chunks is a great way to pace your working time. It makes it easier to work on one task at a time without worrying about what's being neglected, because you have scheduled your time and know what you'll be working on when.

There are two things you need to know if you are to schedule your time:

● how much time you have
● how long each task will take to complete.

A diary will enable you to set aside blocks of time for specific tasks. You will also need to give each task a time estimate. Keeping a timesheet will enable you to record how you actually spend your time. This is important as most people underestimate how long a task will take. They then feel they are very busy but not achieving much. Does that sound familiar to you? It certainly does to me!

Case study

Rupesh hated mornings. At university, life had been fine, but now he was expected to be in the office by nine. What's more, every morning seemed to start with an argument with his boss about what he had not finished the day before.

Rupesh worked in housing and his job was to investigate and respond to enquiries too complicated for colleagues on the help desk to answer straight away. The problem was that people expected to be called back the next morning with an answer, and he was always juggling tasks.

What Rupesh needed was a couple of hours a day to research the complicated cases and write them up without distraction. Starting the day off with a backlog was not helping anyone.

Rupesh discussed the problem with his manager, who agreed to let him come in at 10.30 in the morning and stay until 6.30 in the evening. This gave him some quality time after his colleagues had gone home and meant he could lie in each morning. Because he worked best late in the day, his productivity soared and so did his mood.

Understand what holds you back

If you've read any self-help books, you'll know that defining your dreams and vision for the future is important. You'll also know that what usually gets between you and achieving those dreams is you. The same applies to making best use of your time. To put it simply, good time management means doing what you consider important when you feel best able to do it.

Even if you work on your own, this can be difficult. The problem is that most of us are far too nice for our own good. Our work efficiency and effectiveness suffer because we allow other people to divert us from our priorities. In Chapter 12 we'll look at some techniques to help you avoid distraction, but in this chapter we're thinking about you. Two of the things that might be holding you back from managing your time well are lack of self-confidence and lack of motivation.

Boost self-confidence

If you doubt your ability or value, so will others. If, on the other hand, you have total self-belief, many people will take you at your word and assume that you can do everything you say. Many factors influence our level of self-confidence. You can boost your self-confidence by:

- knowing yourself and valuing the experiences that have shaped you
- recognizing that no one can be good at everything
- not comparing yourself with others, because you'll always focus on what they do better and overlook what you do better than them
- being assertive and not letting others push you around
- not taking criticism personally, but instead treating it as advice.

Boost self-motivation

We all need to be motivated to perform well in our job. A good employer will work hard to give you the clarity of role and support you need to do well. But you also need to be self-motivated. We are all different, and what, to some, might appear a dream job might look truly awful to someone else. Motivating yourself is easier if you:

- believe in what your organization does and consider it worth while
- have not grown bored with your job and keep finding new challenges to excite you
- treat yourself when you do something really well, or complete a task you don't enjoy
- are in control of your workload rather than feeling burdened by others.

Summary

In this chapter you were encouraged to think about your dreams and vision for your future. Only when you know where you want to go can you fully appreciate how your career can help you get there. Managing your time starts with being confident that you're doing the right thing and that, even when it's tough, the end result will make it all worth while.

We also looked at how you work best. Once you know the time of day when you are most effective, you'll appreciate the benefit of doing the most important tasks when you feel most able to cope with them. This means taking control of your working day and doing things in the order that suits you, rather than starting at the top of a list and working your way down it.

Personal factors can also get in the way of good time management. The better you feel about yourself the more you'll be able to assert yourself and feel in control of your work and life. You also need to be self-motivated by really believing in what you do for a living. When your job fits with your personal values you won't feel compromised.

Fact-check (answers at the back)

1. What is a key factor of time management?
   a) It's personal to each of us because we're all unique ❏
   b) It's simply a matter of all of us following the same processes ❏
   c) It's impossible to improve because life's like that ❏
   d) It's difficult because I am just too busy ❏

2. What is Martin Luther King best remembered for?
   a) Being really busy ❏
   b) Not really knowing what he was trying to achieve ❏
   c) Having a dream ❏
   d) Being a really nice guy who always made time for people ❏

3. How should you define your own dream or vision for your future?
   a) Remember what your mother said you should be aiming for ❏
   b) Be able to describe clearly your life as you want it to be in five years' time ❏
   c) Read lots of books and see what other people have done ❏
   d) Ask your friends what they think you should be doing ❏

4. How will you be most productive at work?
   a) By doing things you don't like ❏
   b) By feeling uncomfortable and out of your depth ❏
   c) By being passionate about your work, loving every minute ❏
   d) By being given no direction and left to find your own way ❏

5. If you like mornings but get tired after lunch, how should you start the day?
   a) By doing the most important thing you have to do ❏
   b) By making a list of the day's tasks ❏
   c) By chatting to colleagues ❏
   d) With a cooked breakfast ❏

6. What will happen if you break your working day down into four two-hour chunks?
   a) You'll find the time passes more quickly ❏
   b) Time will seem to drag ❏
   c) You'll constantly run out of time ❏
   d) You'll get more done because you are scheduling your day ❏

7. What's the best way to work out how long things take you to do?
a) Buy a stopwatch ❏
b) Keep a simple paper timesheet and record what you're doing each half hour ❏
c) Ask a colleague to keep an eye on you ❏
d) Download a sophisticated time-recording package on to your PC ❏

8. If you keep a record of how long tasks take, what will you soon be able to do?
a) Demand a pay rise ❏
b) Get promoted ❏
c) Accurately schedule your working day because you know how long you take to do things ❏
d) Pick up when other people are slacking ❏

9. How can you boost your self-confidence?
a) By dressing boldly in bright colours ❏
b) By avoiding conflict because it rocks your confidence ❏
c) By recognizing what you do well and focusing on doing it well ❏
d) By blowing the whistle on the office bully ❏

10. What's an effective way to be more motivated at work?
a) To believe in your organization and what it does ❏
b) To try to pass the day by thinking about your favourite hobby ❏
c) Keeping fit and exercising at lunchtime ❏
d) Being nice to your boss so that (s)he's nice to you ❏

CHAPTER 9

Understanding your job

Although you might lead a hectic social life, it's at work where time management is most likely to become an issue. There's a good reason for this. It's because at work you're being paid for your time and expertise.

We'll start by looking at your relationship with your employer. Get this right and you will feel more in control of your workload. Then we'll look at your job itself and its depth and breadth. Are you doing too much and, if so, why? We'll explore some techniques that will help you deal with this issue.

Finally, we'll look in more detail at the way we make decisions. Sitting on the fence not only hurts, but it also takes up time that you could perhaps better use to get on with the job. We'll also explore procrastination. It's something we all do, so we need to understand why it's so common and what it might mean.

In this chapter we'll answer these questions:

- What is my job and what is not?
- How can I stop myself saying yes to my boss?
- Why are decisions so difficult to make?

Manage your job

We all spend a significant part of our lives at work. Our jobs are important to us, not least because, unless we are lucky enough to be very wealthy, we need paid employment so that we can pay our bills. This, in many ways, is the root of a common problem: many of us feel that we need our job more than our job needs us.

Of course, a lot depends on the job you do. Different kinds of job demand differing levels of commitment from those who do them. A soldier might be expected to take massive personal risks, even risk life to complete a strategically important task. A factory shift worker, on the other hand, can clock off when the whistle blows and not think about work again until the following day.

While, for most of us, our job doesn't endanger our life, it does have a habit of intruding into every aspect of our life. That is because we feel dependent upon it and even subconsciously strive to preserve it.

> *'Give us the tools and we'll finish the job.'*
>
> Winston Churchill

The truth about work

If you are paid monthly, you will receive a cheque at the end of each month for the work you've done. Then you and your employer both start the next month afresh. That is the extent of the contractual commitment you have to each other. Loyalty and respect are important, but only if mutual and equal.

Overcommitting

It is human nature to want to please. This makes it all too easy to overload your working life. No amount of time management techniques can help you squeeze two days' work into one. So here are some warning signs to look out for.

● **Are you volunteering too quickly?**
Make sure you have the time before you agree to take on additional work.

● **Are you straying from your brief?**
As you get deeper into a project, you spot other things that need to be done. Highlight them but don't assume you have to do them.

● **Are you neglecting home life?**
If you work all the time and neglect your personal life, your work quality and work rate will suffer.

And here are some ways to avoid overcommitting.

● Set aside time in your diary for recurring tasks well into the future.
● Confirm exactly what's expected of you when you take on each task.
● Book out personal time in your diary and also time to plan.

Case study

Warren's grandfather had been an ardent trade unionist during the 1970s. As Warren grew up, he'd been told about the way workers stuck to their job and their job alone. His grandfather told him this was called 'demarcation'.

When Warren's boss at the office asked him to take on extra work, he was naturally wary. He remembered how his grandfather had gone on strike rather than accept extra duties for no extra pay.

Warren tried to argue that extra work for no more pay was unfair. However, because he did not schedule or plan his working day, he had no evidence to support his case and so found himself with more work. He started scheduling his time and found his work rate increased. How times have changed, he thought to himself.

Overengineering

You have an eye for detail and want to get every last aspect of a task perfect before passing it on. Remember, however, that to most people, perfection is only a little better than good enough. Furthermore, if your work is being charged on to a client, they may not need or be willing to fund the additional detail you have provided.

Understand your boss

You can dramatically improve your time management if you improve your relationship with your manager. That's not to suggest that you don't already get on with your boss. It's more that he or she is probably also wrestling with their own time management. They may find delegating to you just a little too easy!

Use transactional analysis

This phrase simply refers to the power balance in a relationship. It's important here because the relationship between manager and those managed is often out of balance. That's because your manager has power over you, if only because they are higher up the organization's pecking order.

Transactional analysis teaches that there are three personality states between which we all move:

- **parent** – dominating and using behaviour learned from one's own parents
- **adult** – rational, objective and less emotional behaviour
- **child** – submissive, emotional and reactive behaviour we learned as children.

You don't need to understand the detail of transactional analysis to improve your time management. However, you do need to appreciate that:

- if you respond to your boss emotionally (child), he or she will become more dominating (parent)

- if your boss is unreasonably demanding (parent) and you respond rationally and unemotionally (adult), your boss will also become more rational (adult) and easier to negotiate with
- if you respond emotionally (child) to the demanding (parent) boss, you are far more likely to find yourself with too much to do in too little time.

TIP *Try to avoid responding emotionally to demands from your manager. Instead, ask a question to encourage your manager to think rationally about the wider impact of what they are suggesting. In other words, don't say, 'Oh heck, I don't have time for that.' Instead, say, 'You'll appreciate that I already have a full week. How do you suggest I juggle things to fit this extra work in?'*

Manage your boss and manage your workload

Once you have your relationship with your boss on an even footing, you can become more proactive in managing your workload. In short, you are far less likely to have extra work dumped on you. That's because you engage in adult-to-adult dialogue.

Here are some good ways to manage your boss and your workload.

- **Accept rather than challenge the way your boss is**. Work around your manager's shortcomings and recognize how you can help her or him succeed.
- **Present solutions, not problems**. This enables you to remain in control of your workload and commitment.
- **Ask for advice, not instruction**. You know what needs to be done and have planned the time to do it. Ask for advice about how, not why, when or if.
- **Be honest** and say if you feel you're being overloaded or asked to do things that are really unnecessary. Use a work plan to illustrate the problem.

Be decisive

If you find it difficult to make decisions and procrastinate, time will run away with you. To be effective in how you manage your time at work, you need to be decisive. The more time you spend weighing up the options, the less time you have to follow the path you choose.

Nobody can make only correct decisions. That is because only by looking back after the event can you know whether you chose the right option. Even then, other factors might have also changed so that you can never be certain your decision was the best. All you can do is make your decision based on the situation as it appeared at the time.

Things to avoid

The more you can avoid or manage these behavioural traits, the more decisive you will be:

- **needing to collect a large amount of evidence before making a decision.** As soon as the best option becomes clear, take it. Do not keep looking for further evidence to support what you feel is the right path to take.
- **deciding in an instant and then analysing and doubting the decision after the event.** Sometimes snap decisions are needed. Don't keep going back over things you are no longer able to change.
- **passing the buck.** Too often, people say they need their boss to endorse a decision when actually they don't. Be confident in your own judgement.
- **constantly falling into the same trap.** Over time, you'll get a sense of where you tend to make good decisions and where you make the wrong choice. Learn from your decisions to improve future performance.

Things to do

You'll be more decisive and probably make more good decisions if you try to:

- **listen to your instinct.** Then use the facts to support what feels like the right thing to do or challenge what doesn't.
- **make the decision that benefits most people.** Don't just make the one that simply benefits you.
- **think before following the herd.** Before doing the same action as everyone else, reflect on it and, if you believe it's wrong, prove it by going against the tide.
- **take responsibility for your decisions.** Be prepared to take ownership of them even if they prove with time not to have been the best ones.

Sometimes others will give you plenty of reasons to make a decision they themselves are reluctant to make. If you're going to take the lead, clear your desk of their arguments and base your decision on your own research.

Avoid procrastination

This is one of the biggest challenges we all face. Many of us find it hard to take decisive action over important or difficult tasks, and we put off the jobs we really don't feel like doing. The trouble is, if you always do the jobs that appeal most first, you might lack sufficient time and energy to for the more challenging things you've been putting off.

Procrastination becomes a habit. In fact, in some organizations, people have learned that, if you put something off for long enough, it will eventually become unnecessary. It's rather like a small boy refusing to brush his teeth after a meal. If he can put off the task successfully until bedtime, he might not have to brush them at all.

At work, putting things off because you don't want to do them can be dangerous if the unpopular task relates to health and safety, for example routine equipment maintenance. Alternatively, if people get away without doing something, then perhaps it no longer needs to be done. Sometimes work practices don't adapt quickly enough when new processes or technology make them redundant.

To avoid procrastination:

- schedule into your work the tasks you might otherwise avoid
- don't say you'll wait for the right moment; it might never come
- set aside time for potential distractions such as email and keep your quality work time as just that.

Case study

Charity worked as an administrator at a care home. She loved making sure that everything ran smoothly. She particularly liked organizing visits by people like the chiropodist and physiotherapist. She also enjoyed organizing the shift rotas so that the home was always fully staffed.

What Charity did not like doing was the bookkeeping. She convinced herself that it was far more important to make sure that the needs of the residents were met than those of the group accountant at head office. Invoices were often late going out and the home's cash flow began to suffer.

When the home manager suggested a 'finance for non-financial managers' course to Charity, she agreed. She had now realized how important it was to make her work on the accounts more of a priority.

Summary

In this chapter we've identified the difference that being paid for your time makes to the way you manage that time. It's still your time, but at work you've committed to exchange it for money. We've seen how this means that you have to accept tasks, deadlines and objectives you might not choose for yourself.

That said, you're not going to be a pushover. A brief introduction to the concept of transactional analysis highlighted the importance of maintaining an adult relationship with your boss. Without it you increase your risk of being bossed around and losing control of your workload.

Lastly, we looked at the problems that await you if you become indecisive and put things off. You are now more aware of the dangers of procrastination. You perhaps can now remember instances where, by putting something off, it became far harder to do than if you had dealt with it earlier.

Fact-check (answers at the back)

1. Why does time management matter more at work than at home?
   a) You spend more waking hours at work than home ❏
   b) At work your employer is buying your time from you ❏
   c) Your boss gives you too much to do and at home you like being lazy ❏
   d) It doesn't ❏

2. Unless managed properly, what can your work time do?
   a) Spill over into your private life ❏
   b) Become very boring ❏
   c) Catch you by surprise when it's time to go home so soon ❏
   d) Become dangerous ❏

3. What can our natural desire to please lead us to do?
   a) Waste time with small talk ❏
   b) Buy cakes for everyone every day ❏
   c) Overcommit ❏
   d) Be seen as a soft touch ❏

4. What is likely to happen if you respond to your manager in an emotional, childlike way?
   a) Your manager will become bossier, like a parent ❏
   b) You will lose the respect of your peers ❏
   c) They might give you a tissue to dry your eyes ❏
   d) You'll soon both find yourselves playing games ❏

5. If there are things your boss does really badly, what should you do?
   a) Show them up by telling their boss ❏
   b) Set her or him up to fail at every opportunity ❏
   c) Tell them to go on a course ❏
   d) Compensate for the weak area by doing more yourself ❏

6. What happens when you procrastinate?
   a) You get things done quickly ❏
   b) You put off making decisions ❏
   c) You delegate things you don't like to others ❏
   d) You think too long about things before deciding what to do ❏

7. What will happen if you insist on getting your manager to check every decision you make?
   a) They will respect your commitment to include them ❏
   b) You will be likely to get put forward for promotion ❏
   c) You will be even more highly valued ❏
   d) Neither you nor your manager will get as much done ❏

8. To whom or what should you pay attention when making a decision?
   a) Your instinct ❏
   b) Your mum ❏
   c) Your boss ❏
   d) A counsellor ❏

9. If time proves you to have made a poor decision, what should you do?

a) Dwell on it and make yourself feel bad ❏

b) Stop making decisions until you work out how to get it right every time ❏

c) Accept it and move on, knowing that on the day it seemed right ❏

d) Make sure you ask all your colleagues for their opinion next time ❏

10. Emails are perhaps the biggest distraction in any office. What's the best way to deal with them?

a) Answer them the moment they come in ❏

b) Wait until you've got a certain number and then deal with them ❏

c) Auto-forward them to someone else to deal with ❏

d) Set aside specific times throughout the day and deal with them then ❏

CHAPTER 10

Organizing your workspace

So far we've looked at how you can develop a clear personal vision for your future, which will help you become more focused and make it easier for you to manage your time effectively. We also explored your job and your relationship with your boss, and how to manage the balance of power so that you can influence the work you are given.

Now it's time to focus on some practical ways in which you can work more efficiently. In this chapter we'll take a look at your workspace. You might have your own office or a desk in an open-plan space. You might even have a workshop or work at home. What we'll cover in this chapter is applicable to all these situations.

In this chapter we look at the most basic time management techniques. You'll have heard many of the tips before, but this time we'll try to cover them in ways that are easy to follow. I want you to know how things could be done but I also want to show you how to do them differently.

By the end of this chapter you will have:

- a tidier desk
- simplified your computer desktop
- done some filing and filled the bin.

Your desk

I spend most of my working life at my desk. You probably do the same. It's the place where I put things when I come in from a meeting. It's where I put the day's post when it arrives and where I use my computer. A lot of stuff arrives on my desk. Less of it leaves.

When I look up from my screen, I look out through a glass wall at trees, fields and in the distance, a few houses. I'm lucky to have such a nice view from my desk. I enjoy watching the seasons change, the clouds, vapour trails from passing planes and the cats that play outside my window. It's a wonder I get any work done at all!

> *'I like work, it fascinates me. I can sit and look at it for hours.'*
>
> Jerome K. Jerome

Your field of vision

As you read this page, the centres of your eyes are focused on the line of text. You can see it clearly. However, as I prompt you to notice it, you will become aware of your peripheral vision. You are now aware of objects and movement on either side of the book (or screen) you are reading. If you are reading on a train, you will notice when the person sitting next to you scratches their nose or turns the page of their book or newspaper.

Your peripheral vision is constantly scanning the space around you and alerting your brain to what it detects. It's a defence mechanism because our eyes face forwards, making us vulnerable to prey approaching from the side. It also means that all the clutter on your desk is also literally on your mind. You cannot shut out the distraction, so you have to remove it.

It's simple to improve your view.

● **Put nice things within your field of vision.**
I have flowers, sea shells, a stone from the beach and, if it's dark outside, a scented candle.

● **Remove nasty things from your desk.**
If something annoys you, deal with it or file it away until you can deal with it. In view it will nag at your mind.

● **Keep your desk, keyboard and screen nice and clean.**
Get rid of those coffee stains, bits of Blu-tack™ and crumbs from your lunch.

> ### Case study
> Jonathan has had a lifelong fascination with helicopters. He hopes to learn to fly one before he is 35 and own one before he is 40. On his desk, just to the left of his computer screen, is a model helicopter. It reminds him throughout the working day of his ambition.

What's on your desk?

What do you actually need on your desk? In truth you need very little, yet we almost all have untidy desks. The reason is often procrastination: we leave things on our desks because we have yet to decide what to do with them. They are too important to throw out and too complex to deal with immediately.

Here's how to clear your desk:

1 Start at one side and work across. Pick everything up and put it in one of three places:
   – the bin – because it's not important
   – a file, ideally in a cabinet so you can close the drawer and hide it
   – back on your desk because it is work in progress.
2 Now take a closer look at what you've got left because you're not sure what to do with it:
   – business cards – we all collect them, but add the details to your email address book and you can throw them away. Sync your address book with your mobile
   – work in progress – go through the papers and bin what's no longer relevant. Do not print out copies of emails or

other documents unless you are constantly referring to them; your computer already has the information

- your computer and printer – put the main tower on the floor and the printer on another table, anywhere but your desk. Get longer leads so that all you have on your desk is keyboard, mouse and screen
- Post-it™ notes – keep these handy but only if you promise not to stick notes to yourself around your screen. That will only distract you
- 'homeless' papers – these are the things people have passed to you in case you need them, or you have printed out to read later, but not got round to yet. As a rule of thumb, if these have not been touched in a week, you can throw them out.

Many time management books recommend that you have an in-tray and make sure it's empty at the end of each day. I prefer an in-pile on the corner of the desk. That's because, if it gets too high, it will slip off on to the floor, reminding you to stop hoarding!

TIP Phone management
- *Programme in all your current project contacts so that you can speed-dial out and recognize inbound calls before you pick them up.*
- *Keep a small notebook and pen by the phone. Discard the note as soon as you've acted on it.*
- *If your main work phone is a mobile, sync it with your contacts database.*
- *Use voicemail when you're busy and return calls later.*

Your computer

Many people use a laptop at the office so that they can take it away with them and work from home and elsewhere. Smartphones and tablets are even easier to carry and enable you to keep in touch on the move. If you use a laptop or tablet, invest in a docking system so that you can still use a full-sized keyboard, mouse and screen.

Use two screens

My own efficiency leapt as soon as I started using two screens. Most computers can support two monitors and those that can't need very little adaptation. Using two screens means you can:

- view two applications at once
- easily cut and paste words, images and figures to and from documents
- keep working while an application is loading
- video conference using Skype while viewing the documents you're discussing at the same time.

This might seem like an invitation to become distracted, but actually it works really well. Here's how I use my two screens. I use my left-hand screen for things I want to look at and my right-hand screen for things I'm going to write. This also means that, whenever I cut and paste, it's from the left-hand screen to the right.

Left-hand screen	Right-hand screen
• Google	• Email
• Excel	• Word
• Skype	
• Viewing PDFs	

Organize your computer desktop

There are many ways to organize your computer desktop. It might be that your organization has an intranet and its own systems and applications. Or you might simply use the usual Microsoft applications or their freeware rivals. Whichever applies to you, there are some quick and easy ways to manage your computer desktop.

- **Keep it clear** – file or delete stray files and keep your desktop blank.
- **Start it easily** – add the things you use regularly to your Start menu in the bottom left-hand corner of your screen. This will save time.

- **Set your Internet browser** to open with your most commonly used tabs. Mine, for example, opens with my Google homepage, my Google Calendar and Twitter.

Additionally, my Google homepage has been set up to show me a number of newsfeeds and alerts. This means I can easily keep an eye on what's happening in my work world at a glance. Then I don't feel the need to surf and search unless it's for something I'm specifically researching.

Always make sure your PC backs up regularly and that you know how to retrieve your back-up if your PC fails or your laptop is stolen. No amount of good time management can compensate for the needless loss of your work.

Make your computer faster

You are probably not a computer expert. If you work in a large organization, there'll be someone who maintains your PC for you. But that doesn't mean it's not helpful to know the questions to ask to make sure your PC is as fast and efficient as possible.

Here are some useful tips.

- **Do a weekly clean-up.**
  Use a specialist program to clear out all that digital clutter. Computers pick up lots of 'temporary' files and others bits and bobs. A weekly purge will stop them building up and slowing you down.

- **Check security settings.**
  Be realistic about security. Anti-virus software can slow your machine down but is essential. Beware over-zealous spam filtering and password protecting files. This will hit your efficiency too.

- **Make history history.**
  Set your web browser to keep only your recent history. A bursting web history will slow your browser down, so bookmark things you want to go back to.

Use voice recognition and commands

There are some really useful voice recognition packages available now. These will learn the way you speak and even remember the way you most usually use words. This makes them remarkably accurate. If your keyboard speed is slow, dictating to your PC will be considerably faster.

TIP *When using voice recognition software, pause after each paragraph to check and edit what's been written. This will stop you rambling and keep your writing tight. It also makes it far less likely for word errors to slip through to your final document.*

Your filing

How often do you look at all the pictures you took on your last holiday? Digital cameras make it really easy to take plenty of photos but, if you're like me, you'll rarely make the time to go back and look at them later.

Your work files may be much the same. We all like to keep stuff and it's an easy thing to do. But perhaps less than 10 per cent of it is ever needed or looked at again. We keep stuff because we've always kept stuff.

Filing or archiving?

Filing is not the same as archiving. Archiving is retaining documents you don't need but must keep. In many business sectors, some documents and files need to be retained for as long as seven years. This may be a legal requirement or, if the work you're doing is publicly funded, a condition of contract. This is so that all of the detail can be audited if necessary.

Filing...

- is for documents you need again
- needs to be convenient for your desk.

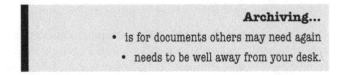

- is for documents others may need again
- needs to be well away from your desk.

How to file

In your filing cabinet as well as on your computer, files need to be arranged in a logical and sensible way. Only those that relate to your current project load need to be near and handy. If, for example, you have a three-drawer filing cabinet, you could label the drawers (from the top) as follows.

Current projects	Proposed projects	Recent projects
• One folder for each • Filed alphabetically.	• One folder for each project you are likely to work on soon • Filed with the soonest at the front.	• Thinned-out folders of projects as you complete them • Filed with the newest at the front.

Unless you are obliged to retain files for a certain period, keep only a fixed number of recent projects on file. Each time you add a new file to the drawer, remove and throw away the oldest one.

Files are best kept in card wallets, with the contents in date order and all the same way up. If you are left-handed, you will want to file papers the opposite way up from right-handed people.

What to file

A filing system is like a vegetable plot: unless you keep on top of the weeding, the success you are cultivating will become choked and lost. The simple fact is that if you keep too much paperwork, it will become increasingly difficult to find the important documents you do need.

As a rule of thumb:

Keep	Do not keep
• Contracts	• Draft contracts
• Important letters	• Routine letters
• Meeting notes (always date them)	• Printed copies of emails
	• Anything you have on your computer

File management

Every time I take out a file I flick through it. This enables me to:

● quickly remind myself what I'm keeping, and why
● pull out and bin documents I no longer need.

TIP *Always label the hanging files in which you keep your papers. Then if you cannot find the file card wallet when you want to add a document, you have somewhere to put it. This avoids the danger of creating a new second file for the same project.*

The paperless office

People have long talked about the paperless office. Originally the idea was that documents would be scanned when they arrived and the originals destroyed (or archived). Few made it work successfully.

Today, however, it is far easier to operate a paperless office. Indeed, some people dispense with an office altogether and work wherever they happen to be. The paperless office is easier to achieve than ever before because:

● 'cloud computing', or web-based personal filing systems, enable you to recover documents and information anywhere you have Internet access
● smartphones and tablet computers are giving us permanent Internet access wherever we go
● online file sharing means you can create a virtual office and limit access to documents to those you want to share them with.

Summary

In this chapter we've looked at where you work and how you organize the space around you. We've looked at your physical space and your virtual space, both in your computer and online.

You were reminded of the importance of removing distracting clutter from your field of vision, and then encouraged to fill in some of that space with things that make you feel good and make you happy. Even if you don't sit near a window, you can bring the outdoors into your office.

I made a plea for you to consider using two screens with your computer. This might mean asking your boss to spend some money, but my experience says that the investment will be quickly recouped in increased efficiency. We also looked at how to simplify access to the programs and content you use the most. Use your common sense and a little time to get your own computer in order.

Lastly we talked about paper. We all keep too much of it for far too long. You now have some tips and techniques to take you closer to a paperless office. This is something we will all achieve one day.

Fact-check (answers at the back)

1. At your desk, why is it good to keep your field of vision uncluttered?
a) Because even stuff you can only see peripherally will distract you ❏
b) Because you'll lose things if you leave them on your desk ❏
c) Because your boss will think you're more organized if you have a tidy desk ❏
d) Because people will borrow things if you leave them lying around ❏

2. What's a good thing to have close to your computer where you can easily see it?
a) A list of all the jobs you haven't got round to yet ❏
b) An object that reminds you of a life ambition or goal ❏
c) Your lunch ❏
d) Your wallet or bag ❏

3. What should you do with a document that has been lying on your desk unread for a week?
a) File it away with other papers you'll read when you have time ❏
b) Throw it away ❏
c) Give it to someone else to worry about ❏
d) Hide it where it can't distract you ❏

4. What will using two screens on your desk do?
a) Make you look important ❏
b) Make you feel important ❏
c) Make you more efficient ❏
d) Confuse you ❏

5. What should your computer desktop screen have on it?
a) All your current project files ❏
b) Holiday photos ❏
c) Webcam images so you can see what's happening at home ❏
d) As little as possible ❏

6. How can you make your computer work more efficiently and swiftly?
a) Download some clever freeware when nobody's looking ❏
b) Avoid spilling coffee on the keyboard ❏
c) Get rid of temporary files and other junk at least weekly ❏
d) Don't turn if off at night ❏

7. Where should you keep archived files?
a) Close to your desk ❏
b) In a bank of filing cabinets along the office wall ❏
c) Where you can get at them but nowhere near where you work ❏
d) With all your other files ❏

8. If you can't find the right file for the document you need to put away, what should you do?
a) Keep it where the file should be ❏
b) Create a second file ❏
c) Search the place for the missing file ❏
d) Throw it away ❏

9. What do cloud computing and tablet technology mean for tomorrow's office?
a) It will be just as cluttered as today's ❑
b) It will be almost entirely paperless ❑
c) It will be full of screens and computers ❑
d) It will be full of plants and flowers ❑

10. What will you have if you do even half the things suggested in this chapter?
a) A better-organized workspace ❑
b) A headache ❑
c) The envy of your colleagues ❑
d) No need to read any more of this masterclass ❑

CHAPTER 11

Managing your workload

Now that you are almost halfway through this masterclass, you will have already improved your time management. Your tidy desk and the beginnings of a filing system are outward signs of the progress you're making. Others will be starting to notice.

But work keeps piling up. Even though you're more confidently challenging the assumption that you'll do whatever you're asked, stuff keeps coming your way. In this chapter we'll look in detail at how you manage your time. We'll strike at the very heart of your time management issues and make it easier to cope with the flow.

In this chapter we'll focus on practical techniques, putting into action many of the principles I've already introduced to you. Much of what we cover is little more than common sense. That's because, at times, we all need encouragement to step back from our day-to-day routine and see what would be obvious if we weren't so busy.

When you finish this chapter, you will have:

- discovered how to manage the size of your workload
- become more proficient at scheduling your time
- developed your own way of prioritizing tasks.

Your workload

Cyril Northcote Parkinson described perfectly a phenomenon you probably recognize only too well. He said that 'Work expands so as to fill the time available for its completion.' People call this 'Parkinson's Law'. In practical terms this means that, however much or little people have to do, they always seem busy. The solution to managing your workload is therefore not to work harder but to work smarter.

> **'Choose a job you love, and you will never have to work a day in your life.'**
>
> Confucius

Work SMART

SMART is an acronym that stands for Specific, Measurable, Achievable, Relevant and Timed. The more you define your workload in SMART terms, the easier it will be to define and manage.

Let's take this masterclass as an example. If my editor had simply said, 'Go and write a masterclass on time management', I would have struggled with the task. Who is the masterclass aimed at? How complicated or detailed must it be? When is it needed and where will it fit in the marketplace? We actually agreed some SMART objectives. These enabled me to work efficiently and effectively. It also means that my editor will get the masterclass he commissioned, not something completely different. Here's what we agreed:

● **Specific**
I would write a practical guide to time management for people who probably work in an office.

● **Measurable**
The masterclass would be less than 25,000 words with a structure common to all masterclasses in the series.

- **Achievable**
  We both knew I could do it, not because I am a time
  management guru, but because I can relate to the subject
  and recognize the need.

- **Relevant**
  The growing economy can easily tempt us to take on more
  than we can realistically handle. Good time management is
  now even more important than during the last recession.

- **Timed**
  I had a deadline by which the masterclass had to be
  submitted. It's no coincidence that that was also the day I
  finished writing it!

I therefore knew precisely what was expected of me. Had
this not been the case, I could have spent months researching
the subject in too much detail. By sticking to agreed SMART
objectives life's been easier and the masterclass more
successful.

When you agree to accept any project, make sure you agree
SMART objectives. Then and only then can you schedule the
task and be confident you'll deliver what's expected.

TIP When your manager gives you a task, discuss with her or
him the SMART objectives. This will encourage her or him
to think in SMART terms too.

Schedule your work

We have already looked at the value of splitting your day into
quarters. For most of us that means dividing it into two-hour
chunks. Now that you are starting to view your work in SMART
terms, you can see that there's potential to plot your workload
in far more detail.

Many organizations use specialist project management
software to schedule complex projects. This produces what is
effectively a diary upon which tasks are mapped. By breaking
the project down into tasks, each with an expected duration
and deadline for completion, you can construct a matrix that

shows what needs to be done when. This is called a Gantt chart and enables a project manager to share out tasks and coordinate their delivery efficiently.

You can do the same thing using your diary. If you use an online diary, you can link it to a task list. Each task needs to be relatively short, so that you don't simply set aside a whole day to work on 'the project'. By breaking a project into tasks, you will know whether you are on schedule.

I scheduled my work in this way when writing this masterclass. I set aside time to do the research, then time to write it. I also allowed time to plan what would be on each page so that the finished work covered everything I wanted to share. Finally, knowing how quickly I write and the need for breaks, I blocked out days for writing in my diary. Only then did I know when to start and when I would finish.

Case study

Jane managed a popular flower shop specializing in funeral wreaths. Although she loved her work and her customers loved her flowers, she had a real problem with meeting deadlines despite having a number of part-time assistants.

She always put the date of each funeral in the diary, but was not good at planning ahead. This meant she often didn't have the right flowers at the right time. Too often, she'd be at work early in the morning to finish wreaths needed later the same day.

Her boss sent her on a time management course. Jane realized that she needed to schedule not only the funerals but also the date by which she had to order the flowers and book her assistants' time to come in and help her.

She bought a new diary and used different-coloured highlighters to schedule when to start each task. She gave each funeral a job number and noted this in the diary too. As a result, Jane no longer had to go in to work at the crack of dawn.

The 80:20 rule

This is also called the Pareto Principle. In 1906 Vilfredo Pareto noticed that 80 per cent of the land in his native Italy was owned by 20 per cent of the people. Research showed him that this was also true elsewhere. Later, people began to see that the 80:20 rule applies to almost any situation. For example:

- 80 per cent of profits come from 20 per cent of your customers
- 80 per cent of the time you wear clothes from 20 per cent of your wardrobe
- 80 per cent of photocopier breakdowns are caused by 20 per cent of the users.

More relevant to how you spend your time is the fact that probably just 20 per cent of your time produces 80 per cent of the results. Conversely, 80 per cent of your time therefore delivers just 20 per cent of your work output.

Set priorities

To make the best use of your time, you need to spend as much of it as possible on the most valuable projects. These will be those that:

- deliver the most financial return to your organization
- are of the greatest strategic importance
- take you closer to your own personal and career ambitions.

In a large organization, where perhaps you feel like a small cog in a very large wheel, setting priorities can be difficult. You may not always know the full significance of the task you've been asked urgently to complete. That's why good managers will explain the bigger picture.

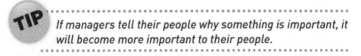

TIP *If managers tell their people why something is important, it will become more important to their people.*

It will help you set priorities if you sort your work into one of these four categories.

1 Very urgent Very important	3 Less urgent Very important
2 Very urgent Less important	4 Less urgent Less important

It's obvious that you need to complete the tasks you've placed in box 1 first. You might label these red, so you know they are both the most important and the most urgent.

Next you have to decide between tasks in boxes 2 and 3. You might label these blue and green. In the abstract, deciding if urgency or importance is more significant is impossible. In reality, when you are looking at real tasks, the choices become much easier. That's because few tasks or projects occur in complete isolation – they all form part of a perpetual flow of activity.

As you schedule your time, you will clearly focus on those from box 1, marked red. Then you will fill in your time with those from boxes 2 and 3, blue and green. So now you should be eager to push away anything that is not important or urgent.

Deal with 'stuff'

You might think that you can ignore the less urgent, less important tasks altogether, but unfortunately this is rarely the case. Yes, some can be dumped in the bin and others delegated, but many will still need your attention eventually. For one thing, they might not be urgent or important now but they may become so with time, as with the following examples.

- Updating policy and procedure documents might not seem important or urgent until an audit or inspection finds you are no longer compliant with legislation or, worse, are in breach of a contract.
- Routine equipment maintenance can be put off when you are busy with important and urgent tasks, but leave it too long and a breakdown will play havoc with your scheduling.
- Requests for information from students doing project work can be ignored. But what if your organization wants to recruit talented graduates? Might some of these be the very young people you are ignoring right now?

There will be days when you are not in the mood for intense, challenging tasks, perhaps because you feel tired or under the weather. These moments are an ideal time for setting aside half a day to clear a backlog of odd jobs, as a break from more demanding tasks.

Always make time for 'stuff' and keep on top of it.

> *'I recommend you take care of the minutes,*
> *and the hours will take care of themselves.'*
>
> Philip Stanhope, 4th Earl of Chesterfield

Free up more time

Author and lateral thinker Edward de Bono said, 'The brain's ability to set up routines is its most important function. Life would be impossible without routines. To go through all the ways of getting dressed with eleven items of clothing could take years, as there are 39,916,800 ways of getting dressed. Like trains on railway tracks, our thoughts and feelings are predetermined paths.'

I guess you did not take years to get dressed this morning. It's also probably true that many of the routine tasks of your daily life are conducted as if by clockwork, following an established routine. For example, I always read the sections of the Sunday newspaper in the same sequence. You too will have routines you follow without thinking.

We also create routines at work. The tasks we habitually need to do are usually done without much thought at all. However, circumstances change and the need for those routine tasks changes also. But habit means that we carry on as before.

Case study

Every Saturday morning I would visit the office building I own and empty the tenants' wastepaper baskets. The cleaner did this on Tuesdays and Thursdays, so my weekly round with a bin bag neatly filled the gap.

Then the cleaner's routine changed so that she visited on Wednesday and Sunday. It was only when she commented on how tidy the place was on Sundays that I realized I no longer needed to empty the bins on Saturday. The task had become a fixed part of my Saturday routine, so that, even though I knew the cleaner had changed her days, it had not occurred to me to stop emptying the bins on Saturday.

In business, habitual behaviour can reduce the cost saving of investment and innovation. A new machine in a factory might mean that an earlier process is no longer required. Often, though, that process will continue, quite simply because it always has.

Are you doing things by habit? Think about everything you do in a typical day and make a list of the things you probably don't or no longer need to do.

Summary

In this chapter we've looked at managing your workload by working SMART. Agreeing and using SMART project and task objectives is perhaps the best way to manage expectations. If your manager or customer expected more – or less – whatever you've actually done will not be appreciated. Working SMART will make life easier: you will not go on beyond the point at which you did as much as was expected, and you can more accurately schedule your work.

We also looked at prioritizing so that you include in your work programme the most important, most urgent tasks first. We then justified the need to make time for all the assorted 'stuff' that inevitably needs doing, even though it's not particularly urgent or important.

Lastly, we reflected on the idea of habits. Habits create activity shortcuts, so that you can complete routine tasks quickly and effectively in the same sequence each time. However, the danger of habits is that you'll continue them after they cease to be necessary. We need to think about changing them, to avoid situations that are like walking to the local school every afternoon even though your child has grown up and gone to university.

Fact-check (answers at the back)

1. What does Parkinson's Law say?
   a) The more work you have, the more time you will find ❏
   b) Work expands to fill the time available for its completion ❏
   c) Time expands to accommodate the work you have to do ❏
   d) However little work you have, you will always find plenty to do ❏

2. What does the S in the acronym SMART stand for?
   a) Specific ❏
   b) Successful ❏
   c) Simple ❏
   d) Sensible ❏

3. What does the M in the acronym SMART stand for?
   a) Measurable ❏
   b) Marvellous ❏
   c) Meaningful ❏
   d) Me ❏

4. What does the A in the acronym SMART stand for?
   a) Accessible ❏
   b) Available ❏
   c) Achievable ❏
   d) Anywhere ❏

5. What does the R in the acronym SMART stand for?
   a) Rational ❏
   b) Replicable ❏
   c) Responsible ❏
   d) Realistic ❏

6. What does the T in the acronym SMART stand for?
   a) Troublesome ❏
   b) Timely ❏
   c) Timed ❏
   d) Tense ❏

7. What does the Pareto Principle state?
   a) 80 per cent of the activity delivers 20 per cent of the result ❏
   b) 20 per cent of the activity delivers 80 per cent of the result ❏
   c) 80 per cent of the time is wasted and 20 per cent is not ❏
   d) 20 per cent of my work achieves as much as 80 per cent of yours ❏

8. When setting priorities, what will be the most important tasks?
   a) Those that are very urgent and very important ❏
   b) Those that are less urgent and less important ❏
   c) Those that are very urgent and less important ❏
   d) Those that are less urgent and very important ❏

9. When is the best time to deal with unimportant stuff that isn't urgent?
   a) When you're at your very best and can conquer anything ❏
   b) When you need a break and it won't be too taxing to do ❏
   c) When you're off sick and feel the need to do some work ❏
   d) When someone's shouting because suddenly it's become more urgent ❏

10. Why is it good periodically to challenge the tasks we do through habit?

a) Otherwise we might take them for granted ❑

b) We want to do them really well ❑

c) We might forget how to do them if we don't think now and then ❑

d) They may no longer be important ❑

CHAPTER 12

Coping with your colleagues

None of us works in complete isolation; we all have to rely on other people to help us achieve our work goals. But other people can also hinder our efforts to manage time effectively. We need to strike a happy balance. Too serious and work-focused and people won't want to help you. Too playful and easily distracted and you'll get nothing done. It's something we all have to cope with.

In this chapter we're going to explore how you can work more effectively with your colleagues. You will learn some useful techniques that will help you better manage your interactions with others. We all need each other if we are to succeed, so don't be selfish and overlook the needs of your colleagues. They may need your help to see the benefits to them of managing time better.

As you read through this chapter, try out the tips and techniques. Not all will be relevant and some will be tougher to do than others. By the end of this chapter you will be better able to:

- manage delegation, both ways
- avoid distraction
- make meetings more effective.

Make delegation work for you

A good way to get more done is to get other people to help you. If you line manage others, they will expect you to delegate work to them. But you also need to delegate to colleagues, both within your team and often across the wider organization. At times you may also need to delegate to your manager.

> *'We wander for distraction, but we travel for fulfilment.'*
>
> Hilaire Belloc

Earn the respect of others

People will do more for you if they want to help you. Even if you're someone's boss, you'll get more done if they respect you than if you simply issue orders. Here are some ways you can make it easier for others to respect you at work.

- **Respect yourself.**
  Self-respect is not a given; we all doubt ourselves from time to time. Self-criticism and doubt can be harmful. It's difficult to respect someone who doesn't respect themselves.

- **Respect others.**
  Being respectful to others will encourage others to respect you in return. Respect their views, priorities and prejudices even if they differ from your own. You don't have to agree with people in order to respect them.

- **Be realistic.**
  Don't expect too much of yourself or those you delegate to. Don't lose perspective or objectivity. Agree what is to be done and by when.

- **Be selective.**
  Distance yourself from bullies and other toxic people. If you let others push you around, you'll be tempted to do the same yourself.

People have short memories. If you change, others will respond to the way you are now and forget how you were before.

Rules for delegation

If someone reports to you and you are delegating them tasks, there are some basic rules that will help you.

1 **Right person**
Make sure you ask someone with the skills and knowledge to do the job.

2 **Right task**
Explain clearly what you want done, why and by when.

3 Right resources

Ensure that whatever's needed to do the job is available. This applies as much to information as equipment.

4 Right support

Make sure people know how to get help if they encounter a problem or need more resources. If you are the support, how will they contact you?

5 Right reward

Unless people can see what's in it for them, the tasks you delegate will feel like a burden.

> **TIP**
>
> *If you are delegating to someone who does not report to you, explaining 'what's in it for them' is even more important. You have to 'sell, not tell'.*

Deal with distractions

We all get distracted from time to time. Your susceptibility to distraction will to some extent depend on your personality. Some of us are far more easily distracted than others! Let's look at some of the things that can distract you and how you can minimize their impact.

Time thieves

These are people who seem to have nothing more important to do than stop you working. They are the workplace equivalent of those irritating neighbours who seem to wait and pounce on you the moment you go out of your door. They are often lonely and simply want to chat.

You find this at work too, where time thieves will appear in a number of guises.

● **Negative people** want you to support their latest complaint. Say that while you sympathize, you're busy right now and can't spare the time.

- **Gloomy people** want to explain why in their view what you're doing is not going to work out. Tell them you have to find out for yourself and please can they let you get on.
- **Adoring people** see you as successful and think that, by hanging round you, some of your success will rub off on them. Encourage them to earn your patronage by doing something useful to help.
- **Lost people** have taken on more than they can really handle and now want you to help them with their work. These are difficult to shift if you feel sorry for them. Be firm, point them in the right direction and let them go.

Social media

After email, which we'll talk about in the next chapter, social media are perhaps the biggest distraction in most offices today. In small organizations in particular, websites such as Facebook, Twitter and to a lesser extent LinkedIn are becoming massive distractions. You only have to look at fellow commuters on the train, bus or even on foot to see the extent of the problem. Everyone spends their travelling time online, updating their Facebook and Tweeting their thoughts.

Twitter, in particular, is now widely used in the workplace to research, market and recruit. Journalists, for example, are often most easily contacted via Twitter. You can also use Twitter to follow proceedings at conferences and events, and even to monitor what rival organizations are saying and doing.

As with other business tools, social media websites need to be used sensibly and at specific times. For some of us, me included, the temptation to monitor debate and comment on Twitter about often highly relevant topics is almost overwhelming. The simple fact is, however, that you can't be part of every conversation, read every article or comment on every debate.

The best way to use social media at work is to:

- be very focused about what you want it to help you achieve
- set aside a number of 10- or 15-minute slots each day to use it

- use these slots as breaks between larger tasks, coffee breaks even
- take the trouble to learn how to use it properly so your time spent on these websites is more productive.

Other distractions

Many other things can distract you during the working day. Here are some of them, together with suggested ways of reducing their impact.

- **Yourself**
  If you have ideas for projects other than the one on your desk right now, keep a notebook and jot down a reminder. Go back to it later.
- **Passing traffic**
  If your desk is near the toilets or kitchen you may have lots of people passing by. Position yourself so they don't catch your attention as they pass.

- **Phone calls**
  Use voicemail or divert to a colleague when you need time to concentrate without distraction. There might be occasions when you have time to help colleagues by picking up their calls. Work together and help each other.

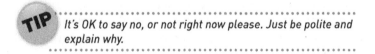

TIP It's OK to say no, or not right now please. Just be polite and explain why.

Make meetings more effective

Next time you go to a meeting, try to calculate how much it is costing. I don't mean for the room, coffee and biscuits, but for the people round the table. What is the salary bill for the afternoon likely to total? Your best guess is likely to produce a surprisingly high figure. Add the time taken to prepare, get there and return home again and you can see why it's so important to make meetings really effective.

Meetings are not all bad. When well managed and attended by the right people, they enable issues to be properly debated and good decisions made. Let's see how you can make sure the meetings you attend make best use of your time.

Why have meetings?

All meetings should have clear objectives. What are the decisions to be made? If the meeting is just to brief people, could this be done differently? The fact that you've always had a departmental meeting on the first Tuesday of the month is not sufficient reason to have one next month. Meetings, like so many other activities, become habit. Understand why you are meeting and state the objectives.

Who should come to the meeting?

If a meeting is to result in decisions being made, you need to have the right people round the table. If you can't get all the decision makers there, make sure they delegate authority to someone who can be there. Without the right people, a meeting can become pointless. Equally, don't assume that just because someone's always attended these meetings they still need to be there. Situations change and people may not always tell you they no longer need to attend.

If when you arrive for a meeting you are missing a key person or are not quorate, it's often better to stop and rearrange than to discuss things just because some of you are there.

What's the meeting about?

The most important document in a meeting is the agenda. This should:

- list what is to be discussed, starting with the most important item and ending with the least important
- have start and end times for each item to keep things to time

- be supported where necessary by short, easy-to-read papers that explain the options. It is often also useful if the paper's author includes their recommendation
- have been circulated, with supporting papers, before the meeting so that people can prepare.

How should we run the meeting?

Good chairing is vital to a successful meeting. The chairperson should:

- check that people understand why they are there
- keep the meeting to time
- briefly set the scene for each agenda item
- invite, then chair, debate
- involve the quieter people who otherwise might not speak
- seek agreement or, if this is not possible, take a vote
- make sure someone reliable and unbiased records action points and, if necessary, full minutes.

Sometimes people get angry or confrontational in meetings. This can be disruptive, but at times it may also be vital if the real issues are to be discussed. Manage conflict sensitively. If the meeting degenerates, insist on a ten-minute break so that people can cool off. Encourage opponents to spend that time discussing their differences in private.

'Laughter drives shouting away.'
Indra Devi

Where shall we hold the meeting?

The best meetings take place where it's convenient for most of those attending. Technology means that far-flung participants can take part over the Internet, using teleconferencing or Skype. It is possible to hold a meeting entirely online, either as voice only or using video too if you have sufficient bandwidth.

Meetings work best when held in a room that is:

- large enough for the number of people attending
- comfortable, neither too warm nor too cold and adequately lit and ventilated
- undisturbed by noise or other distraction
- available for as long as you need it.

Sometimes it can be useful to hold a meeting close to where the issues being discussed are most important. For example, if you're meeting about a factory extension, meet at the factory so you can see the site and get a feel for the context.

TIP *If your meeting ends ahead of time, it's not a problem, providing everyone has had the opportunity to contribute to the debate. Don't stretch a meeting out simply to fill the time set aside.*

Case study

Michael ran a busy sales office. Every morning at nine he called the team together for a 15-minute daily briefing. The meeting took place in the main sales office with everyone standing in a large circle round the room.

Everyone was given the opportunity to say whether they:

- needed particular help with a job that day
- had good news to share from the day before
- had an idea to share that could improve sales performance.

Although up to 20 people sometimes attended the meeting, it never took longer than 15 minutes because everyone was standing up. What's more, Michael's team all felt involved in what was going on in the company.

Summary

In this chapter we've seen that coping with people, particularly colleagues, is one of the toughest time management challenges. The paradox is that we need other people in order to succeed, but those who work with us can also be a distraction.

We saw the importance of delegation, and that it works well only when the person picking up your tasks clearly understands why the work needs doing and why it is to their advantage to do it punctually and well. It also helps if you have the respect of those you are delegating to.

In today's largely open-plan office environment, it's all too easy to get distracted. We looked at how you could minimize distractions, recognizing that some of us are more easily distracted than others.

Lastly, we talked about meetings, which need to be well organized and managed if they are not to become a costly waste of time and resources. You now have a better appreciation of what makes meetings useful. This will help you with any meeting you attend: you don't have to be chairing a meeting to influence its success.

Fact-check (answers at the back)

1. What is the first thing you need to do to win the respect of other people?
   a) Be nice to them ❑
   b) Pay them ❑
   c) Respect yourself ❑
   d) Respect them ❑

2. What does respecting someone else's point of view mean?
   a) Always agreeing with them ❑
   b) Trying to change their views to match your own ❑
   c) Sometimes agreeing to disagree ❑
   d) Getting frustrated when you cannot agree ❑

3. Before you delegate a task to someone, what should you make sure of first?
   a) That they have the knowledge and skills to do the job ❑
   b) You choose someone who won't give you a hard time ❑
   c) You're certain you don't have time to do it yourself ❑
   d) They have the time ❑

4. What should you always do when delegating a task to someone who doesn't report to you?
   a) Make sure their manager doesn't find out ❑
   b) Ask their manager's permission first ❑
   c) Make sure they can see how helping you will help them too ❑
   d) Pay them something, even if it's only lunch ❑

5. Why do time thieves steal your time?
   a) They don't know any better ❑
   b) They don't realize how busy you are ❑
   c) They are thick-skinned or just ignorant ❑
   d) You let them ❑

6. Your boss points out that you're spending too much time on Twitter. What do you say to her?
   a) She's wrong and it's worth every minute you spend there ❑
   b) She has a point and perhaps you need to schedule set times to use Twitter ❑
   c) It's none of her business how you spend your time as long as you do your job ❑
   d) You'll stop using Twitter during work time ❑

7. What should you do if you find there's less and less to discuss at your weekly departmental meetings?
   a) Create agenda items to make the meeting seem worth while ❑
   b) Suggest meeting only when there's enough to discuss ❑
   c) Invite people to offer new subjects they'd like to see discussed ❑
   d) Treat it as a training session and practise your debating skills ❑

8. What should you do if you're chairing a meeting and someone seems too shy to contribute?

a) Not bother to invite them next time ❏

b) Pick on them so they have to say something or look stupid ❏

c) Give them opportunities to comment without putting them on the spot ❏

d) Ignore them and concentrate on everyone else ❏

9. If your meeting is about a single issue about which not much is known, what should you do?

a) Only invite people already familiar with the issue ❏

b) Question the need to discuss it when you probably know the answer already ❏

c) Wait until you have more agenda items ❏

d) Organize a visit or at least a presentation so that people understand the context ❏

10. People are most likely to influence your time management if you are:

a) The boss ❏

b) Bottom of the pecking order ❏

c) Anywhere: we all need people to do our job ❏

d) In an open-plan office ❏

CHAPTER 13

Communicating effectively to save time

One thing that distinguishes us as a species is our communication. We never stop chattering to one another. You only have to go into a bar or restaurant to see the extent to which we all talk all the time. In fact, in a packed bar, we all talk more loudly, trying to be heard above the background noise.

In this chapter we'll look at how you can improve your communication at work. The structured environment of the workplace means that you need to communicate in a more objective and precise way than you would in a social situation. At the same time you also need to remain friendly, because you need to have a good relationship with those working around you. No one wants to work with a surly grump who only speaks when absolutely necessary.

Increasingly, we are communicating online rather than speaking. It may seem more convenient to send an email than pick up the phone, but this can create problems, as it's easier to misinterpret written communication than it is when we simply talk to each other.

By the end of this chapter you will have worked on your communication skills. In particular, you'll find yourself:

- speaking more meaningfully
- writing more clearly
- using email more efficiently.

Speaking

Talking to people is great. In a five-minute conversation you can raise an issue, discuss the options and agree an action. To do this by email would take a lot longer. Yet, too often, we persuade ourselves that email is more convenient than picking up the phone. That's not always the case.

Even something as simple as arranging an appointment with someone is so much faster when you pick up the phone and both open your diaries. So let's look at how, when and where you can use speech more effectively.

> *'Don't write anything you can phone. Don't phone anything you can talk.'*
>
> Earl Long

Face to face

If you're with someone, you can pick up on their body language as well as the words they use. This works in two ways, so the first thing you need to be aware of is that you'll get the decisions you want faster by looking as well as sounding committed. Our body language often conveys our meaning more accurately than our words. This also applies if you are video conferencing or using Skype, although to a lesser degree as cameras usually have a narrower field of vision.

Here are a few tips to help you get more from face-to-face conversation.

- Have a clear objective.
- Have answers to the most likely questions you'll be asked.
- Don't use words or jargon the other person might not understand.
- Listen to what the other person says.

On the phone

The main difference between face-to-face conversation and a phone call is that you cannot see the person you are phoning. This sounds really obvious, but actually makes a big difference. Much of our communication is non-verbal, so when you only have voice you have to work harder to get the same result.

Here are some tips to help you achieve more from your phone calls.

- Start by asking if now is a good time; people answer the phone even when busy doing something else. Get their consent to continue the call.
- Get to the point. You can be more direct on the phone than face to face.
- Have paper and a pen beside the phone and note the key points.
- Summarize what you think has been agreed at the end of the call.
- Follow up in writing to confirm what happens next.

Here are some practical time-saving tips.

- Always leave a message if your call is answered by voicemail. Be sure to leave your name and suggest a good time for the person to call you back.
- Use speed dialling. If you make or receive a lot of calls, use software that identifies incoming numbers and opens the client record automatically.

TIP *Stand up when making important phone calls. It makes the call more focused and businesslike. This really works; try it!*

Writing

For some reason, many people write differently from the way they speak. This is probably due to either a lack of confidence or a lack of practice. The only real difference between writing and speaking is that, when you write, you are not there to answer questions. This means that your writing has to be:

- **clear and easy to read**
  I always assume that English is not my readers' first language.
- **explicit**
  Get straight to the point and say it as you see it.
- **purposeful**
  Say what you want the reader to do next.

Short is sweet

The longer the message, the less likely people are to read and understand it. It is frequently true that the more words you need to use to get your message across, the less you've actually thought about what it is you are trying to say.

Your memos, emails and letters will be quicker to write and faster to read if you:

- have a clear reason for writing before you start
- make no sentence more than 12 words long
- start with a summary, then go on to context, content and call to action.

Taking notes

We take notes to help us remember something. This works because:

- notes capture just the key points that are relevant to us
- the process of writing something down makes it easier to recall.

Make your notes:

- short and simple – what matters rather than all that was said
- personal to you – adding comments, underlines, stars or circles.

Consider creating mind maps. These diagrams enable your notes to build up along a number of strands, one for each theme you want to explore. Google 'mind mapping' to find out more.

Always have a notebook and pen, or even a phone with a notepad facility, in your bag or pocket. You can then jot things down when they occur to you.

Reading

When you first learned to read, your reading speed will have been quite slow. This is because you'll have looked at each and every word. New or unconfident readers also verbalize; they say what they are reading, even if internally.

Fluent readers, on the other hand, scan a line of text and read the shapes of the words, rather than looking at the individual letters that form each word. This is a form of speed-reading. The brain is familiar with word and phrase shapes and so helps your eyes out.

Imagine you have a long work document to read. You want to read it fast enough to get the meaning and slowly enough that you don't miss anything vital. You will read faster if you:

- run your finger slowly down the page and read just above it
- scan quickly but slow down as soon as a key word catches your eye

- highlight key words and sentences to go back to later
- finish the whole document before going back to just the highlighted areas.

TIP *If you are reading on screen, use the 'find' function to take you straight to the words you are most interested in. For example, if you are in the insurance business, you might search for words like 'risk' or 'underwriting'.*

Emailing

Are you old enough to remember the days before email? It's hard for most of us to imagine how we'd operate without it now. Email enables us to communicate with many people round the world quickly and conveniently. It also enables us to send files that once would have had to be posted or taken by courier. Since we all spend increasing amounts of time reading, sending and replying to email, conquering our inbox is one of the most productive ways to improve our time management.

Managing emails

You can't stop people sending you emails, but you could probably manage them more efficiently. Here are some ways you can deal with incoming email.

- Turn off your email alert function so you are not distracted when an email comes in.
- Check emails every hour, not every minute.
- Create folders for each of your current projects.
- Create 'rules' so that emails are automatically filed by project.
- Use a spam filter to intercept unwanted email.
- Don't read emails copied to you unless they're clearly relevant to you.
- Resist the urge to reply straight away. Think first – do you need to reply?

Replying to emails

The subject line and sender should help you decide which emails to read first. You don't have to read them in the order they arrive. Here's what to do when you open an email.

1 If it's clearly not relevant to you, delete it.
2 Speed-read it to find what the writer expects of you.
3 Then do one of the following:
   - click reply and answer concisely
   - forward it to someone better able to deal with it
   - pop it in the relevant project folder if it contains information you will need again
   - delete it.
4 If the message is negative, it might be better answered by phone.

Writing emails

Email is unique, and it benefits from being written in a style that is:

● more formal than if you are speaking face to face
● less formal than if you are writing a letter.

I think this applies even if you are emailing someone you've never met. You might not agree, in which case you need to do what works for you.

Remember, though, that one of the key benefits of email is the intimacy of the medium. Your unsolicited email will appear on the recipient's screen, perhaps sandwiched between emails from his or her colleagues.

When you write emails, try to:

- use the subject line to summarize the message in five or six words
- keep the email short, ideally less than 150 words
- use hyperlinks to relevant web pages to offer additional information
- make clear what you want the recipient to do – and why
- avoid using 'text-speak' like LOL or BTW.

TIP

As a rule, always deliver:

- *good news in writing*
- *bad news verbally, ideally face to face.*

Summary

Effective communication is vital to our success at work, but we can spend too much time communicating at the cost of actually getting things done. In this chapter we learned that by saying more with fewer words we improve our time management. By communicating more concisely and precisely, we convey our message with greater clarity and meaning.

We have learned ways not only to save time when speaking face to face and when using the phone but also in our writing. Short sentences with simple words always work best. Not everyone is a confident reader, but you really can make your writing easy to understand without being patronizing.

Lastly, we looked at how to cope with the flow of emails. Email can be hugely distracting and many of us wrestle with it every day. Managing our inbox using the advice from this chapter is one of the most productive ways there is of improving our time management.

So far, we've covered all the key aspects of good time management. In the final chapter we will wrap up with a compendium of useful shortcuts.

Fact-check (answers at the back)

1. At work, how should we communicate?
   a) Quietly ❑
   b) By being specific and purposeful ❑
   c) By making sure we aren't caught chatting ❑
   d) By talking to everyone ❑

2. What will using jargon and industry acronyms in a work conversation do?
   a) Impress others with your depth of knowledge ❑
   b) Show people that they aren't as bright as you are ❑
   c) Confuse and possibly alienate the person you're talking to ❑
   d) Remind you what they all mean or stand for ❑

3. When you meet someone important, it's useful to be able to say briefly who you are, what you do and why you are worth talking with further. What is this called?
   a) An elevator pitch ❑
   b) A staircase pitch ❑
   c) Showing off ❑
   d) A washbasin pitch ❑

4. Why is it harder to get your message across on the phone than face to face?
   a) The person you're talking to might not hear too well ❑
   b) It might be a bad line and you could be cut off ❑
   c) Neither of you can read the other's body language ❑
   d) You can't tell what else they're doing while talking to you ❑

5. How could you come over as more businesslike and focused on the phone?
   a) Put your feet on the desk and relax ❑
   b) Close your eyes and imagine you can see the other person ❑
   c) Read their website or LinkedIn profile as you speak ❑
   d) Stand up ❑

6. When you write, what should you always try to do?
   a) Be yourself and write largely as you would speak ❑
   b) Be more formal ❑
   c) Make it impersonal as you're writing on behalf of your organization ❑
   d) Be chatty and familiar ❑

7. When writing, what is the maximum length your sentences should ideally be?
   a) 6 words ❑
   b) 12 words ❑
   c) 18 words ❑
   d) 24 words ❑

8. When should you ideally check your emails?
   a) As soon as the 'ping' tells you they've arrived ❑
   b) Every ten minutes ❑
   c) Every hour, when you pause for a break ❑
   d) Daily ❑

9. What is the longest an email should ideally be?
a) 50 words ❏
b) 100 words ❏
c) 150 words ❏
d) 200 words ❏

10. What is the best way to deliver bad news or a complaint?
a) By registered letter ❏
b) By email ❏
c) By putting a poster on the office noticeboard ❏
d) Face to face ❏

CHAPTER 14

Time management favourites

We started the masterclass by focusing on you, your aspirations and your goals. How can your career deliver these? It's important to know why you're striving to get more done and manage your time better. You had to be motivated to work at the techniques in this masterclass.

So far, we've looked at your job, your workspace, your time, your colleagues and finally your communication. That pretty much covers all the bases. What we've not done yet is explore some of the less obvious, perhaps even quirky, things you can do to boost your time efficiency.

This chapter is different from what you've read thus far. It highlights some of the specific time management tips that work for me. I think they'll probably be useful for you too. They may make you frown, smile and then say 'Aha!'

By the end of this chapter you will:

- have considered my own top time management tips
- feel more in control of your life, work and your time
- see how technology can help you.

Reduce stress

I don't know about you, but I get very wound up sometimes. The truth is that we all suffer from stress to some extent. In many workplaces you see the organization's challenges convert into unrealistic goals. Each person in the chain of command simply divides up then delegates the unrealistic goals further down the line. This creates a situation where everyone blames everyone else for the inevitable failure –except, that is, the unfortunate people at the bottom who have no one to blame.

> *'Why does it take me nearly two hours*
> *just to get through the morning*
> *emails? Pah, poo and pants.'*
> Stephen Fry (Tweet, 18.04.09)

One of my pet hates is people dumping stress on others less able to deal with it than they are. Here's how you can stop people dumping their stress on you when they try to delegate jobs with unrealistic goals.

- Ask how your manager came to accept such a tough challenge.
- Offer to help, but don't accept responsibility or make it your problem.
- Retain control of your diary so that others can't fill it brim full with commitments.
- Make time to exercise, even if it's using the stairs rather than the lift.
- If your health starts to suffer, ease off and look after yourself. You're of no use to anyone if you become ill.

However much you love your job, remember that you are responsible *to* your boss, not responsible *for* them. Don't take on what you know cannot be delivered.

Learn to say no

I've got to know the now retired management writer Charles Handy. Before we first met, I had to persuade his wife it was worth while for him to meet me. She had a reputation for being hard to get past and very protective of her husband's time. When I met him, I realized why. He's such a lovely chap he finds it really difficult to say no. Liz, his wife, acts as gatekeeper and says no for him.

I also find it hard to say no. Too often I find myself helping people with things I frankly should not have got involved with. It could be that you are something of a soft touch too. It's all too easy to sell yourself the idea of helping someone else. The danger is that you end up helping them and neglect your own work as a result.

Try these ways to say no without hurting anyone's feelings.

- 'I'm sorry, but I have a big workload and simply have no capacity for more.'
- 'I'm pretty busy, but if you could send me a short email saying exactly what you want and how you feel I can help, I'll take a look at it.'
- 'I really don't think I'm the right person for this. Why don't you ask...'

As a rule, the longer you delay saying no, the harder it is to do. Get tough.

Deal with tiredness

We all get tired, particularly if we are trying to pack a lot into our lives. It's one of the problems people encounter when they are studying while working. It's also a problem if you are trying to keep up with people far younger and fitter than you.

Being tired reduces your work rate. I sometimes find myself staring at my computer screen but doing nothing. That's a sign that it's time to switch off and take a break. Here are some effective ways to keep alert at work.

- **Drink water**
  I always have water on my desk and drink lots.

- **Eat fruit**
  I also have fruit on my desk as a great, non-fattening energy boost.

- **Move about**

  I rarely sit still for too long. When I need to think, I pace about; it gets the blood flowing.
- **Sleep well**

  I'm an early bird, so refuse to stay up late at night. I need my full eight hours of sleep and make sure I always get it.
- **Keep fit**

  I recently turned 60, but still run, go the gym and am reduced to a sweating wreck once a week by my personal trainer. Fitness becomes even more important as you get older.

Tiredness can also be a symptom of stress, as I know only too well. Understand why you feel tired and then do something it about it. Your life won't change on its own!

Question well

I had the advantage of formal sales training early in my career. This taught me how to control the flow of a conversation. The techniques help me encourage people to tell what I'm trying to find out. It also makes it easier for me to get their commitment. Consequently, I am often well informed and usually persuasive.

Here's how you do this.

Open questions

Open questions make it easy for people to give you information. For example, 'How has your time management improved since you read my masterclass?' Open questions require more than just a yes/no answer.

You direct the question towards the subject you want to hear about. This is great when trying to gather information. It's also a good way to get your children to tell you about their day. Here are two options.

- 'How was school today?' will probably receive the answer 'OK.'
- 'What did you do at school today?' will probably receive a longer answer.

You can focus your open questions by 'funnelling' the person you're talking with towards the area you're most interested in.

For example, 'That's really interesting; can you tell me more about the green ones?'

Closed questions

Closed questions enable you to check understanding or gain commitment. They encourage yes/no answers. In sales, they often offer two alternatives, neither of which is no. For example, 'Can we meet to discuss this on Monday at ten, or is Tuesday afternoon better for you?'

Imagine you are delegating a task. You've explained what has to be done and by when. By asking open and closed questions you can make absolutely certain the person understands what it is you want them to do.

- Open question: 'Can you tell me in your own words what it is you are going to do?'
- Closed question: 'And you are confident you can complete the task by Thursday?'

Minutes, not hours

Most people arrange meetings to start at the top of an hour, say at ten o'clock. Diary systems block out time in full hours, so you all sit down expecting to be there for a full hour. The meeting stretches to fill the time available. I like to start meetings at odd times – say, quarter to the hour – and schedule them to finish at quarter or half past. You'd be surprised how much faster a meeting flows when time is limited.

Do it now!

I sometimes shock consultancy clients when they tell me that a customer is resisting their sales approach. I ask for their number and ring to ask why. It's much easier to do things when they're on your mind than to procrastinate. Don't leave things for later; do them right now.

Challenging or embarrassing things are almost always better done straight away. Of course, there are some things for which you need to prepare, so please don't become impulsive. However, you'll find plenty of situations where it's timelier to do something immediately than to delay. Here are some good office examples.

- Always keep a spare loo roll beside the toilet. Replace the spare when you start the last roll, not when someone has used the last square.
- Keep spare toner cartridges and, again, replace them when they are fitted, not when you run out.
- When you see that things need to be forwarded to someone else, do it straight away. Don't put stuff down only to pick it up again.
- If you drive a lot, fill up with fuel when the level drops below a quarter full. Then you won't be in a rush when the dial hits red.

Sleep on it

We all face conundrums from time to time at work – the challenges for which there is no clear-cut answer. They can take hours to work out and, even then, you are rarely sure you have made the right decision.

I tend to summarize the possible options on a piece of paper and take it home. I read it late in the evening and start my brain ticking. It's surprising how often I wake in the morning with an answer I've not thought of before.

I'm no neuroscientist, so I don't know how sleeping on challenges works. All I know is that it does. I think it's because my subconscious mind whirrs away at it through the night. Doubtful? Give it a try and see if it works for you.

Talk as you drive

I changed my car recently. Now I can plug my phone into the car and make calls without taking my hands from the steering wheel during the one or two long car journeys I make a week, thus combining the two tasks.

I also always have a list of people I want to talk to, when I can find the time. What I do is arrange phone calls with them in advance, booked at 30-minute intervals, for the duration of my planned journey. Immediately after each call, I phone my office to list what's been agreed. Because I have a very able assistant, sometimes the actions I've agreed have been done before I complete my journey.

Work on trains

I only drive when it's not possible to use the train. Trains can be great places to get some work done. Surrounded by people, you can't really make work phone calls. Internet access is usually sporadic so you're less distracted by email.

Rail journeys enable me to do quality writing without distraction. Sections of this masterclass were written on train journeys. I also try to travel off peak and book my tickets in advance. Often this enables me to travel first class at a lower fare than the regular standard class fare. And finally, pre-booked tickets mean no queuing at the station!

Use visual filing

You've already read about the importance of keeping your office neat and tidy. However, one exception to the minimal paperwork rule that I allow myself is a row of plastic trays in one corner of my office. Each is labelled with a day of the week. I put in these trays anything I know I need to do the next time that day comes round. I also drop in things that come in that I can't deal with or dump straight away. This means little waits more than a week to be done.

Summary

In this chapter we covered several varied time management tips. You may not find them in other time management books, because they are less obvious but still useful time management ideas that you can apply in all areas of your life.

Some of these tips took us back to the subject of you and your well-being. You are not a machine, and do get tired, upset and stressed. Equally, you have a remarkable brain that can work away on problems when you are asleep. Time management always comes back to you, your motivation, determination and commitment.

Only you can change you. It's easy to blame others for the predicaments we find ourselves in. Often we unwittingly project on to others responsibility for what we actually do to ourselves. And that really does bring us back to the beginning. Only you know what you want to be and how work can help you get there. Take time to know yourself and then the tips in this masterclass will be far easier to put into action. Good luck!

Fact-check (answers at the back)

1. When we lose control of what we are committed to, how can we reduce our stress?
   a) Challenge those who ask you to do what looks impossible ☐
   b) Get plenty of sleep before you attempt the impossible ☐
   c) Make sure people know it's not your fault ☐
   d) Cry when you want to get your own way ☐

2. If you find it impossible to say no, what should you do?
   a) Ignore people when they ask you things ☐
   b) Say yes and live with your shortcoming ☐
   c) Get someone else to say no for you ☐
   d) Work harder to get it all done ☐

3. What is the best way to deal with tiredness at work?
   a) Ignore it and plough on regardless ☐
   b) Have a nap and hope the boss doesn't catch you ☐
   c) Drink water, eat fruit or take a quick walk ☐
   d) Vow to party less in future ☐

4. What can using open and closed questions help you do?
   a) Trick people into doing what you want ☐
   b) Maintain control of a conversation ☐
   c) Be really annoying ☐
   d) Get a date with that nice boy/girl in the next office ☐

5. When is the worst time to start a meeting?
   a) Half past the hour ☐
   b) Quarter past the hour ☐
   c) Five to the hour ☐
   d) On the hour ☐

6. What should you do after putting the last loo roll in the holder at work?
   a) Be glad someone put a spare in the room ☐
   b) Use what you want, then hide the rest as a joke ☐
   c) Not even think about this stuff as it's not part of your job ☐
   d) Replace the spare before you go ☐

7. If you go to sleep thinking about a particular work conundrum, what will happen when you wake up?
   a) You'll feel tired ☐
   b) You'll find you've overslept ☐
   c) You'll have some surprising answers to your conundrum ☐
   d) You won't get to sleep at all ☐

8. What's the best way to spend a long work car journey?
   a) Try to arrive ahead of your satnav's prediction ☐
   b) Listen to music and chill out ☐
   c) Have some scheduled phone calls that you can make hands-free ☐
   d) Eat lots of boiled sweets ☐

9. What are train journeys great for?
a) Reading or writing without being distracted ❑
b) People watching ❑
c) Chatting to strangers ❑
d) Sleeping ❑

10. If you have a box file for every day of the week, what should you put in it?
a) A daily treat ❑
b) Your newspaper ❑
c) Stuff you need to get done on that day ❑
d) Nothing ❑

7 × 7

1 Seven key ideas

- The more clearly you have defined your objectives, the easier it will be to focus your effort on what's most important.
- Keep work in perspective. Sure, it's important, but your health and relationships are even more important.
- Don't try to change everything all at once. Instead, improve your time management bit by bit.
- No is a shorter word than yes, and yet we all find it harder to say, so practise!
- Be realistic when setting deadlines and don't wait until the last minute to make a start.
- Make it easy for those around you to manage their time, too. Don't just pass work on.
- Remember to remain human. Make yourself more efficient, yes, but don't turn into a machine.

2 Seven things to avoid at all costs

- **Addiction** – Work can become an addiction, just as alcohol and drugs can be addictive. I became a workaholic; make sure you don't!
- **Over-committing** – Always, always, allow time for projects to slightly overrun. You also need to leave yourself time to think.
- **Doing more than enough** – it's always good to do a little more than you promised, but stop as soon as you're confident you've done enough. To do more can be pointless.
- **Getting overloaded** – We all like to help others when they find themselves overloaded, but to overload yourself in the process is counterproductive for everyone.
- **Blind obedience** – It can be tough to challenge your brief if you have a pushy boss but, unless you do, she or he may

just keep piling on more work. Become assertive while remaining positive.
- **Neglecting the kids** – Too many people look back and say they wish they'd spent more time with their kids when they were small. Don't be one of those people.
- **Losing perspective** – Few of us work in 'life or death' situations, so, however much you feel pressured, keep your perspective.

3 Seven of the best resources

- **Google** – Keeping your diary on Google means you can set reminders, share across devices and link to your current tasks. Put all your stuff into your diary and stick to it.
- **Voicemail** – Phones are intrusive and demand attention when they ring. If you're busy on something, ignore the phone, email and online chat. Respond when it suits you, not others.
- **Two screens** – as I mention earlier, adding a second screen to my PC changed my life. I no longer have to keep switching between programmes, and I have whatever I need to view at the same time in front of me.
- **iPad** – I use my iPad all the time when I'm not in the office. It means I can deal with email on the train, the sofa or even the toilet. I also use it to take notes in meetings and then I can share them with those I need to before I leave the table.
- **Piano** – I find it vital to have something outside my work I treat as an equal priority. For me it's my piano as I recently started learning to play. Having something you must do other than work will help you balance your life.
- **Notepad** – I keep a notepad on my desk and list the key tasks for each day. I prioritize them and then cross them off as I complete them. This stops me getting distracted by 'urgent' stuff that actually isn't.
- **Clocks** – I keep a couple of small clocks in my office, carefully positioned so I can see the time when talking with visitors or holding a meeting. Clocks will help you to be in control of your time too.

4 Seven inspirations

- **The Prime Minister** – Whoever's in office, see how they have others to brief them before any meeting. They go in prepared and knowing what's it's possible to achieve.
- **Stephen Fry** – He lives with bipolarity and predicts when he's likely to be down and, I'm told, keeps those weeks clear of commitments. Be realistic and practical about your time.
- **Richard Branson** – He's developed a strong brand and identifies, then supports, talented people to run the different businesses he sets up. He's clear where he adds value and appears to delegate and empower people very effectively.
- **Chris Woodhead** – The former head of OFSTED died when this edition was being written, but he was an excellent example of how, when struck by a terrible, debilitating illness, it's possible to remain active and engaged in the things you care about.
- **Michelle Obama** – She manages to balance being the partner of a world leader with leading positive change in her own right. That takes both willpower and outstanding time management.
- **Angela Merkel** – She was brought up in communist East Germany and uses her past experience to inform her decision-making as one of Europe's political leaders. We should never forget our past, but build on the foundations it creates.
- **Your dog** – who knows that life is actually for living and not to be spent entirely at work!

5 Seven great quotes

- 'Better three hours too soon than one minute late.' William Shakespeare
- 'The only reason for time is so that everything doesn't happen at once.' Albert Einstein
- 'The time you enjoy wasting is not wasted time.' Bertrand Russell

- 'Hide nothing, for time, which sees all and hears all, exposes all.' Sophocles
- 'We must use time creatively.' Martin Luther King
- 'Friends are thieves of time.' Francis Bacon
- 'Your time is limited, so don't waste it living someone else's life.' Steve Jobs

6 Seven things to do today

- **Clear your desk** – This is always the best place to start. Piles of paper just don't help.
- **Prioritize** – Take time to reflect on what is really most important to you and your success.
- **Become more elusive** – You need to regain control of your time and that means not being available to others quite as much.
- **Bounce things back** – We all assume that if we're asked to do something, it's for a good reason. But asking 'why?' and 'why by then?' will help you prioritize and control the flow.
- **Make shortlists** – It's no good if your to-do list never gets done. It's better to list only what's possible in the day, then make a new list for tomorrow.
- **Define 'enough'** – You only need to do enough of anything, or perhaps just a little bit more. Knowing when to stop will really help you out of 'overworking'.
- **Have daily treats** – I make sure there's something I know I'm going to enjoy built into every day. It might just be ten minutes sitting in the sun or a slice of chocolate cake, but every day you need something.

7 Seven trends for tomorrow

- **Flexible working** – More of us will find ourselves working remotely and possibly for ourselves. Technology makes it easy to work 24/7. The challenge is to manage that!
- **Goals, not hours** – I rarely work at a day rate these days. People pay me to achieve a specific goal and it's up to me how long I let it take. Try not to think nine to five.

- **Messaging** – I can find my landline ringing, mobile ringing, Skype ringing, email pinging and someone messaging via Facebook or Twitter all at the same time. It's going to become harder to retain control of your time as opportunities to interrupt you increase.
- **Retiring later** – If, like me, you've reached the age when your parents retired, you'll realize that most of us are working for much longer these days. It's even more important to manage your time well as you grow older, if only because you've less time left than you had!
- **Specializing** – A benefit of easier communication is that you can afford to specialize and still keep busy. The more you specialize in something, usually the better and more efficient you get. This helps you manage your time.
- **Retro can be good** – Just as handwritten invitations now have greater impact because they're rare, so, too, will there be things you can do that have the impact of novelty. Face-to-face meetings, rather than always just emailing or phoning, are one example.
- **Keeping in touch** – You can never know enough people and social media like Twitter make it easy to keep tabs on those who interest you. Follow me @robertashton1 and let me know how this masterclass has helped you improve your time management. I'd really like to know.

PART 3
Your Speed Reading Masterclass

Introduction

When people think about speed reading they often narrow it down to simply reading fast. This, however, is only a small part of the overall process. The key to truly effective speed reading is first being able to identify what you really want or need to read and then reading that carefully selected material – fast.

Take a moment to mentally review all the information that passes in front of you in a typical day: at home, at work, in the papers at the local coffee shop. How much of it do you ignore because it looks like too much to take on, leaving it instead to build up and stack high until you're so behind you need days or weeks to catch up – if you ever manage to at all?

If you had a simple process to follow that allowed you to quickly and easily identify the information you need and eliminate that which you don't need, this backlog of information wouldn't happen and you'd have more time to live your life instead of worrying about what you might be missing because you think you're overloaded.

The aim of this masterclass is to give you the tools you need to get up to date and stay that way.

The key to this masterclass is practice. You don't have to set aside an hour a day, simply use what you learn here on everything you read – from books to newspapers and manuals to cornflake boxes. The more you use it, the more natural it will become so, eventually, you'll wonder how you ever read any other way.

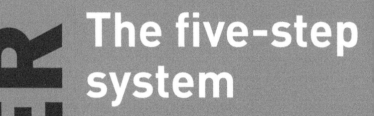

CHAPTER 15

The five-step system

This chapter is the key to effective speed reading. If you only have ten minutes to read one chapter in this book, then make it this one. In it you'll learn a strategy that addresses one of the primary fears people have when it comes to dealing with information: missing something important.

Have you ever been part of a conversation where people are discussing a document or project, only to find that you haven't a clue what they're talking about? Have you ever met people in your field who are talking about new trends that you've never heard of?

The frustration and overload created in situations like this comes from 1) not being able to identify what's relevant and what's not, 2) reading the information but not remembering it and/or 3) not having a strategy for getting through volumes of material in a short amount of time.

This first day outlines a strategy that gives you a solution to these challenges. The skills to identify what you need to read and eliminate what you don't need to read while being certain that you've missed nothing out.

This technique is much like making a good cup of tea; if you follow the instructions, you'll get the result. Only one step of the five-step system needs practice and that step we'll explore in more detail in Chapter 16.

How to use this book

This book is designed to be a workbook for your speed-reading skills and a reference for you as you practise.

Each day may be referred to independently. This makes it easy for you to locate the information you need. Becoming accustomed to moving freely around a book instead of reading it from front to back is an important habit to develop since most authors don't put the information in precisely the right order to suit *you*.

Which brings us to a most important rule of effective reading: *make your own reading rules*.

Here's a quick guide to reading this book fast and effectively:

1 Flick through the book to get a feel for its structure.
2 Read this chapter carefully so you know and understand how to apply the five-step reading system.
3 Apply the five-step reading system to this book.

As you learn new techniques, practise them here. You will find that you get through the book much faster than you would have imagined and you will have had the opportunity to try out new skills.

Speed reading raises questions

● What's the fastest possible reading speed?
● How do I remember what I read – when I need to remember it?
● How do I read dry or technical material and maintain concentration?
● Is speed reading easy to learn?

Firstly, we do not know the limit to the speed at which people can read. As an example, Anne Jones read *Harry Potter and the Deathly Hallows* in 47 minutes (4,251 words per minute), then offered to write book reviews for the media to prove her comprehension, comprehension being the most relevant part of the exercise. Why spend precious time reading if you don't plan to remember and perhaps use what you read? Remembering the information long after you have read it, whether fact or fiction, will be explored in Chapter 17.

Speed reading is easy. It's the one part of this process that needs some practice but it reflects only one fifth of the reading strategy presented in this book. The rest of the system works simply because you use it.

The five-step system

There are five stages to the strategy. By the time you complete them you will have:

- explored the material at least three times
- read what you need to have read
- integrated the new knowledge into what you already know
- found the information you need.

And, most importantly, you will have spent a fraction of the time you might otherwise have spent.

To avoid slipping back into old reading habits, accurately follow the five-step process as outlined in this book. Once you are familiar with the system, you can adapt it to any type of reading (articles, newspapers, memos, books or magazines) by combining and omitting steps.

The five-step system has one overriding rule: *always know why you are reading something.*

Whether the reason is 'I want to', 'it looks interesting', or 'because Joe says it'll be a good read' doesn't matter, as long as you have one.

The five steps are:

1 Preparation
2 Structure
3 Language
4 Content
5 Purposeful selection

This system is based on the process of *highlighting* and *eliminating*. As you use the system, your aim is to highlight areas for further study and eliminate those that you are certain you do not need.

Depending on how much you want from the book, steps 1 to 4 could take between five and 40 minutes for a book of 300 pages. The time you spend on step 5 depends on the amount of detailed information you want from the material.

Steps 1 to 5 will now be precisely detailed. Read through this section once, then, using this book or another non-fiction book, try the system out. At this point don't worry about reading fast (as in more 'words per minute') – we'll discuss that in the next chapter.

Step 1: Preparation

One reason that reading can be frustrating is due to a lack of focus and concentration. The preparation stage helps you stay on task.

First:

● Write down what you already know about the subject: key words will be sufficient.

Next:

● Decide what you want from the book – general information, enough information to write a report or simply the answer to a specific question?

Always ask yourself these three questions:

● Why am I reading this in the first place?
● What do I already know?
● What do I need to know?

Step 2: Structure

The purpose of this stage is to become familiar with the book's *structure*:

● What does it look like?
● Are there summaries or conclusions?
● Is the book all words or are there any pictures?
● What size is the print?
● Is the text broken up into sections?
● Is it a series of paragraphs?

For a 300-page book, this step should take about five minutes.

- *Read* the front and back covers, inside flaps, table of contents, index, and scan the bibliography.
- *Determine* the structure of the book; chapter headings, sub-headings, pictures, graphs, cartoons and images.
- *Eliminate* the parts of the book that you are sure you don't need.
- *Highlight* areas you think you do need.
- *Reaffirm* your decision about what you want from the book.

If it becomes clear that the book does not contain what you need, put it away. You will have saved yourself hours of work.

Step 3: Language

You have prepared yourself and you know the structure of the book. This next step will familiarize you with the language in the book. Is it full of jargon? Do you need a dictionary even before you begin? Is the language so complex that you decide, at this stage, to get a more basic book on the subject? This step works well if you have completed step 1 (preparation) thoroughly.

A 300-page book should only take between five to ten minutes to review for language.

- Scan the pages at a rate of about a page every few seconds.
- Look for words that stand out and highlight them. They might be names, long or technical words, or words in **bold** or *italics*.
- Study the language: is it technical, non-technical, user-friendly, are you familiar with it?
- Do you need to refer to a dictionary (technical or otherwise) before you carry on?

The bonus of going through this step is that as well as getting familiar with the language, you'll also pick up some of the key ideas, putting you in good shape for step four.

> ## An important note
> If you know *why* you are reading the book you will know *what* you are looking for and words related to your area of interest will stand out. Try this now: look around the room for everything red. Only red. Notice how much and how many shades of red there are in the room. Now, close your eyes and try and remember everything blue in the room ... what did you notice? If you know what you are looking for, you will find it.

Step 4: Content

This is the first time you will be doing anything close to reading. Most well-written material will outline the aim or core of each chapter in the first paragraph and the contents of each paragraph will be made clear in the first sentence of that paragraph. So, for more detail:

● read the first paragraph of every chapter; and
● the first sentence of every paragraph (and the last if the paragraph is very long).

As you read – cross out, highlight, underline, circle, take notes and mind-map. The more thoroughly you do this, the more effective the final stage will be.

Step 5: Purposeful selection

Here is a thought experiment (don't actually do this unless you want to fall foul of mountain rescue).

Imagine you are to take a trip from London to Edinburgh. You are to use country roads as far as possible. Imagine you have never taken such a trip before, but still you decide not to use a map. On your arrival in Edinburgh, check your time, which will include all the detours you had to take and the stops you had to make to ask for directions. Make the trip a second time with a map, then compare the ease and speed of the two journeys.

The same principle applies to reading. Steps 1 to 4 create a map for you to follow. Once you know where you are going and how you are going to get there, the task is much easier to accomplish.

The aim of the first four steps is to allow you to select what you need or want to read with purpose.

During the first four steps you have decided what it is you want to read, what answers you are looking for and what you are interested in about the subject. You have studied the structure of the book, you are familiar with the language, you have read approximately one third of the content and you have an excellent understanding of what information the book contains. You are now in a position to select the sections you really need to read without worrying whether you have missed anything out or not.

To do this most effectively:

● Review the notes you made in step 1.
● Add to your notes any information you have gained as you have been reading.
● Ask: 'Have I found what I'm looking for?'
● If you have what you need, stop.
● If not, review the key words you have highlighted in step 3 and repeat the question: 'Do I have what I want yet?'
● You made notes in step 4: review them and again ask whether you have what you want.
● If you decide that you need more information, then go through the book and read the sections you identified as relevant during the first four steps.
● If you do decide you need to read the entire book you will find you will be able to read it much faster, because, having completed the first four steps, you will know what the book contains and what to expect.

TIP *If you know nothing about a subject it is almost impossible to remember what you read. The five-step system helps you build a framework of knowledge, making retention and recall easier.*

Summary

By the time you've applied the five-step system to any non-fiction material, you will be familiar with the layout, the key ideas in the book, the language and a good deal of the content. By step 4 of the five-step system you will have been able to delete sections that have no relevance and highlight areas that you need to study in more depth (step 5).

How much more time you spend on the material will depend on exactly what you want from it. It might be that you've identified the page and paragraph that contain the answer to your question, or you might have decided that you still need to read it all. Whatever you choose, it will be an informed decision and you'll be spending your time reading material you are sure you want to read.

The best way to learn anything new is to use it. Take a few minutes to apply the five-step system to a book you are reading. Review the steps and give yourself a target of 20 minutes to get as much as you can from the book. Once you've identified the sections of the book you want to focus on, then read those using the speed-reading techniques outlined in Chapter 16.

Fact-check (answers at the back)

1. What is the fastest possible reading speed?
   a) 500 words per minute ❏
   b) 1000 words per minute ❏
   c) 25,000 words per minute ❏
   d) Who knows? We're learning more about what the human brain can do every day! Our only limits are the ones we place on ourselves. ❏

2. Is speed reading easy to learn?
   a) No – it takes a lot of practice. ❏
   b) Yes – after hours of practice. ❏
   c) Yes – if you have Einstein's IQ. ❏
   d) Yes – if you apply these techniques to anything you read. ❏

3. The purpose of reviewing the structure of a book is to:
   a) get an overview of the book. ❏
   b) eliminate parts of the book you are sure you don't need. ❏
   c) highlight areas you think you might need. ❏
   d) All of the above. ❏

4. What is the overriding rule of the five-step system?
   a) Always know why you're reading something. ❏
   b) Always wear rubber-soled shoes in a thunderstorm. ❏
   c) Whenever you read anything boring, have plenty of strong coffee to hand. ❏
   d) If you're going to read anything after midnight, do 50 press-ups first. ❏

5. What should you do if you discover (in step 2) that the book won't give you the information you need?
   a) Finish the book because you've started it. ❏
   b) Put down the book and move onto something else – you've saved yourself hours of work. ❏
   c) Put down the book until later, then review it again. ❏
   d) Redo the five-step process in case you've missed something. ❏

6. During the 'language' stage, what are you looking for?
   a) Jargon ❏
   b) Unfamiliar terminology ❏
   c) Any words or phrases you don't understand ❏
   d) All of the above ❏

7. What is the greatest challenge you'll face in step 4?
   a) Pulled eye muscles ❏
   b) Flea bites ❏
   c) Being trapped in old habits and reading more than the first sentence and first paragraph of every section ❏
   d) Falling asleep ❏

8. By the time you've completed steps 1 to 4, you'll have read approximately:
   a) 90% of the book ❏
   b) 10% of the book ❏
   c) 33.3% of the book ❏
   d) None of the book ❏

9. Why is it important to know why you're reading something?
a) It's easy to find what you're looking for when you know what it is. ❏
b) It saves time. ❏
c) It gives you focus and motivation. ❏
d) All of the above. ❏

10. How does the five-step system improve memory?
a) It builds a framework of knowledge. ❏
b) By the time you get to step 5, you've gone through the information four times and repetition aides recall. ❏
c) The five-step system increases your reading rate, which helps keep you alert. ❏
d) All of the above. ❏

CHAPTER 16

Speed reading

There are a number of factors that will influence the speed at which you can read, and these are covered in this chapter, followed by speed-reading techniques that will help you through any challenges you might face.

The key to success in this chapter is to enjoy it. If you allow yourself to get frustrated and uptight, then no amount of practice will increase your reading rate. Instead, follow the instructions through steps 1 to 4 of the five-step system; when you reach step 5, you will have a vastly reduced amount to read. You can then choose how fast you want to read based on the type of material, its complexity, how much detail you need and how much time you have.

If you're under too much pressure, you're likely to go mentally blank and won't be able to read at all. Relax, breathe and read at the most appropriate speed for the material and what you want from it.

The more you read, the better you will get at recognizing when to read fast and when to slow down. The more flexible you are with your reading, the faster the overall session will go and the more you'll retain. The good news is that this is the only part of the five-step reading process that needs practice.

The more you read the better you will become at recognizing when you can read fast and when to slow down.

Factors contributing to speed

Factors contributing to the speed at which you can read are:

- **Familiarity with the subject-related terminology** – if you are already familiar with the subject you will already have a framework on which to build and you will be able to read quite quickly because you will not have to stop to think about what key words mean and how the ideas fit together.
- **Clarity of purpose** – remember step 1 of the five-step system. The clearer your purpose is, the faster you will be able to read. Always know why you are reading something.
- **The difficulty of the text** – some material is difficult to read even if you are familiar with the terminology and content – this includes anything technical or industry specific like legal or medical texts.
- **Urgency and stress levels** – have you ever noticed that when you absolutely have to read something immediately you find that you can't read it fast? Stress will slow you down. Stress will be considered in Chapter 17 in conjunction with concentration and memory.
- **Mood** – if you are feeling tired, restless, impatient or irritable, you may find that you will be unable to read as fast as when you feel alert, fresh, happy and relaxed. You may not always be alert, fresh, happy and relaxed when you have to read so, if you can, learn how to manage your feelings so that you can concentrate regardless of how you might be feeling at the time.

What you need to improve speed

Many of us are taught that in order to be fully informed we need to read every word in the book or article we've chosen. But in reality, with so much information available to us, it makes more sense to select what we need at the time and leave the rest. The first four steps of this system will help you with that selection process giving you the time and mental focus to speed-read the relevant content.

To improve your reading speed you will need:

- good background knowledge of the subject or, if you do not have that yet, a strategy for building the background knowledge quickly
- familiarity with the language related to the subject
- a good vocabulary
- a desire to learn how to improve your reading
- a good attitude towards reading – ask yourself the question: 'What is it that I get from speed reading?'
- practise – if you use these techniques every day you will find that the speed at which you read, your recall, comprehension and the flexibility of your reading will quickly improve.

Increasing your basic reading rate

The main reason that we tend to read slowly is because we read with our ears instead of with our eyes (more about this in Chapter 18). The second reason we read slowly is because we are easily distracted by what's on the page and by what's going on around us.

Using a pacer

A pacer is a tool that will help you to eliminate most of your speed-reading problems. A pacer can be your finger, a chopstick, a pencil or pen, or even speed-reading software.

A pacer helps to eliminate most distractions, and it includes an extra sense (touch) in the reading process. Using a pacer adds a kinaesthetic, physical dimension to your reading. You are actually *doing* something instead of simply reading. You are involving your hands as well.

Using a pacer helps your reading in several ways.

- It increases your reading rate by encouraging your eyes to focus on more than one word at a time.
- The pacer focuses you on what you are reading instead of allowing your eyes to jump around the page at anything that attracts your attention.

Here is an experiment for you to try. Find someone willing to take part. Ask that person to draw a circle in the air using their eyes. Notice the eye movements – are they smooth or jerky? Do they create a full circle or does it look like they are making corners? Next, ask them to draw a circle in the air with their finger and this time to follow their finger with their eyes. Watch their eyes. Do you notice that the second time their eyes move smoothly, quickly and deliberately?

The pacer also

- helps you move to new lines smoothly and easily
- prevents you losing your place
- prevents sub-vocalization (the voice inside your head caused by reading with your ears) by speeding up the pace at which you read and allowing you to see more than one word at a time.

How to use a pacer

You can use a pen, a chopstick, a finger, anything you like, as a pacer. To begin, place your pacer on the first word on the line and move it smoothly across the page or screen to the end of the line, then return it to the next line.

Use your pacer to read the next paragraph. Place the pacer on the dotted line and move it smoothly across the line. Re-read the paragraph several times until you feel that you have the rhythm smooth and fast – also, move the pacer just a little bit more quickly than you think you can 'read'.

It is important that the pacer moves smoothly and steadily across the page. If the movement is hesitant your eyes are dictating the pace at which you read and your reading rate will not increase. If the pacer moves smoothly, your eyes, with practice, will learn to keep up and your brain will learn to absorb the meaning of words in a new way.

What was different about reading with a pacer? How did you feel? How much faster did you feel you read? How do you feel about comprehension?

Are you still reading with your pacer? For the duration of this book read using a pacer. By the time you finish the book you will find that it has become second nature and you will be well on the way to becoming an expert speed-reader.

Different types of pacing

The pacing you are using now is one basic method for guiding your eye across the page. There are different methods of pacing for different types of material and different readers' needs.

Technical material with which you are not familiar

Place the pacer under every line and move it steadily across the page from the beginning to the end of each line. This method ensures that you miss nothing.

Technical material with which you are familiar

Place your pacer under every second line. This method encourages you to read more than one line at a time and ultimately to understand the meaning much more quickly.

Material with which you are very familiar

If you are very familiar with the material and you only need to have a general idea about what you are reading you can run the pacer down either the side or the middle of the page.

Ultimately, the more you experiment and the more flexible your reading becomes, the easier you will find it to change from one technique to another.

Practice box

Novels are the best source of practice to develop flexibility in pacing. At the start of the novel you might find that you pace under every line, then as you get familiar with the plot you might pace under every two lines. When the story really gets going and you are looking for the exciting bits in between the description, you might find that you run the pacer down the middle of the page until you find the sections of the book that really carry the story. Your enjoyment of the book is not lessened in any way at all – in fact you might find that you actually finish more novels than you used to.

Hints to increase your speed:

- **Push yourself quite hard.** It is easy to stay in the comfort zone of reading slowly. Once you break through the barrier of believing that you can only remember what you read when you hear every word, your enjoyment of reading and your pace will increase.
- **Practise – often.** Use everything you read as a practice medium. Speed-read the instructions on the back of a bottle or the sales blurb on the back of a cereal packet. Instead of just reading as you have previously, read with the purpose of going as fast as you can for good comprehension. Use a pacer when you do so.
- **Build the context first.** The first four steps of the five-step system will make speed reading anything easy and several times faster than if you were reading it for the first time.
- **The faster you go the less you will vocalize.** Later on in this chapter, we will discuss ways of building speed and maintaining it – play with these exercises daily until you feel that they are a natural part of your reading strategy.
- **Eliminate or decrease distractions.** In Chapter 19, we look at different distractions you are likely to encounter and some solutions to them. The more you are able to concentrate, the faster you will be able to read.
- **Read actively.** Take notes, mark and highlight relevant sections, make comments as you read, build reading maps and think about the arguments as you read. If you must

do any talking inside your head while you read, choose to make it a debate or dialogue on aspects of the topic with the author. The more actively you read, the better your understanding and long-term comprehension will be.

It is important to remember that speed reading is not about reading fast all the time. The technical content of the material, the print size, your familiarity with the subject, and, particularly, your purpose for reading can affect the speed at which you read. The key to speed reading is having the choice to read as fast or as slow as you wish.

Skimming and scanning

What is the difference?

The difference between skimming and scanning is that when you scan for information you stop once you have it. With skimming you don't stop, unless you want to.

When are they used?

Scanning is used when you are looking for specific information; an answer to a particular question or a telephone number in a directory.

Skimming is used during step 3 of the five-step system. You use skimming when you know what you are looking for and want a general impression of what the text contains.

There are different types of skimming depending on what your purpose is:

- **Skimming to overview** – the purpose of this method is to get an outline of what the document is about. You will be looking more at structure than at content. This method is used mostly in the second step of the five-step system.
- **Skimming to preview** – this is when you know you are going to re-read the material. Your purpose is to gather as much background information as you can on the subject without spending too much time on it.

● **Skimming to review** – you would use this method when you have already read the material and your purpose is just to refamiliarize yourself with the content.

Successful skimming

Skimming for information is easier when you know where the information is likely to be within the overall scheme of the piece you are reading. While you are speed reading, look for the core information. Once you have stated your purpose for skimming and you know what you are looking for, you will be able to identify trigger words that hold the relevant information:

● who
● what
● where
● why
● when
● how.

Other key words are those that distinguish fact from opinion. An author might spend the first half of a paragraph giving fact, then you may find words like:

● but
● nonetheless
● however
● yet
● on the other hand.

These key words signify that the author may be drifting from fact to opinion. If you are looking for an author's opinion on a subject, look for these words.

Practice box
Practise this by going through newspaper or magazine articles with the purpose of identifying the *who*, *what*, *where*, *why*, *when* and *how*, as well as the author's opinions, as quickly as you can.

Getting the message

When you read, you convert the information embedded in groups of words into ideas, images, thoughts, feelings and actions. One of the purposes of reading is getting the message that the words carry. This does not necessarily mean that you have to read all the words. When you speed-read – especially when you start to get used to reading more than one line at a time – you might at first get confused because the words may be presented to you in a different order to the one that was intended. When you read with your eyes, you will find, however, that this does not present a problem because your brain works out what the sentence means regardless of what order the words are in.

Your brain is always trying to make sense of information it receives. When the information you are reading is not complete your brain will naturally fill in the blanks and organize the information so that you can make sense of it. First, read the following sentences out loud and work out what they mean:

We'll 20 minutes in be there.
Let's dinner for tonight go out.
Reading visual activity done slowly is only the.

Now, look at the next batch of sentences and get the meaning from them as quickly as you can by looking at the whole sentence and identifying the key words:

Speed reading have if you a purpose is easy.
Have yet holiday you been on this year?
The improve is to best way to practise.

Which was quicker – reading with your ears or reading with your eyes?

You don't have to have the words in the right order to get the message.

'It's all in the words' – developing a good vocabulary

The bigger your vocabulary, the faster you will be able to read. Hesitating at words you are unfamiliar with wastes time. Unfamiliar terminology makes you think about the whole passage, not just the word. Several questions might go through your head. What does this word mean? Does it change the context? Is it important to my understanding of the text? These questions go through your mind very quickly, but the problem is that once you have answered them you may have forgotten what you have been reading. The real time-waster is when you have to return to the beginning of a passage and start again.

Solving the vocabulary problem is relatively easy. Some vocabulary will become clear to you within the context of the paragraph; the rest you should look up before you begin step 5.

> **TIP** *During steps 3 and 4 of the five-step system look for unfamiliar words as part of the skimming exercise, then look them up before you begin step 5.*

Ways of increasing your vocabulary:

- Pay attention to new words.
- Keep a small notebook where you write down new terminology (with meanings) that you come across in reading and in conversation.
- Use your new vocabulary.
- Become familiar with the roots of words. If you understand the root, you will be able to work out the meaning of many words. All good dictionaries will show you the roots.

Reading exercises

Here are some exercises to increase your speed-reading rate.

Stretching speed and comprehension

This quick exercise will help improve your memory and increase your speed.

1 Using a pacer, read one page as fast as you can.
2 Stop and write down everything you can remember.
3 Read five pages like this every day, gradually increasing the number of pages you read before you stop to recall what you read.
4 Start with a familiar subject, then, as your ability, confidence and comfort become more apparent to you, move on to more challenging material.

Stretching speed – the one-minute trip

1 Read for one minute and count how many lines you have read.
2 Continue reading for another minute, reading two lines more than you did the first time.
3 In the next minute, read four lines more than you did before, then six, then eight, then ten.
4 Always read for good comprehension and recall. As soon as you feel you are not understanding or remembering the text, consolidate at that level until you are comfortable. Then speed up again gradually.

Reading quickly requires concentration. If you don't understand or remember what you read you may find your concentration drifting because you are becoming disappointed and perhaps bored.

As your concentration improves, stretch the one-minute trip to two minutes, then four minutes, then six, and eight ... and so on.

Mostly reading

This technique is good for the parts of the text with which you are already fairly familiar and when you want to be sure you have missed nothing out.

1 Read the *first* sentence of the paragraph.
2 Skim the rest of the paragraph for key words and, if necessary, read the *last* sentence of the paragraph.

Metronome pacing

You can buy a small electronic metronome at any music shop quite cheaply – it will be a good investment.
Do this exercise for two minutes, then relax for five minutes.

1 Set the metronome at its slowest speed and read one line per 'tick'.
2 Every page or half page increase the pace of the metronome by one, or by as much as you are comfortable with, until you reach the fastest speed on the metronome.
3 Then relax.

The metronome will reach a speed at which you will not be able to read every word. This exercise 'pushes' your eye and brain to see and absorb more than one word at a time, and gradually stretches your ability.

If you drive on a motorway at 70 miles per hour and, as you approach a town, you suddenly have to reduce your speed to 30, you might slow down and think you are travelling at 30 until the police stop you and inform you that you were travelling at 40 or 50 – much faster than you thought.

The similarity between driving and speed reading doesn't stop there. Travelling at 70 miles an hour you have to concentrate and don't have time to look at the scenery. When speed reading you are reading so fast that your mind doesn't want to wander as much as it can at '30 miles per hour'.

Summary

Most habits are subconscious, so they're pretty hard to fix. The first step to changing a habit is working out you have it and admitting to it!

The challenge with learning to speed-read is that your new reading habits will compete with old habits that you've been enforcing every day since you learned to read. As a result, reading fast is the only part of the five-step system that will take a bit of time to get used to and practice to get right.

The key is to reduce vocalizing and sub-vocalizing.

● To stop yourself vocalizing (mouthing the words), put a pencil between your teeth while you read. You'll soon notice if you start moving your lips.

● With sub-vocalizing (saying the words in your mind), the faster you read, the less you'll sub-vocalize.

Be patient – you've been reading to yourself for many years and your memory strategies are well established. The more you practise, the easier it'll get. Make the job easier by focusing on the first four steps of the five-step system and reducing the amount of unnecessary information as much as possible. Then take the time to practise speed reading techniques on the remaining material knowing that if you need to, you can slow down and you'll still have read the book faster than you would have previously.

Fact-check (answers at the back)

1. What factor(s) can help increase your reading rate?
   a) Familiarity with the subject ❑
   b) Clarity of purpose ❑
   c) Mood ❑
   d) All of the above ❑

2. What do you need to increase your reading rate?
   a) A 21-speed bike ❑
   b) Someone standing over your shoulder ❑
   c) Focus and attention ❑
   d) A lot of caffeine ❑

3. What should you use as a pacer?
   a) Your finger ❑
   b) Anything as long as it works ❑
   c) A pen ❑
   d) A chopstick ❑

4. A pacer will help you:
   a) move to new lines easily ❑
   b) keep you eyes on the page ❑
   c) prevent excessive sub-vocalization. ❑
   d) All of the above. ❑

5. Speed reading needs practice because:
   a) you're working on breaking an old and engrained habit. ❑
   b) anything new needs practice. ❑
   c) it's difficult. ❑
   d) it seems like something that'll be fun to do on a Saturday night. ❑

6. What is skimming?
   a) A technique to use when you know what you want and just want a general overall impression of the material. ❑
   b) Bouncing rocks over water. ❑
   c) Taking the best bits off the top of a chocolate pudding. ❑
   d) All of the above. ❑

7. What is scanning?
   a) Finding specific information like a phone number or the answer to a particular question. ❑
   b) Digitizing a document. ❑
   c) Running your eyes across a view looking for something specific. ❑
   d) All of the above. ❑

8. Why is developing a good vocabulary useful?
   a) It's fun to confuse your friends. ❑
   b) Fancy words make you seem smart. ❑
   c) The easier it is to recognize new words, the faster you'll read them. ❑
   d) If no one else understands what you're saying, they won't ask questions you can't answer. ❑

9. What is sub-vocalizing?
   a) Saying the words in your head while you read. ❑
   b) An underground train. ❑
   c) Noises rabbits make in their burrows. ❑
   d) The language you use when you're telling your boss where to go. ❑

10. What might be the best way to stop you moving your lips while you read?

a) Putting a pencil between your teeth ❏

b) Taping your mouth shut ❏

c) Have someone tug your ears every time you do it ❏

d) Any of the above, as long as it works ❏

CHAPTER 17

Remember what you read

The most common complaint people have about reading – fast or slow – is their ability to remember what they read. This concern isn't linked just to remembering something a week, month or year later, but ten seconds later!

Have you ever got to the end of a paragraph or page and had to go back to the beginning because you can't recall anything you've read? Even worse, have you ever studied for an exam and gone back to revise only to realize you don't even recall seeing the page (despite your handwritten notes all over it), let alone remember the content? Memory is fickle. There are all sorts of physical, mental and environmental distractions that can contribute to you forgetting something as soon as you've looked at it.

Conversely, you might read an odd and interesting fact that has no relevance at the time, but you'll remember it forever.

We'll probably never fully understand human memory, what we're capable of and how to tap into it to get more consistent results, but there are certainly a few strategies we can employ to help ensure that when we read (with purpose in mind) our chances of remembering are greatly improved.

The key to all these memory techniques is to follow the primary rule of the five-step system: have a clear purpose. With that in mind, in this chapter we'll look at the memory process, how it works and how to get the best from it.

Memory myths

There is the danger that modern living is overloading the human memory system. There is much more for us to remember than there was for our grandparents. With mass communication growing, more paper being printed than ever before and the emphasis of success moving from physical strength to mental power, we have to develop skills that help us keep up before we can get ahead. The main factor contributing to this overload, however, is not necessarily the amount of information we are faced with but rather our *attitude* towards it.

When faced with a huge amount of information, the real damage is done by the stress it induces rather than the data itself. So when you're faced with an overload of information, deal first with your attitude. Calm down, relax, get some perspective, then apply the five-step system. If you're not careful, stress will creep up and cripple you before you start.

Normally, we're only aware of our memories when we forget something. It's a big issue for reading because most people find remembering what they want to remember when they read challenging. This is mainly because they are not using an appropriate method for retaining the text.

There are some myths and false assumptions about memory that need to be countered first.

- Memory is *not* a stand-alone system. It relies on perception, attention and reasoning. Each of these areas will be discussed further in this chapter.
- Memory is *not* a system that is based on isolated facts.
- Everything you remember *is connected* to other pieces of information in your memory.
- Memory retrieval relies greatly on *association*. The more connected your memories are, the easier it will be to recall information.
- New information is *not* stored separately from old information. Old knowledge helps make sense of new

information and vice versa. That is one reason why it is easier to read material you know something about.

● Memory is *not only* designed to store information; it is also designed to *use* it.
● We speak about memory as if it is an *object*. We tend to describe ourselves as having a good, bad or average memory, just like having good or bad lungs. But your memory is not a *thing*. It is certainly not a *single* thing. It's a series of processes that take place throughout your brain, *all the time*.
● Your memory *can* be trained. It has been said that there are no good or bad memories, just trained or untrained. With very few exceptions, and barring organic damage, everyone is born with a memory that can be developed.

The more you use your memory, the stronger it will get. Many of the problems people have with their memories when they grow older are due to lack of mental exercise, lack of physical exercise, poor nutrition, excess stress and/or poor coping strategies.

The basic guideline for improving your memory and ability to concentrate by focusing on physical and mental health is that what is good for the body is also good for the mind.

How memory works – and when it doesn't

There are many models for how the memory system works. Basically, your memory is divided into three functions:

● acquisition – absorbing information
● retention – keeping it in your head
● retrieval – getting it out again.

A memory can become unavailable at any point. The trouble is that you only know it is unavailable when you try to retrieve it: you are standing in front of a person whose name you have forgotten, trying to introduce him to someone else whose name you have also forgotten.

There are some basic memory rules to follow at each phase to help you remember.

Memory acquisition

The first rule of acquisition is pay attention. Most of the time we 'forget' something because we didn't have the opportunity to remember it in the first place. Have you ever been told someone's name only to realize two seconds later that you have 'forgotten' it? Chances are your attention was elsewhere. The same phenomenon occurs when you read.

If you have internal talk going on inside your head, asking yourself whether you are likely to remember what you are reading or not, the chances are you will not remember much at all.

The second rule of acquisition is plan. Before you begin, think of when you are likely to use the information you are reading. Then, decide which memory tool (to be discussed later on in this chapter) will help best when the time comes to use the information in the future.

The third rule of acquisition is be interested. Even if the material seems dull, find something in it that interests you. If you are bored, then parts of your brain will go to sleep and you will find paying attention even more difficult.

The final rule of acquisition is be active. Read actively. Think about what you read. When you follow the five-step system and you *prepare* to read, take some time to think about what you already know on the subject. As we saw from the 'myths and assumptions', your memory does not work in isolation. The more connections you make between the new and old information the easier it will be to understand what you are reading. Understanding is the key to remembering.

Memory retention

Keeping information in your head is one thing, keeping it there in such a way that you can retrieve it later is a different matter.

Your memory thrives on association. The better connected your memory is the easier it will be to retrieve information when you need it. Also, you don't have to keep everything in your head. You can be just as connected on paper as long as you know where to find the information when you need it.

These simple memory tools will help you organize your reading so that retrieval is easy.

Memory retrieval

One reason we have difficulty retrieving information is that we use the wrong method of retrieval. Memories are stored in several parts of your brain. When you try to remember what your front door looks like several areas of your brain will be activated. You might:

● see an internal picture of what your door looks like (visual)
● hear the sound of it closing (auditory)
● recall the last time you walked in or out (kinaesthetic and proprioceptive)
● remember the feeling of the last time you locked yourself out (emotional)
● smell the fresh coat of paint from when you painted it last (olfactory).

When we try to retrieve information we often use only one access point. If you can recreate the whole experience as you remember it, you will be able to recall it more easily.

The importance of concentration

Without concentration there is no memory. Remember the first rule of acquisition – pay attention. Ideas on how to concentrate and avoid the distractions that break up your concentration will be discussed in Chapter 19.

Concentration does not come easily to many people for two reasons:

● We are very easily distracted.
● There is much to distract us.

Improving concentration isn't always easy. We don't always have the time or the desire to meditate and practise absolute concentration for several hours each day. Fortunately, there are other ways of getting results.

Improving concentration

Interest and motivation

The more you are interested in what you are doing, the easier it is to concentrate. Remember the last time you were so engrossed in what you were doing that you lost all count of time. Nothing else distracted your attention. You were totally interested and motivated towards a goal. There are two words to take particular note of – motivated and goal.

When you know what you are after (a goal) and why you are doing it (motivated) then the desire (interest) to complete the task successfully makes for total concentration.

However, if the job is particularly boring and it is hard to find either motivation or interest, then make the *process of reading* the challenge. Make a decision that, for example:

● Your *goal* is to finish this task as quickly as possible.
● Your *motivation* is that you can get home sooner or get on with another more interesting task.
● Your *interest* is developing a system that will allow you to get through boring material faster and more effectively every time you are faced with it.

Mental numbers

You will be surprised at how easily you can be distracted without realizing it is happening. Try this simple experiment: count from one to 26. Notice at what number another thought comes into your head.

Many people will have another thought in their minds by the time they reach five. When you count, it is easy to think of other things and still keep going because counting from one to 26 is a simple exercise. When you are reading, the mental energy needed to focus your attention increases and these drifting thoughts contribute to lack of concentration.

You might like to use the following experiment to increase your concentration.

Simultaneously count from one to 26 and go through the alphabet from A to Z, thus: 1 – A – 2 – B – 3 – C – 4 – D – 5 – E ... and so on. Imagine the numbers on the left side of your brain and the letters on the right side. Then switch sides, imagine the numbers on the right side of your brain and the letters on the left.

How fast you can go? How far can you go before you realize your attention has drifted? Once you can go through the alphabet and up to 26 fluently going forwards, try it backwards.

When you feel that your concentration is dipping, do the exercise a few times. It can be quite meditative and relaxing.

Techniques for remembering what you read

There are many ways to remember what you read. Some are listed below. The aim is to be comfortable with all of them and be able to use the right one for the material you are reading. Everyone is different, so experiment with all the approaches.

Linear

Make notes as you read or after each section. These should include your own thoughts, ideas and cross-references. The more you include your own ideas the stronger your long-term memory will be.

Key words

Highlight the words that carry the message. If you do make notes separately, ensure that the key words are correct, so as to avoid having a list of words that make no sense to you when you review the information in the future.

Margin reading

Many people are brought up to believe that books are to be kept in perfect condition. However, a book is just a form of communication from the author to the reader. You start to take ownership of a book by writing in it or marking it. Underline, circle, highlight essential areas, note your opinions, whether you agree or disagree, and mark what you do or don't understand, and do something about that 'not understanding'. This should only be done if the book belongs to you and is not a priceless antique!

Mind-mapping

- Place the key idea in the centre of a horizontal (landscape) page.
- Main ideas form thick branches from the centre.
- Secondary ideas flow from the main ideas.
- Tertiary ideas flow from the secondary ideas.
- And so on until you reach the finest relevant detail.
- Use colours and symbols.
- Use one word or idea per line.

Multi-sensory reading

Do you remember your front door? Do you remember what it sounds like when you close it? What does fresh paint smell like? What does it feel like to be locked out? What colour is it? Multi-sensory reading uses as many of your senses as possible to help you make sense of and absorb the information. Here are some ideas on how to involve your other senses while you read:

- **Sight** – imagine what you are reading in your mind; create a film of the story you are being told.
- **Hearing** – speak to people about the subject; ask questions as you read, teach someone else, make up rhymes and stories.
- **Touch** – draw pictures and symbols representing the information. If the information is something you can do – do it instead of just reading about it.

The more senses you involve in learning new information the easier it will be to recall it because the information will be accessible via more than one function of your brain.

The five-step system and memory techniques work if you simply use them. The more you practise and the more you become aware of memory, the better you will become.

Revision

A basic guideline is to revise seven times in ten days. To remember what you read in the long term, use the information. As mentioned under 'Memory myths', the memory process is designed for use as well as for storage.

Summary

Like many deeply held beliefs, a lot of what we believe about memory is based on myth and old information that makes sense on the surface but doesn't really stand up to serious investigation.

We use those beliefs to explain faults in our capacity to remember, which is why people say, 'I have a hopeless memory for names/faces/numbers/facts/figures/what I read ...' – take your pick – and everyone nods and agrees that they have the same issue.

The truth is, if we have these 'issues', we're either not applying ourselves to the task of improving our memory in that particular area, or we're not interested in names/faces/numbers/facts/figures/what we read ...

If there is any type of information that you seem to magically absorb, no matter what format it's in or what the environment in which you read it, then you'll know that your memory works fine.

Take time to consider why some information is easy to remember. You'll probably find that you're interested, or think it will be useful to you personally.

If you could find a degree of interest or usefulness in the information you struggle to absorb, you'll find that your ability to retain and recall that information will increase exponentially.

Having a purpose and applying the five-step system to such material (knowing why you're reading something and when you'll use it) will go a long way to helping you.

Fact-check (answers at the back)

1. Why do we struggle with our memories so much?
   a) Too much information ❏
   b) Too little time ❏
   c) Not enough focus ❏
   d) All of the above ❏

2. What myths and assumptions do we make about our memories?
   a) It's a standalone system. ❏
   b) New information is stored separately from old information. ❏
   c) Memory can't be trained. ❏
   d) All of the above. ❏

3. What are the general elements of our memory process?
   a) Remember, forget, give up ❏
   b) Acquisition, retention, retrieval ❏
   c) Try to remember, fail hopelessly, pretend we know people we don't ❏
   d) All of the above ❏

4. The rules of memory acquisition are:
   a) try, try harder, try again. ❏
   b) pay attention, plan, be interested, be active. ❏
   c) listen once, give up, don't bother again. ❏
   d) cry. ❏

5. Why is concentration so important when you read?
   a) There's no memory without it. ❏
   b) The better you focus, the faster you'll read. ❏

   c) It allows you to get through your in-tray faster. ❏
   d) All of the above. ❏

6. Which of the following techniques will help you remember what you read?
   a) Highlighting key words ❏
   b) Mind-mapping ❏
   c) Multi-sensory reading ❏
   d) All of the above ❏

7. Multi-sensory reading is:
   a) reading using all your senses. ❏
   b) reading actively. ❏
   c) being engaged. ❏
   d) questioning the author. ❏

8. Basic guidelines for frequency of revision are:
   a) read it once a day for the rest of your life. ❏
   b) read it once and only once. ❏
   c) read it seven times in ten days. ❏
   d) read it five minutes before you need the information. ❏

9. Why can concentrating be so challenging?
   a) We're easily distracted. ❏
   b) There's a lot to distract us. ❏
   c) When it comes to work, we're probably not that interested in most of what we have to read. ❏
   d) All of the above. ❏

10. When are we most aware of our memory challenges?

a) When we forget something. ❏

b) When we're talking to someone who seems to know everything about us but whose face we don't recognize. ❏

c) When the word we need is right there, on the tip of our tongue, but just won't come out. ❏

d) All of the above and a whole lot more. ❏

CHAPTER 18

Your eyes and effective reading

The most important tools you have for reading are your eyes. Any discomfort or strain will affect concentration immediately. When you are tired, or if the lighting is wrong, you are likely to experience discomfort in your eyes. If your eyes hurt, a headache may follow quickly. Soon, you may find you have lost concentration and it is difficult to read. It is easier to look after your eyes continually, than it is to have to treat them when something goes wrong owing to bad habits.

The exercises in this chapter will give you an idea of what your eyes do while you read.

How the eyes work when you read

Speed-reading basics

The main reason people read at an average reading rate of 150–250 words per minute is because that is approximately the rate at which people speak.

While you are reading this paragraph listen to what is going on inside your head. Do you hear a voice inside your head while you are reading? Are you saying the words inside your mind while you read? This happens because of the way most people are *taught* how to read.

When we are first taught to read we learn to recognize one letter or sound at a time; then, when we have mastered that we move on to recognizing one word at a time. The next step is being able to read out loud so that your teacher can see that you have learned to recognize the words accurately. Then you are left to read 'to yourself'.

That is how the inner voice most of us have in our heads while we read becomes a habit. Instead of reading out loud we read silently. So when we talk about reading with your ears instead of your eyes – that is how it happens. You learn that you have to *hear* the words rather than see them to understand what you are reading.

At the beginning of your education, reading 'to yourself' was slow because you were still learning to recognize the words fluently. As you read more and got further into the education system your reading rate increased because your vocabulary increased. But your reading strategy didn't change.

As long as you are reading by saying each word to yourself in your mind, you will only ever be able to read as fast as you can speak – which for most people is between 150 and 250 words per minute.

You can only hear or say one thing at a time but you can see millions of things at a time. Learning to speed-read is about learning to read with your eyes instead of your ears.

Reading is the slowest visual exercise we do. Look outside the nearest window for three seconds then close your eyes and say what you saw. How long did it take you to see what you saw and how long did it take you to say what you saw? Speaking to yourself when you read is the same as looking at a spectacular view or watching a film and, instead of visually understanding it, translating what you see into words that take several times longer to form, communicate and understand.

Visual and auditory memory are in different parts of the brain. When you first start to learn how to read with your eyes instead of your ears, your comprehension will diminish. This is perfectly normal. After a few hours of practice (in the beginning) and maybe 15 minutes a day for a few days you will find comprehension returning to what it was, and more long-term and integrated than you ever had it before. The same happens, for example, when you learn to touch type instead of looking at the keyboard and typing with one finger.

Reading for comprehension

The aim of speed reading is to learn how to 'read' more than one word at a time. This leads to reading *phrases* rather than isolated words which goes a long way to helping you make sense of what you read. Meaning is in *groups* of words, so the more you are able to comprehend at one time the better your comprehension, understanding and subsequent recall will be. You understand more because you are reading in terms of ideas, thoughts and images rather than isolated words that mean nothing in themselves.

An exercise later in this chapter will help you increase your confidence in reading with your eyes instead of your ears.

The biological challenge

Your eyes move very fast. They can process large amounts of information rapidly. If you read slowly, your eyes will tend to wander. The pacer will go a long way to help prevent that. Remember the exercise you did in Chapter 16 that showed you how differently your eyes moved when they had something to follow? Go back and refresh your memory if you need to.

Some eye movements you can do something about, some you can't.

Fixation time

Your eyes need a certain amount of time to be able to absorb information. Try this experiment next time you are a passenger in a car. As the vehicle moves down the motorway, keep your eyes fixed on one point, not letting them settle on anything flying by the window. Does your view become blurred? Next, pick out certain parts of the landscape and follow them briefly. You might notice that what you look at becomes clear while the background is blurred. The same applies to reading. Your eyes need to rest – albeit it briefly – on groups of words, to be able to see them. The more words you can see and recognize in a single visual 'byte' the faster you will be able to read.

Peripheral vision

Try an experiment: place your finger on the middle of the page and see as much as you can – where you are sitting, the room you are in, your surroundings. Your peripheral vision gives you the ability to see an enormous amount in a single visual byte. Now, without moving your eye from middle of the page, try to read the words on the edges of the page.

How did you do?

You will find that although you can see the words, you might not be able to 'read' them. When you were taught how to read you were taught to focus on one word at a time and not a whole line. Being able to expand what you can recognize within your peripheral vision takes practice. There are some exercises later in this section that will help you increase peripheral perception – you can do some of them while walking down the street.

Regression and progression

These are visual tics. They are the result of poor concentration and lack of confidence in your memory.

Regression refers to the habit of going back to previous words or paragraphs to make sure you have understood them or remembered them accurately. *Progression* refers to the habit of jumping forwards for no particular reason.

Studies were done in the USA on how people's eyes moved when they read. Groups of people were given texts to read. At the bottom of the test piece was the figure $3,000,000.00. Every single person's eyes moved to the bottom of the text before they had read half the page to see what the $3,000,000.00 figure was all about. In terms of wasting time several things happen when you do this.

- You forget what you have just read.
- Your comprehension drops because you are reading something out of context.
- You lose time when you have to track back to find where you left off before the distraction.

Reading with a pacer and following the five-step system will help to reduce these reading habits. The following exercises will help you further.

Increasing your span of recognition within your peripheral vision

Exercise directions

In the pyramid of numbers and letters on the following pages, focus on the hash mark down the centre of the pyramid. The aim is to see how much you can read in your peripheral perception. Write down what you can see. Note: don't move your eyes from the centre column. You will be tempted to focus on the end of each row, but for the purpose of the exercise try to keep your eye on the centre hash. You might notice several things.

- You might not be able to see some of the letters and numbers on the longer lines. This is quite normal. Your optic nerve enters your eye at that point creating a 'blind spot'.
- If your eyes are of equal strength, you may find that you can see more to the right of centre than you can to the left. This is because we read from left to right and our eyes are conditioned

to look in that direction for new text. If you were brought up reading Arabic or Hebrew, you might find that you will be able to see more to the left instead of the right of centre.

Exercise 1

Place your pacer on the hash and move it down the hash marks in the centre of the pyramid. Keep your eye in the centre. Write down what you see on either side of the hash mark without moving your eyes away from the centre.

```
            S # p
          2 E # 7 e
        d R 8 # E 5 a
      D 2 5 l 5 # n G 5 8 9
    6 B 2 9 o 6 3 # R 8 3 4 2 N l
  3 9 g 9 2 E 5 4 n # 8 5 2 i 4 u S 7
```

Exercise 2

Follow the instructions in exercise one. Keep your eye on the central column of letters and write down what you can see on either side.

WG	H	PF
KD	T	OL
VS	K	DA
YO	E	NL
PZ	R	NJ
5S	l	B9

Exercise 3

Repeat the above instructions, with the following columns.

only if	armbands	existed but
once a	bee	swam in
a three	legged	race he
got half	way	to the other
end of the	beer glass	but was

Did you find the words any easier to read than the random letters? The words didn't make much sense either. Try this next exercise.

Exercise 4
Beginning to read more than one word at a time: read the text as quickly as possible, keeping your eyes in the middle of the pyramid.

Winter
should be here by now
to seize the trees, our knees, the bees,
But every living breathing being
from bats to cats to sows to cows
Is basking in this balmy breeze
when normally man and beast should freeze.

Summer
might be looking down
So bright the sight with such delight,
And think her warming job is done
Courtesy of the winter sun,
So come mid year when nights should glow
We might be deep in cold white snow.

Reading with your eyes instead of your ears

This next exercise will illustrate to you the difference between reading with your ears or your eyes. The more you practise it the better you will get at trusting what you see without having to hear it.

Exercise 5
Recognition exercise:

1 Cut a piece of fairly thick card about 2 cm square.

2 Cover the letters and 'flash' them as fast as you can, then make a note of what you see.

3 Try to keep the pace at which you reveal the numbers and letters to yourself constant.

143	Emc2	tdp	inki
146	Lsp5	3Pq	blt9
Heg	wini	olp	wom8
37R	rQwg	3owm	286r
63l	6The	tap	unlw
53L	Hare	cim	te4q
Jo4	M23p	536	wim2
ThR	Luck	592	241y
2h7	7play	per	tolp
Jon	u89Un	ith	154r
8Em	Pking	kin	tosi
Em2	43Jub	min	90Pp
492	krimb	map	76yz
hEp	HatrP	43T	jipx

● For the third and fourth columns, note down two sets of letters and numbers at the same time (i.e. only write what you see every other line).

● Which column was easiest to do?

● Did you find that sometimes you mistook an 'S' for a '5'?

● Did you find the double lines more challenging than the single lines?

● Most important – did you find that the letters that most resembled words were immediately recognisable and easy to recall?

When you read with your eyes you don't need to hear the whole word in your mind to know what it says. Your brain only needs a portion of the word to be able to make sense of it.

Develop your own eye exercises and practise them as often as you have time to. If you are going to choose one exercise to develop your visual reading for your 21-day programme (see Chapter 21) then exercise five should be it.

Peripheral vision and awareness

As you walk, look straight ahead and try to 'see' as much as you can in your whole visual range. Try to see what is to the extreme left or right, top or bottom of your visual field.

As you go, articulate what you see. After you have done this for a while sit down and read, using your guide, as fast as you can and see the difference in the speed and ease of your reading. This is an excellent exercise to do while you are walking through town or a park.

How to prevent and cure eyestrain

Your eyes need rest. The more relaxed they are, the longer you will be able to read. Here are a few simple things you should do to prevent and cure eyestrain.

1 Even before you feel tired, rest your eyes by closing them for a few moments every ten or 15 minutes.
2 As often as you remember to, palm. Palming is an excellent eye-relaxing exercise. Rub your hand together until they are warm, then close your eyes and cover them with your hands so that no light gets in. Do not press against your eyeballs: if you were to do so, you could damage them. Cover your eyes like this for as long as you have the time.
3 Blink – The scratchy feeling in your eyes is probably there because they are dry. Many people who have eye problems compound them by not blinking and watering the eyes. While you are reading (especially from a PC monitor) be aware of your eyes and blink often. If it helps, put a sign above your PC reminding yourself to blink.
4 If your eyes feel particularly tired, there are a number of very good eye washes you can get from any pharmacy. Follow the

instructions carefully when you use them. Check with your optician or your doctor.

5 If you wear contact lenses, it is even more important to take care of your eyes while you are reading. If you have a lot of reading to do, it might be advisable to take your lenses out. Carry a pair of glasses with you so that you can swap.

6 When you read, your eyes are limited in how much they can move. An excellent way to relieve stress is to practise some eye-robics. First, look straight ahead, then look up as far as you can, down as far as you can, to the left and to the right. Then, look to the top left, top right, bottom right and bottom left. Hold each gaze for only a second or so. When you have done that, squeeze your eyes shut and, if you want to, repeat the exercise. After you have completed the exercise, palm for a few minutes.

TIP *NEVER rub your eyes directly on the eyeball. There is nothing to protect the eye from damage when you do that.*

Reading from a PC monitor without straining your eyes

There is much you can do to make reading from a monitor less stressful on your eyes. Here are a few tips.

- **Font size and type** – if someone has sent you a document and the font is difficult to read either due to its size or type, change it.
- **Screen contrast** – make sure the background contrasts the text on the screen. Sometimes a white screen might be too strong and a blue one too dark. A pale blue screen is quite a good one to read from.
- **Screen interference** – have as little around your screen as possible. Sometimes it is tempting to have all the icons on display. The more you have around your screen, the smaller the screen space is. Only have what is necessary for the work you are doing.

- **Screen savers** – there are screen savers on the market now that remain active all the time. The one that held my attention for quite some time was a sheep that ran around my screen while I worked. Not only does it help to relax your eyes and prevent you from staring at the screen, but a sheep chasing frogs across the screen is good for your sense of humour and anything good for your sense of humour is good for your stress levels, which in turn is good for concentration.
- **Screen position** – keep the screen a comfortable distance away from you. It should be at least an arm's length away. Also, avoid having the screen right in front of a window. The contrast in light can be uncomfortable and the activity outside can be distracting.
- **Comfort** – working at a PC means that the only part of your body that gets any exercise are your fingers. Stop, stretch your body and do the eye-robics every 20 to 30 minutes.

Summary

A pacer will help you increase your reading rate by keeping your focus where it should be and your eyes moving across the page. Your aim is to gather the information you need without relying on the voice in your head or saying every word because, for as long as you hear each word in your head, you'll never be able to read any faster than you can speak.

When you start learning to speed-read you will probably find that the first thing that happens is the voice in your head starts talking really quickly. This is fine, but with practice you'll break the barrier and learn to understand what you're reading based on what you see rather than what you hear. At that point, the speed at which you read will increase rapidly.

This is not a technique you use while reading fiction or poetry or even when relaxing with the Sunday paper.

It's important to remember that applying speed-reading strategies to work-related material through this Part won't affect your ability to enjoy a good novel in the evening and at weekends, a quality poem over coffee or the papers over breakfast. You can choose when to apply these techniques and when not to.

Give yourself time, be patient, but more important, be persistent. Use a pacer on all non-fiction you read, no matter where you find it. If people look at you strangely, it doesn't matter – you're the one increasing your reading rate.

Fact-check (answers at the back)

1. What are your most important tools for reading?
   a) A spade to bury the book ☐
   b) Your eyes ☐
   c) A match ☐
   d) A pillow ☐

2. What is the average speed at which people will read if they haven't learned how to speed-read?
   a) Less than 100 words per minute ☐
   b) Between 150 and 250 words per minute ☐
   c) Between 250 and 500 words per minute ☐
   d) Between 500 and 750 words per minute ☐

3. Why do we read one word at a time?
   a) That's how the brain works. ☐
   b) It's easy. ☐
   c) It's how we were taught. ☐
   d) It makes sense. ☐

4. For as long as you have the voice in your head, what's the fastest you'll be able to read?
   a) Between 250 and 500 words per minute ☐
   b) Between 500 and 750 words per minute ☐
   c) Between 750 and 1000 words per minute ☐
   d) As fast as you can speak ☐

5. Without training, what is the slowest work our eyes carry out?
   a) Star gazing ☐
   b) Watching a movie ☐
   c) People watching ☐
   d) Reading ☐

6. Fixation time refers to:
   a) length of time you're able to concentrate. ☐
   b) length of time it takes to fix something. ☐
   c) length of time your eyes need to focus on something before you see it clearly. ☐
   d) a small coastal town in Texas. ☐

7. On the subject of reading, 'regression' refers to:
   a) a visual tic that sends your eyes back to the start of the page. ☐
   b) something you do to remember your early childhood. ☐
   c) a visual tic that sends your eyes ahead looking for anything on the page that interests you. ☐
   d) something that happens when you get really angry. ☐

8. On the subject of reading, 'progression' refers to:
   a) a commune in California that attracts forward thinkers and visionaries. ☐
   b) a visual tic that sends your eyes ahead looking for anything on the page that interests you. ☐
   c) a visual tic that sends your eyes back to the start of the page. ☐
   d) thinking about something else rather than concentrating on what you're reading. ☐

9. The best way to prevent eyestrain is:
a) plenty of rest. ❏
b) plenty of good light. ❏
c) palming your eyes. ❏
d) blinking. ❏

10. What can you do to your PC to avoid eyestrain?
a) Increase the font size. ❏
b) Avoid clutter on your screen. ❏
c) Avoid dark backgrounds. ❏
d) All of the above. ❏

CHAPTER 19

Distractions and solutions

Although sore eyes leading to a headache can be one of the biggest distractions, there are any number of personal and environmental factors that will distract you from focusing on what you're trying to read. In an ideal world we would read only what interests us, in a perfect environment, with as much time as we needed, when we wanted. However, life isn't like that. We sometimes have to read material we aren't particularly interested in, at a time and place not suited to our reading style and, all to often, with a deadline looming.

External distractions like a ringing phone, too much noise in an open office or bright sun shining through your window can be switched off or blocked out relatively easily, but what happens inside your head is far more challenging to deal with. Thoughts about your weekend, upcoming holiday or dinner tonight won't stop you seeing the words on the page, but they'll guarantee you don't remember them. Add to that the idea that you might be reading a jargon-packed technical document that you've got little or no interest in and you might as well pack it in, put your feet up and plan the holiday you've got going in your imagination.

Or, you can learn to refocus your mind despite your distractions.

Lack of concentration

If your attention drifts easily, inconsequential things distract you and you find it hard to concentrate, an easy solution may exist.

We discussed concentration and focus in Chapter 17. If you think it might be helpful to go back to refresh your memory, try one of the concentration exercises in Chapter 17. The following tips will help increase your concentration and your ability to focus on one task.

- If you're reading a single document and need peak concentration to get through it, then take breaks often – approximately five minutes every 30 minutes. If you are reading a number of different texts and taking notes as you go, you can stretch your reading time to 45 minutes or an hour before you take a five or ten minute break. Pay attention to your body as you read. When you start yawning, making mistakes, re-reading passages or developing a headache it is time for a break. If you work through the symptoms of tiredness, your concentration, ability to remember and to understand what you are reading will diminish rapidly. Taking a break does not mean lying down and going to sleep for 20 minutes (although that does help) – go for a walk, drink some water, do something different.
- Know your *reasons for reading*. In Chapters 15 and 16, we discussed the importance of knowing why you are reading something. The clearer your purpose, the easier it will be to concentrate. As with many things in life – if you know what your reasons are for doing something, it is easier to do it, even when you don't really want to. If you have no reason, however, you are likely to give up fairly quickly.
- *Read actively* using a pacer, especially if you're feeling tired or if the material is challenging. The more senses you use, the more alert you're likely to remain. Imagine eating a meal and all you could do was see it. You couldn't smell it, taste it, feel the texture of the food or hear the sounds of cutting and slicing a juicy dish. All you could do was see it and eat it. How much do you think you would enjoy it? 80 per cent of the enjoyment is in

the sensory appreciation of the meal: the taste, smell, texture and presentation of the food. The same applies to reading. Unfortunately, we are taught at a very early age to appreciate reading only through one sense. When you start building mind-maps, taking notes, thinking, discussing and actively reading, you will find that reading becomes more like the meal you can see, taste, smell, hear and feel. You almost always remember a good meal when the company is entertaining and the surroundings are pleasant. Treat reading like a good meal – you'll be surprised.

● Set a definite *time limit*. Break your reading into chunks. The chunks should be small enough to feel easily manageable and big enough to feel that you are achieving your goal. Be realistic. If, as you read, you find that the size of the chunks are too big or too small, stop and reassess. Be flexible.

External distractions

Some people can concentrate because of the noise and chaos around them and some people can concentration in spite of it. If you're not one of them, do everything you can to minimize the noise around you.

● *Use earplugs* – if you get the right type they can be very comfortable and effective. Most good chemists will supply them. Try out a few makes and then keep a few sets on your desk.

● Wear headphones to *listen to appropriate music* – music without words and not too loud. Baroque music is best for maximum concentration; approximately 55–60 beats per minute. Make sure it's not too melancholy and only play music you enjoy. Experiment with music. Put one composer on for 20 minutes, change to another and then compare how you feel or how well you concentrate.

● If you work in a truly open-plan space – no dividers between the desks – *creating* a *visual barrier* between you and the people around you will help cut out distraction. You do not have to build a wall around you; this is not always desirable or possible. All you need do is place something on your desk that reaches eye level. This will provide a psychological barrier between you and the distracting environment, making it easier to cope with.

- If at all possible, leave the noisy environment and *find a quiet space* to read in. A delegate in one of my workshops would go into the cleaning closet when he had a very important document to read that needed all of his attention. He would go into the closet, jam the door shut, read the document, take the notes he needed and when he was finished he would come out. It worked for him and he was lucky enough to have a cleaning closet nearby with plenty of light and a bit of space, a supply of fresh air and no fumes.

Internal distractions

Internal noise is caused by your mind wandering, perhaps because you have not fully and consciously committed to spend the time on a particular task. The guidelines on concentration will help you here. But what will help most is the decision to take the time to read.

If you don't make a firm decision to sit down and read, the type of internal talk that goes through your head might sound like this: 'I don't have the time for this ... X really needs to be done now ... Y will have to move to this afternoon ... I should be doing Z ...' There will be so much 'noise' in your head that you will be unlikely to remember one word you have read and will be wasting time.

- Make a decision to allocate a certain amount of time to read a set amount of material. If you can plan it into your day, do so. Some reading cannot be planned for. In this instance, instead of diving into the text without thinking, take time, go through the first two steps of the five-step system. Then, if you feel that the document does need to be read, decide when you are going to do it and put the time aside.
- When the decision is made, most internal talk will disappear and you will be able to focus.

Physical distractions
Tiredness

When you are tired you will find it almost impossible to concentrate. If you can take a break and go for a short nap or walk in the park, do so. If you can't do this, there are several other strategies open to you.

- Cut the time you spend reading down to ten- to 15-minute chunks.
- Use multi-sensory reading.
- Drink plenty of water
- Do aerobic exercises during your breaks – jump up and down a bit to get the oxygen flowing.
- Breathe deeply and stretch every few minutes.
- If you have music playing make it upbeat and energetic.
- Make sure you have a very good reason for reading through your tiredness.
- Do not go on more than you have to – stop when you are finished and take a good rest.
- Avoid working through the night.
- Avoid sugar.
- Avoid too much caffeine. For optimum performance you want to be alert not jittery.
- Reading at the right time of day can go a long way to preventing tiredness. You may notice that you can concentrate better at certain times of the day. Your results will be better if you read at those times.

Sore eyes

Any kind of physical discomfort is a distraction. Your eyes are your primary tool for reading, so take care of them. For more details on eye care while reading, go back to Chapter 18.

Stress and reading

If you are stressed it is better to stop for a moment even if you feel you don't have the time. Stop, breathe, relax, evaluate the job, have a cup of tea or water and carry on. Being stressed does not make you read any faster or more effectively.

Hunger and thirst

Hunger is a serious distraction. Similarly, if you eat too much, your concentration will be badly affected. If you have a large amount of reading to do, avoid eating too much at once and avoid excess sugar. Another cause of poor concentration is dehydration. Your body needs to be constantly replenished. When you feel thirsty, you are already dehydrated, so drink even if you don't feel you need to.

Environmental issues

Comfort

Ensure that you have fresh air and adequate light. Make yourself as comfortable as possible without feeling sleepy.

Light

Daylight is best. If there is none, then there should not be too much contrast between the levels of light under which you are working and the rest of the room. This helps prevent eye strain. The main source of light should come over the shoulder opposite to your writing hand.

Desk and chair

Make sure your desk and chair are the right height. When you are on your chair you should be able to sit back, with the chair supporting your back and your feet flat on the floor. If you cannot reach the floor place a block at your feet. Your desk should be large enough to take everything you need for the work you are doing.

Work distractions

- **Plan your day.** Distractions come easily when you don't know what you want to achieve. At the start of your day write down everything you want to get done including what you want or need to read. Set aside a realistic amount of time. Add time for leisure reading! When you consciously put time in your day to read what you really want to read you will find that you enjoy the time, still get everything done and improve your speed reading by reading more.
- **Set ground rules.** When you start something, *finish it*. This will not only improve the quality of your work, it will increase the quantity of what you can achieve. You will also feel more relaxed and at ease because the job has been done and won't plague your mind as unfinished business.

People demanding your attention

Few people have the luxury of being able to work without interruptions. There will always be someone, somewhere demanding your attention at some point, whether by phone, in person, by email, social media... the list goes on.

If you can, set aside the time you need to read and put up a 'do not disturb' notice.

If you are unable to do that, and most of us are, deal with interruptions like phone calls and people wanting to see you by consciously breaking off from your reading task and paying attention to the interruption.

If the phone rings or someone comes up to you while you are reading:

- finish the sentence or paragraph you are on, if at all possible
- place a mark on the place where you stopped
- briefly revise in your mind or on paper your understanding of the last sentence you read
- then, give attention to the next task.

Once the interruption is over, you can return to your reading, by:

- sitting for a moment to recall your understanding of the last sentence you read
- reaffirming your intention and purpose for reading
- setting the time again for a manageable chunk
- then, continuing to read.

Habit dictates that when we are interrupted we are very likely to 'hop' from one task to another. Taking a brief pause between tasks will ensure that you don't waste time trying to find where you left off. When you go back to your reading you will be able to begin immediately instead of having to sort out your ideas and remove confusion from your mind.

Clearing your desk of distractions

- **Mail** – If you get a lot of mail at the beginning of the day have a routine of 20 minutes maximum each day to open it all and file it, deal with it or bin it. Don't let anything get in the way of doing that. It might not seem an important job at the time but when a week's mail piles up on your desk undealt with, it can be very distracting and waste more time than a short stress-free period set aside every day.
- **Desk space** – Every piece of paper on your desk will distract you several times every day. To minimize this type of distraction, make sure that the only things on your desk are those that have something to do with the project in hand. If you have your 'in' and 'out' trays on your desk, find another place for them for a week. At the end of the week, assess how differently you spent your time. When the tray is on your desk, all you have to do is look up and you will see everything else you have to do instead of being able to focus on one job at a time.
- **Clutter** – If your desk tends to be full of paper, clear it of *everything* other than the job at hand – for just one day – and see the difference. At the end of each day, make sure you leave your desk totally clear. In the morning you will feel far more relaxed and able to choose what you want to deal with instead of having to deal with whatever happens to be on the top of the pile.

● **Other people's reading** – Do not let anyone put anything on your desk that you haven't seen or agreed to have there, especially if you have to read it. When someone gives you something to read ask them to clearly explain why they think you have to read it and then decide if you want to accept it as an activity in your schedule. If they cannot give you an answer, think carefully before you accept it because once you have, you will be committed to doing it.

Vocabulary

The better your vocabulary the faster you will be able to read. For more details see the section on speed reading in Chapter 16.

Summary

The number of distractions around you – internal or external – is infinite: aches and pains, itchy feet, tired eyes, stress through the day, tight deadlines, an over-demanding boss, memories of your last holiday, plans for your next holiday, ideas for the weekend, too much noise around you, too little noise around you, ringing in your ears ...

You could deal with the distraction by eliminating it – but this might create a new problem because eliminating it might mean booking the holiday you're thinking about, calling the friend you can't get out your head or dropping down to the local coffee shop for a brew and turning what was a mere distraction into procrastination.

The real solution is (I might have said this before!) to have a clear purpose, which could be anything from finding the answer to a specific question to wanting to have a general understanding of the subject in 20 minutes. By applying the five-step system you will not only get through your reading in record time, you will also be able to remember what you read and apply it when you need to.

If you find you are still distracted despite applying the five-steps then put your reading away, go and do something else and come back to it later.

Fact-check (answers at the back)

1. What are the most difficult distractions to deal with when we read?
   a) Other people ❏
   b) Outside demands ❏
   c) Deadlines ❏
   d) What goes on inside our own head ❏

2. What can you do to ensure peak concentration?
   a) Take breaks often ❏
   b) Have a reason to read ❏
   c) Read actively ❏
   d) Set a time limit ❏

3. What are the best ways to minimize external distractions?
   a) Wear earplugs. ❏
   b) Create barriers around you if you're in an open plan environment. ❏
   c) Do difficult work away from the office. ❏
   d) Listen to your type of music. ❏

4. When your mind keeps drifting while you read, what are your options?
   a) Take a break. ❏
   b) Focus on what you're reading, get it done, then move on to whatever is drifting through your head. ❏
   c) Deal with the distraction and get back to work. ❏
   d) All of the above, depending on what's drifting through your mind and how important it is. ❏

5. What do physical distractions include?
   a) Sore eyes ❏
   b) Tiredness ❏
   c) Stress ❏
   d) Aches or pains ❏

6. What can you do to ensure your work environment is designed for maximum concentration?
   a) Cover the floor with beanbags. ❏
   b) Pipe whale sounds into the office. ❏
   c) Make sure your desk and chair height are comfortable and adjust the lighting to suit. ❏
   d) Wear a kaftan into the office and soak your feet in bath salts. ❏

7. What are the most effective ways to avoid distractions at work?
   a) Plan your day. ❏
   b) Set ground rules. ❏
   c) When you start something, finish it. ❏
   d) All of the above. ❏

8. How can you avoid distractions from people while you read?
   a) Finish the sentence or paragraph before you engage with the person speaking to you. ❏
   b) Place a mark where you left off. ❏
   c) Take a second to run mentally through what you just read. ❏
   d) Pay attention to the person demanding it, when you're ready. ❏

9. How can you clear your desk of distractions?
a) Clear your mail every day. ❏
b) Clear the clutter off your desk. ❏
c) Make sure everything on your desk has a reason to be there. ❏
d) Don't let anyone else's reading become your priority (unless it's your job). ❏

10. Does what you eat through the day impact your ability to concentrate?
a) No, I can eat anything and I have tons of energy through the day. ❏
b) A heavy lunch knocks me out for the afternoon. ❏
c) I need sugar to keep me going. ❏
d) I don't know... I'll take a week to carefully consider what I eat to see how it affects my moods, energy levels and concentration. ❏

CHAPTER 20

Reading different types of material for different reasons

Most people will learn one reading strategy when they're at school – left to right, beginning to end, one word at a time – and apply that to everything they read from newspapers to novels to technical documents ...for the rest of their lives.

However, if you follow the five-step system you'll soon realize that your reasons for reading a newspaper or novel or technical document are different and, as a result, the strategy you apply to each should also be different.

You might want to apply the full five-step system to a work-related document, but you certainly won't want to apply it to a novel. Likewise, you'll read a Sunday paper differently based on whether it's over breakfast or is part of your PR job.

Now that you've learned the five-step system, you can bend it and reshape it to suit any type of reading material, no matter what your reasons for reading it.

The same applies to the memory techniques you use. If you're reading something for general interest you'll use a different memory technique from when you read material you might be examined on.

The challenge you face as you learn to apply the five-step system is falling into the bad habit of using one technique for everything. Be flexible, use different strategies and you'll find you'll want to read more because the time you spend reading effectively will be time well spent.

Reading different types of material

The way you approach a document (book, newspaper, memo, email etc.) should be driven by your purpose.

Technical material

This type of reading can be fairly easy because most technical writing is well structured. Also, it will be rare that you have to read and remember everything about the text without being able to refer to it later on when you need to. For this type of reading apply the five-step system in its entirety and use a memory system that works well for you. Use mind-maps. If you don't like mind-maps, try a process map. This technique, similar to a flow chart, allows you to see how information, ideas and practices are linked and what effect they have on each other.

Non-fiction for leisure

This is probably the easiest of all reading simply because you are interested in the subject. Most non-fiction, like technical writing, is also fairly well structured so the five-step process can be readily applied.

It is easy to become absorbed in 'work'-related reading and not put time aside for leisure reading and knowledge gathering. Once you are comfortable with speed reading and the five-step process, you will find that non-fiction is the ideal material to practise on. Enjoy taking the time for this type of reading. If you have 'work' to do, you might feel uncomfortable or guilty about taking time out for leisure, albeit non-fiction, reading. A good way to get around this is to make part of your purpose increasing your reading skill so that you will be able to read 'work' material more effectively. Besides, if you only ever read text that bores you, your passion for reading will soon be subdued. Make the time to read what you want to read.

Reading for study

More and more people are studying as well as coping with a full-time job. Here is a way to structure your reading so that you succeed without causing yourself undue stress and giving up on life for a few years.

- Determine how many study days you have before the exam or end of the course. Be realistic about this. If you are working full time as well as studying, then remember that you will only have mornings, evenings and weekends and that you also have to fit a life in somewhere.
- Establish exactly how much material you have to get through to complete the course or module. Generally you will have a number of books, perhaps a few CDs or DVDs, a few television or online programmes, and some notes from lectures. Gather all the material together into one place so that you can see that the amount of information you have to learn is finite. This does the soul good.
- Go through the course notes and make a list of all the different sub-topics you have to cover. This allows you to break the overall subject into manageable chunks.
- Under each sub-topic write down the chapters, CDs, DVDs and lectures (all sources) you have to refer to for information.
- Organize the sub-topics into an 'information order'. Some will serve as good background for others so cover those first. The order you study each sub-topic in is entirely up to you and dependent on your current knowledge base.
- Once all sub-topics are identified and sources are gathered you will be able to create a realistic and achievable timetable.
- The timetable you create should not have you waking up at 4 a.m. and going to sleep at midnight. You will burn out. Make space in your timetable for Quality Recover Time (QRT). Have plenty of it.
- Create a good study space. This space should only be used for study if possible.
- Enjoy the learning process by rewarding yourself for each accomplishment (at least once a day).

Reading for research

The good thing about reading for research is that your purpose is very clearly defined and you are looking for something quite specific. Apply the five-step system and follow the guidelines for 'reading for study'.

Reading for work (especially mail, emails and memos)

The rule here is 'be selective'. The trouble with reading that you do for work is that there will probably be a resulting activity for each document. Before you read anything, especially if it is likely to take you a while or if it seems to land on your desk often, ask a few questions first:

- ● Who wants you to read it?
- ● Why do they want you to read it?
- ● What do you have to do with the information once you have read it?

Once you have ascertained that there are good reasons for you reading the documents, take the following steps:

- ● Decide how much time you are going to spend reading incoming mail, emails, articles or reports.
- ● Scan the documents for structure and key ideas with one thing in mind – can any of them go in the bin? Then sort them into two piles – one of which goes straight into the bin, the other which requires further attention.
- ● Skim all of the documents that need further attention and ask one question of each – can this be filed or does it require action? Put the pile for filing aside to file.
- ● Actively read the remaining pile and, using post-it notes or writing directly on the letter or document, write what actions need to be taken.
- ● Finally, plan the actions into your day or week and file the documents so that you can retrieve them easily when you need them.

TIP
Remember the clear-desk policy – only have papers on your desk for the job you are currently working on.

Newspapers

NOTE – this does not necessarily apply to the casual, relaxed Sunday morning reading of the paper, unless you want it to. Reading a newspaper should be approached with as much consideration as reading anything else. The five-step system works very well for papers, but it is not necessary to go through the entire five-step process in order. You can read a paper very quickly by following three very simple steps.

● State your purpose – are you reading to get an overview of the whole paper or are you looking for a particular story?
● Glance through the paper looking for key articles you're interested in. Read the headlines and first paragraphs. Go through the entire paper, circling the articles you would like to return to.
● Finally, speed read selected articles for the information you want.

TIP
REMEMBER – these are only suggested guidelines. If you find another way of reading a paper even faster, then use whatever works for you.

Magazines

Reading a magazine (particularly a special interest or trade magazine) is slightly different to reading a newspaper. A newspaper is one of many sources of news. If you miss anything from the paper, you could get the story from the television, radio or Internet. Most magazines only come out once a month or once a quarter. A magazine should thus be treated like a small textbook. Follow all the steps of the five-step reading system to get the best out of a magazine. If there is information you are likely to need again there are several things you can do to make it easily accessible.

- Read the magazine with post-it notes to hand. As you find articles you are interested in, note the page number, title and brief summary (just a sentence or two) on the post-it note. Stick the post-it on the front page of the magazine and file it in a file dedicated to 'interesting articles'.
- If you don't want to keep the whole magazine then tear out the pages or photocopy the articles you want and file those away with a brief summary of what the article is about and what you might use it for later.

Emails

Emails are a blessing or a curse depending on who is sending them. Rule one with emails is to do to others, as you want them to do to you. If you don't want a huge amount of junk in your in-box – don't send it! If you have someone who keeps sending you emails you don't want, whether it's jokes or stories, be firm and ask them not to. Like traditional mail, if you can see it is junk before you open the envelope – bin it.

A good way of viewing email is to have the feature on your system where your inbox screen is split. One half has a list of all the messages, and the other half lets you read the email without actually opening it. This saves time.

If there are attachments to the email and you need to read them fast then it might be better to print them out or use a piece of software like Spreeder.com. If you prefer to read from the screen there are some ideas in Chapter 18 on how to do that without straining your eyes.

Novels

The more you read the faster you will become. Reading novels is excellent practice for speed-reading skills. Your reading rate will automatically increase when you are aware of your reading strategy and practise the reading system on non-fiction.

Making the most of your available time

The most important thing about reading (for work or study, this does not apply to leisure reading unless you want it to) is planning. Here are some simple guidelines on how to make the most of your time.

- Read when you are feeling alert and refreshed. If you have to read and you are tired, drink plenty of water and take regular breaks.
- Plan what you have to read and set aside a little more time than you think you will need.
- When someone puts something on your desk expecting you to read it, find out whether it is really necessary. Perhaps someone can summarize it for you, rather than reading the whole document yourself.
- Make the bin the first option when you are sorting mail (including email).
- When you are going through your mail decide what you have to read and put non-urgent documents aside. If you have time at the end of the day to read them, then do so.

How to get the message in the minutes before a meeting

'I only have five minutes and I have to sound like I know what I'm talking about.' Have you ever been in the situation where someone gives you a document and tells you that you are expected at a meeting in five minutes to discuss it with others who have probably had a day to read it?

Do you find that your mind goes blank and for some reason words and letters don't make sense anymore? This has more to do with stress and a lack of strategy than it does with time. When this happens, ask the document-giver:

- what it has to do with you – ask for background information.
- why you only have five minutes – this gives purpose and focus.
- to briefly summarize the text for you – this gives you content.

Once you have done that, complete steps 1 to 4 of the five-step system:

- State your purpose – why do you have to read this? What are you going to do with the information?
- Flick through the text reading any summaries and conclusions.
- Read through it again, this time looking for key words, significant figures or words in bold or italics.
- Read the first and last paragraphs of each section.
- Finally, if there is time, fill in the gaps by reading as much as you can, beginning with the first sentence of each paragraph and any bullet points (see step 4 of the five-step system).

TIP *It is very important to remember, as you go through steps 1 to 4, to take notes, preferably on the document itself. The thoughts you have as you read will probably be what you would want to contribute to the meeting. If you don't write them down you might forget and lose valuable insights.*

Going into the meeting

Before you go into the meeting, stop at the door, stand up straight, breathe in deeply and smile (relax). Once inside:

- Don't profess to be the expert on the subject.
- Listen first to what others have to say.
- Ask questions before you make statements.

You could bluff if others know less than you do but eventually you will be caught out. It's easier to find a reading strategy that gives you a chance of absorbing as much information as possible rather than struggling to look as if you know what you are talking about.

Once you take control you will relax and be able to concentrate successfully on the task.

Finding the right information fast

When you have to find information fast, use steps 1, 2 and 3 of the five-step system.

- Be very clear about what you are looking for.
- Write your purpose down.
- Begin step 2 (structure) by highlighting any chapters or sections that look like they could contain the answers to your question. Use post-it notes to mark the relevant pages with a comment on them as to what you expect to find there.
- Once completed, begin step 3 by restating and reclarifying your purpose. What exactly are you looking for and what are the key words that would alert you to the answer?
- Skim or scan the pieces of text you identified during step two, looking for language and key ideas.

Stop as soon as you find your answer, unless you decide to continue.

When you read a document for the first time, read it with the intention of going back to it to find information at a later date. Mark relevant pages or take referencing notes. Writing a brief summary of each section in the margins is an excellent way to help you access information later. It is also a very good technique for remembering what you have read.

The real world – reading under pressure

Sometimes there is not enough time to read what you have to. When this happens (and for some people it could be happening every day) you have to be disciplined about what you read and develop excellent prioritization skills.

A deadline can be one of the biggest distractions. Becoming wound up and stressed only defeats the object. When you have such a situation:

- Make a realistic assessment of the available time.
- Decide what you have to know.

- Decide what the best and fastest source of information is.
- If it is something you have to read, complete steps 1 to 3 of the five-step system and be very clear about cutting out what is not essential.
- Speak to someone who already knows something on the subject and gather as much information as possible.
- Find out exactly why you have such a tight deadline and find out whether it can be changed.
- After your questions have been answered, divide your reading into the amount of time you have, and focus, relax, breathe deeply, make sure you have a good supply of water.
- Take plenty of breaks. When you are under pressure it is more important to sit back and take stock than when you have all the time in the world. If you are under pressure and not taking care of yourself, stress will counteract all the work you are doing.

To avoid this happening repeatedly, it is important to be able to prioritize your reading and other tasks all the time, not just in an emergency.

Summary

You'll now be able to apply the five-step system to every type of reading material and under any conditions, regardless of the tenacity of the distractions around you.

Have some fun with this and put yourself to the test. Take your reading into busy, noisy, difficult places, decide what you want to get out of it, set an amount of time and get through it regardless of what goes on around you.

Ultimately you want to be able to read any technical document in any high-stress environment, even if people are literally waiting in front of you for your response.

Your success will be a culmination of having a clear purpose (have I mentioned that before?), using the five-step system and having command of your mind and your emotions to ensure stress doesn't get in the way and slow you down.

No matter how much pressure you're under or how much you have to read, take the time to plan your reading and prioritize what's important. In the long run, it'll be the shortest route.

Fact-check (answers at the back)

1. You should use different reading strategies on different types of reading material.
   a) True ❏
   b) False ❏

2. Reading for pleasure will not be ruined when you learn to speed-read.
   a) True ❏
   b) False ❏

3. What time of the day is best for reading difficult, technical material?
   a) Early morning ❏
   b) Late afternoon ❏
   c) When the office is empty ❏
   d) When you feel most energized and alert, no matter what time of day it is or what's going on around you. ❏

4. What should be your first option when you're sorting mail (snail or e-mail)?
   a) Read everything to make sure it's not important. ❏
   b) File everything for later. ❏
   c) Bin it. ❏
   d) Pass it on to someone else to read. ❏

5. When you have only a few minutes to get to a meeting and you have to read something before you go in, you should:
   a) hide in the restroom. ❏
   b) panic. ❏
   c) leave the office for the day. ❏
   d) apply the five-step system. ❏

6. If you're at a meeting and you've only just familiarized yourself with a new document, you should:
   a) start talking and not stop until someone kicks you out. ❏
   b) hope no one has read it and wing it. ❏
   c) keep quiet and listen. ❏
   d) act mysterious if someone asks your opinion and pretend to know everything. ❏

7. When you need to find information fast, you should:
   a) get someone else to do it. ❏
   b) use the five-step system. ❏
   c) make it up and hope no one notices. ❏
   d) panic. ❏

8. When prioritizing your reading, you need to consider:
   a) what's important to you and your outcomes. ❏
   b) what you can do in the amount of time you have. ❏
   c) when and for what you need the information. ❏
   d) All of the above. ❏

9. If you need answers to questions and don't have a lot of time to get them, you should:
   a) use the five-step system on every form of written material you can get your hands on (paper and electronic). ❏
   b) speak to experts. ❏
   c) use every source. ❏
   d) All of the above. ❏

10. The key to successful speed reading is reading everything in detail.
   a) True ❏
   b) False ❏

CHAPTER 21

What next?

Whenever you learn something new there is a period when you know how to do it but haven't quite got it right yet. This is a most fragile time in learning. Receiving the information is easy – you read a book, go on a course, listen to a recording. Once the information is in your head, it's up to you whether you use the information or not. Do you put your course books on the shelf until 'later'? Do you put the book back on the bookshelf and think, 'Hmmm, interesting', and fall back into your old habits? What you do with your new information is entirely up to you. You can forget about it, or you can integrate what you have learned into the way you live, work and study.

It takes decision and action. The decision takes a split second. Are you going to become the best you can be?

After you make the decision it is important to build a plan.

Sometimes, when we are about to start something new, we believe that it is the only way to go and everything else in our lives must change to suit the new way. The problem is that when you try to change old habits, they fight back. One way of making the change process easy is to create a daily plan. Instead of doing everything in one day and being overwhelmed, complete the task a bit at a time.

Guidelines for a 21-day programme

The first time I created one of these programmes I put aside four hours a day to the new task. The day started at 5 am and at 9 am I would have breakfast, go for a run and get on with the day. I lasted two days. I started too early, spent too long at it, crammed too much into the time and spent the rest of the day half asleep and irritable.

Rules for the 21-day programme are based on general commonsense.

- **Make your programme not too easy, not too difficult.** The programme you create must be easy enough for you to know it is achievable and challenging enough to excite you.
- **Select topics that interest you.** The material you read to develop your speed-reading skills should be interesting to you. During your normal working day you may come across plenty that you have to read that isn't too interesting.
- **Have variety.** On one day, practise speed reading with a novel, the next day, try a newspaper, after that practise with magazines you have wanted to read for a while. Each time the aim is to read as much as you can, using the most effective technique possible.
- **Put aside 20 minutes each day to practise speed-reading exercises (see Chapter 16).** Twenty minutes is a guideline. If you only have ten minutes then that would do fine, as long as every day you are spending some focused time working on your new skill. The best time to do this is in the morning because it will remind you to pay attention to your reading as the day goes by. If you can only put 20 minutes aside in the evening then remind yourself in the morning when you plan your day that you have put that time aside and that you will be aware of your reading throughout the day.
- **Integrate your new knowledge into what you already do during the day.** Use your new skill every time you read something: your mail, letters, newspapers, books, emails, memos, the backs of cereal boxes – anything.

- **Keep your purpose clear.** If you do not have a purpose you will quickly lose interest. Keep in mind why you are learning how to read fast. What else do you want to do with the extra time you have? What will speed reading give you?
- **Practise daily.** The more consistent your practice is the better you will become. If you speed-read on one day and forget for the next few, the chances are that the number of days between practices will just increase.
- **Teach someone else.** When you can teach someone else what you have learned, you have learned it well. If you have children, teach them – any time is a good time for them to learn. If you can't answer all their questions use the five-step process to find the answers.
- **Read in groups.** Developing a reading group is an excellent way to ensure you practise. Meet once a month or more often if you like. Make the purpose of the group twofold; firstly, discuss the contents of the book, articles or papers you read, and second, discuss the reading methods you used or had trouble with. Also, begin to explore other ways of reading effectively and bring that to the group. This way, group motivation will drive your learning forward. The more people you involve in your learning the easier it will be to stay motivated. It helps if there is someone there to help you along when you are having difficulties.
- **Learn something new every day.** No matter how small, learn something new. Keep a notebook for your mini lesson of the day and you will be surprised how fast your general knowledge grows.
- **Learn a new word every day.** The better your vocabulary is the faster you will be able to read.
- **Be flexible.** If you find that your programme is too easy or too difficult, change it.
- **Don't stop after 21 days.** After your first 21 days you will have integrated the basics of speed reading successfully. After that, take your reading to another level. You have already developed the habit of putting aside time to practise a new skill: keep that time available. Keep reading.

Opposite is a table you can use as a template to design your 21-day programme.

Day	Reading material / purpose	Time	What did I learn?	New word
1	The morning paper in 20 minutes or less. To practise five steps and gain information.	20 min (0600–0620)	[In this column write the most interesting thing you learned.]	[At least one new word and its definition.]
2				
3				
4				
5				
6				
7				
8				
9				
10				
11				
12				
13				
14				
15				
16				
17				
18				
19				
20				
21				

Another useful tool is to keep a small notebook (together with your 21-day programme) to write down comments on the day's reading activities. What did you feel or think as you read?

What was easy? What was difficult? What would you change about the way you read that day? What questions do you have?

A to Z of effective reading

A **Active reading** – Take notes, write in margins, circle, highlight, underline, think, argue, debate your way through whatever you read.

B **Believe** – You are capable of phenomenal things. Make this only your first step to effective reading. Look constantly for a better way of doing what you do.

C **Concentration** – Practise concentration techniques; remember that without concentration there is no memory, whether you are reading or remembering names.

D **Determination** – Frustration is a natural part of the learning process. Learn to enjoy it.

E **Enjoy** – The more you enjoy reading the less stressed you will be and the better you will remember what you read.

F **Flexibility** – Remember that you don't have to read fast all the time. Develop the skill of being able to identify when you can read fast and when you have to slow down.

G **Groups** – Sometimes a group of brains is better at staying motivated than one working alone.

H **Harassed** – If you are feeling stressed or tired your effectiveness will diminish. Stop and take a break especially if you feel you do not have the time.

I **Ideas** – Cross-reference, combine and elaborate on ideas between texts.

J **Justify** – Always ask yourself why you have to read it and what call it will have on your time.

K **Knowledge** – Make increasing your knowledge of yourself and the world around you a daily goal.

L **Learn** – Make it a habit to learn something new from your reading every day.

M **Manageable chunks** – Avoid reading for more than 30 minutes at a time.

N **Novels** – Using the five-step system for novels could spoil the ending. You will find, however, that the speed at which you can read novels will increase as a result of your speed-reading practice. You will not lose any of the enjoyment, in fact, you might find you finish more of the novels that you begin.

O **Organized** – Clear your desk of everything other than what you are working on at the time.

P **Purpose** – Have a clear and definite purpose whenever you read anything.

Q **Question** – Always ask questions. Just because what the author has said is in print, does not mean that he or she is right.

R **Revise** – Refer to notes you have made previously whenever you have the opportunity to do so. Sometimes what we think at the time we only appreciate later.

S **Stretch** – Your body is involved in your reading as well as your mind. Reading is physically passive. When you read for any length of time your body will become stiff and sore. Stretch whenever you take a break.

T **Time** – Take time to develop any new skill. Enjoy the gap between knowing you don't know how to do something and achieving success. Be patient with yourself.

U **Use** – The more you use the information you learn the better you will remember it and will be able to apply it when you need it.

V **Vocabulary** – Use steps 2 and 3 (structure and language) to identify words you don't understand. Look them up before you continue. If you encounter a word you don't understand while you are reading, take note, keep going and look it up at the end of the paragraph or section. You might find that the meaning becomes clear in the context of the text.

W **Work is play with a suit on** – Make whatever you do fun and you will be able to carry on longer and perform more effectively.

X **X-plore** – Find information from as many different sources as possible. Sometimes what you are looking for in a text you can get more quickly from a phone call to an expert or a friend.

Y   **You** – Reading and learning is a personal skill. Make sure that the techniques you use work for you. Try a variety of different ways of reading and learning and create a set of tools that suits you.

Z   **ZZZ Sleep** – Avoid reading and studying at the expense of a good night's sleep. Take breaks whenever you need them. Read something enlightening, but light, before you go to sleep and think of what it means to you.

Summary

You should by now:

- have learned, applied and practised the five-step system
- have increased your reading rate by learning to read based on what you see rather than what you hear
- have started to use a variety of memory techniques based on what you're reading and when you'll need to use the information
- be treating your eyes with more respect
- be learning to adjust how you read based on the material and your environment
- be integrating what you have learned in this masterclass into how you think and work and read until this new habit replaces the old, and effective reading becomes 'how you do things'.

Do yourself a favour and have one last big sort through old magazines, documents, manuals and newspapers that you have allowed to build up, and then throw your in-tray away.

Don't let unread material build up. There's no need. You now have the skills to get through the reading that lands on your desk as it comes in. If you really want to read it later, spend a couple of minutes doing steps 1 to 4 on the material, put a note on the cover outlining why you're keeping it and how it might be useful later, then put it away with the intention of picking it up and doing step 5 when you actually need it.

Take control of your time, your knowledge and how you action it. In doing so you'll be taking control of your life.

Fact-check (answers at the back)

1. The best way to fully integrate the new skills learned in this masterclass is to use them in your everyday reading.
   a) True ❏
   b) False ❏

2. Your 21-day programme should include:
   a) topics that interest you ❏
   b) daily practice ❏
   c) reading in groups ❏
   d) all of the above. ❏

3. Your 21-day programme should:
   a) be not too easy and not too difficult. ❏
   b) integrate new knowledge with what you already know. ❏
   c) include about 20 minutes to simply practise speed reading (step 5). ❏
   d) have plenty of variety. ❏

4. You should learn a new word every day so that you can:
   a) mess with your friends. ❏
   b) increase your reading rate. ❏
   c) improve your general knowledge and understanding of language. ❏
   d) All of the above. ❏

5. It's important to create a work environment you like to be in.
   a) True ❏
   b) False ❏

6. There is a known limit to the speed at which you can read.
   a) True ❏
   b) False ❏

7. The key to the five-step reading system is:
   a) having a purpose (even if it changes). ❏
   b) applying it to everything, no matter how long or short, fact or fiction. ❏
   c) using it when you remember to. ❏
   d) using it only for work. ❏

8. You should be flexible in your reading – read to suit the material, what you want from it and your environment.
   a) True ❏
   b) False ❏

9. You have to practise steps 1 to 4 of the five-step process or you'll never get it right.
   a) True ❏
   b) False ❏

10. It's important to take breaks while you read because:
    a) it helps maintain concentration. ❏
    b) it relaxes you, and the less stressed you are, the easier it'll be to concentrate. ❏
    c) it allows you to think about what you read. ❏
    d) walking around and stretching your body is as important as taking care of your eyes. ❏

7 × 7

1 Seven key ideas

- Always have a purpose. Know why you're reading something – even if it's just because you want to.
- Use the five-step system to identify what you want to focus on and eliminate what you don't need. Don't fall into the trap of thinking you need to know everything all the time – you'll never keep up.
- Know what you will be using the information for before deciding which reading or memory technique to apply.
- Share the load. If you can, split the required reading between a few people then get together and share the knowledge.
- When reading technical material keep a list of acronyms, key terms and definitions handy. It will save a huge amount of time as you read.
- Read a book a week by dividing the number of pages of a book by seven and reading those pages each day. You'll be surprised how quickly you can get through 50 or so pages a day. By the end of the year you'll have read 52 books!
- Challenge yourself. Read books you'd usually avoid.

2 Seven best resources

- Software to help you read digital content faster: http://ereflect.com/
- Stretch your mind. Try photoreading: http://www.photoreading.com/
- Tony Buzan is great for information on mind-maps, memory techniques and speed-reading in general: http://www.tonybuzan.com/
- Get to grips with time and how you manage it. Brian Tracy's *Eat That Frog* (Berrett-Koehler, 2007) is a good start.

- Join a local book club or, if you don't have one, join the Goodreads book club (www.goodreads.com). It's a great collection of people who read a huge variety of books. You can of course, start your own book club.
- Subscribe to a 'book summaries' site. Do a search for those key words and choose one that suits your needs. These are sites where you can find summaries of some very amazing books.
- If you have any questions visit www.tinakonstant.com and get in touch through email, twitter or Facebook.

3 Seven great quotes

- 'Knowledge Management is expensive – but so is stupidity!' Thomas Davenport
- 'The more that you read, the more things you will know, the more that you'll learn, the more places you'll go.' Dr. Seuss
- 'Learn from yesterday, live for today, hope for tomorrow. The important thing is not to stop questioning.' Albert Einstein
- 'If you only read the books that everyone else is reading, you can only think what everyone else is thinking.' Haruki Murakami
- 'To read without reflecting is like eating without digesting.' Edmund Burke
- 'There is more treasure in books than in all the pirate's treasure on Treasure island.' Walt Disney
- 'It is what you read when you don't have to that determines what you will be when you can't help it.' Oscar Wilde

4 Seven things to avoid

- Avoid reading work/research material from beginning to end.
- Avoid reading what you don't want or need to read. If a book doesn't meet your needs, ditch it! You don't have to finish a book just because you started it. Your time is too valuable.
- Avoid overload. Prioritize and deal with information as it comes in.
- Avoid taking on information you don't need just because someone says you must.

- Avoid buying into the idea that information from a specific source is a 'cure all'. Get what you need from all angles and perspectives. It will give you greater depth and detail.
- Avoid forgetting what you read by having a purpose, applying an appropriate memory technique and applying the knowledge you gather.
- Avoid falling back into old habits by using every opportunity to read faster and more efficiently.

5 Seven inspiring people

- Sir Richard Branson grew up with dyslexia yet gathered the knowledge and information he needed to build an empire.
- Nelson Mandela: 'Education is the most powerful weapon which you can use to change the world.' Need I say more? Here is a man who never ceased to learn and grow despite undeniable hardships.
- Howard Berg is in the 1990 *Guinness Book of World Records* for reading 25,000 words a minute.
- Einstein was spectacular at turning accepted beliefs on their heads. His take on reading (too much): 'Any man who reads too much and uses his own brain too little falls into lazy habits of thinking'. Read all you like, but if you don't think...
- Malala Yousafzai – shot for wanting to go to school, then standing up to an entire culture for her rights and the rights of others to be educated.
- Robert E. Kahn and Vint Cerf – 'the fathers of the Internet' which in turn led to the technology we have today to create and share more knowledge (and nonsense) than ever before.
- The person who read to you as a child.

6 Seven things to do today

- Use the five-step system on a non-fiction book you've been avoiding.
- Practise speed-reading using a guide.
- Enhance your digital reading by trying out speed-reading software.

- Commit to using the information you read.
- Clear your desk. Just do it. Get the clutter out of your workspace once and for all.
- Choose a book you really want to read (fiction or non-fiction) and read at least 50 pages – then do the same tomorrow and the next day.
- Get through your reading as quickly as possible, then go play on the beach... in a park... up a mountain... in your garden...

7 Seven trends for tomorrow

- With the surge in self-publishing, mass opinion and information is only going to get bigger. It will get more difficult to identify qualified information from amateur contributions. Research the author for credibility before taking what they say as gospel.
- Reading is only one way to gather information. Make use of audio books, speedreading software and other technology.
- Teach your kids to manage information and read effectively. The better they handle information in the future, the better they'll do.
- Get practical. With so much information coming at us at such a pace, it's easy to get stuck in our heads and forget to use our hands. Pick up a practical hobby.
- As we become more independent of each other at work (working from home or on the road) the flow of information and knowledge will become more critical. Do your colleagues a favour and share what you have in a way they can easily understand.
- With so much amateur information spilling out through the internet, do the world a service and make sure what you contribute has great value.
- The speed of the world is increasing. There will be conflicting movements to slow things down. People will be looking for the simpler things in life which includes reading a good book by an open fire as the sun sets over the hills. Get in there early. Don't let the information age drag you under its wheels.

PART 4
Your Managing Stress At Work Masterclass

Introduction

It has been said 'employees join great organizations but leave because of bad managers' and from my own experience I can testify to the truth of the statement.

A number of factors, such as recognition, variety of work, achievement and prospects for promotion play an important role in job satisfaction and help good managers retain their staff. However, stress can be one of the most significant reasons for employees leaving or if not in a position to leave, at least wishing they could.

Some see stress as a problem for the individual or even a sign of some defect in character. Yet most forward-thinking managers and organizations see the effective management of stress as an essential part of their business practice, benefiting both employees and the business or organization.

Arguably anyone who comes into contact with another person needs to manage stress. Whether in the workplace, socially or at home, human interaction can create pressures, conflict and stress. Even when free from the influence of others we can often generate our own stress through our own desire to succeed or through innate fears and concerns.

Ultimately how you handle stress personally and as a manager will vary depending on a number of factors: types of people, the organization, inherent pressures of a job and specific economic factors. This Part of the book aims to provide you with information that you can use in assessing what is appropriate for you, your team and organization.

CHAPTER 22

What is stress?

We have all heard people saying they are stressed – you may even have said it yourself. Perhaps you have had a lot on at work or too much to think about or maybe others are making unreasonable demands on your time. In this chapter you will learn that the response to stress is hard-wired into our biology and has played an important role in the survival of the human race. We will look at how the modern world can confuse or trigger our natural response to danger and understand that what we call stress today isn't always bad, isn't the same for everyone and that stress can exist even if there are no visible signs of it.

We will also look at how to assess stress in the workplace, and consider the causes of stress that can be generated by organizations, other circumstances in our lives and even by our own outlook and expectations. Finally, we will examine some of the impacts stress can have on both individuals and organizations and in turn demonstrate the real value of the effective management of stress.

What is stress?

If you ask a group of individuals what they mean by stress, you will find some people talk about the causes of stress, giving responses such as 'too much work', or 'too much pressure', while others will respond citing the effects of stress, with responses such as 'feeling tired or depressed'. For clarity, throughout this Part we will refer to the causes of stress as **stressors** and the effects as the **response.**

The stress response

Stress is a commonly used word but one that means different things to different people and lacks a single coherent definition. At a basic level stress relates to the biological response of our body to certain situations.

Throughout prehistory people faced life and death situations on a daily basis with strong competition for survival. Since the earliest days of the human race, an inbuilt stress response has proved an effective means of protection in situations of extreme danger.

So from a biological perspective, stress is the natural physical reaction to events that make an individual feel threatened in some way. Sometimes the threat is real, such as coming face to face with a predator, or sometimes the threat is imagined – e.g. the wind moving the bushes may cause you to believe there is a predator hiding, ready to pounce. Stress is the body's way of helping to deal with the situation. In the emergency situation stress can save your life as your body automatically adapts to stay focused, alert and highly energized. This acute stress response, often referred to as **fight or flight** (or sometimes the 'fight, flight or freeze response'), prepares the body for fending off an attacker or rival or for running away. The response can also result in freezing to the spot, unable to move.

The response is triggered by a threat, excitement, noise, bright lights or temperature and is characterized by physical changes in the body including the release of hormones such as adrenalin and cortisol. Adrenalin regulates heart rate and the flow of blood and air, by altering the diameter of blood vessels and air passages, while cortisol increases blood sugar, suppresses the immune system and increases metabolism. This chemical/hormonal change triggers the physical changes in the body. Once the threat has passed the body returns to its normal state ready for the next time.

The fight or flight response is directly associated with the autonomic system, which controls both the physiological and psychological changes in the body in response to a stressor. We will look at this system in more detail in the next chapter.

General adaptation syndrome

Stressors lead to stress and some form of physiological or psychological reaction. In 1936 Austrian-born physician Dr Hans Selye defined his general adaptation syndrome (GAS) as comprising three stages:

1 the **alarm reaction stage**, where a shock stimulates the body's defences
2 the **resistance stage**, where the body either resists the stressor or adapts to the effects of the stressor
3 the **exhaustion phase**, where if the stressor continues but the resistance or adaptation is lost, the body is overloaded, the alarm stage returns and if the stress is prolonged, damage will occur.

Stress in the modern world

Some see GAS as over-simplistic and have developed their thinking to consider a more interactional approach, considering the individual in more detail. Whereas GAS seems to imply an automatic response, research has shown that individuals balance the demands made on them considering a variety of factors and this approach leads to a definition of stress as more of an imbalance.

Factors associated with the interactive model of stress that affect an individual's response include:

- **cognitive appraisal** – an individual's perception of a situation or event
- **experience** – familiarity, previous/historical exposure to similar events, relevant learning or training and any reinforcement or conditioning (what is seen as success or failure to cope)
- **demand** – perceived demand, actual ability to meet demands
- **interpersonal influences** – background and influencing factors
- **state of stress imbalance** – between actual and perceived demand and the ability to cope.

The interactive model provides a useful foundation for the management strategies detailed in later chapters.

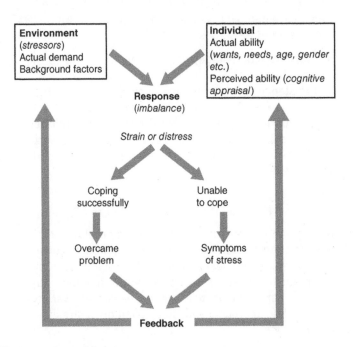

The interactive model of stress

Fight or flight evolved for dealing with physical danger in the modern work environment. Today, the situation is more likely to result in psychological danger, anticipation of events such as losing a job, failing to meet a deadline as well as actual danger from bullying or harassment. The world has moved on from the threat of being eaten by a tiger but as yet our biology has not caught up; it doesn't distinguish between physical and psychological threats – just think back to the last time you went to see a horror movie.

So from a work or organizational perspective, what we mean by stress today is more accurately described as *the negative effects or response to excessive pressure or other types of demands placed on people.*

Stress isn't always bad

Stress can be both positive and negative. Much of this Part focuses on management of the negative aspects of stress. However, the benefits of positive stress or pressure should not be overlooked. Positive pressure can be motivating and create a sense of team that helps get the job done.

The effects of positive stress, such as the 'butterfly feeling' you get in your stomach, link back to the basic biological response of fight or flight and the response to hormones in the bloodstream. In small doses this can help you perform under pressure and motivate you to do your best. Think of feelings you may have had before a job interview, a critical presentation or a looming deadline or target. Positive stress can make you feel pumped up and ready to succeed. Managed effectively in the workplace it can improve performance and bring a team together and improve overall wellbeing.

Like all stress though, people's thresholds vary and beyond a certain point stress stops being helpful and can start to damage the body. If you are continually performing under pressure your body and mind will ultimately pay the price.

The human performance curve shows the relationship between stress and performance and is adapted from the Yerkes-Dodson Law, originally developed in the early twentieth century by psychologist Robert M. Yerkes and John Dodson. The law states that performance increases with physiological or mental arousal, but only up to a point. When levels of arousal become too high, performance decreases. The adapted human performance curve illustrates how the same variation in performance is related to the amount of stress to which an individual is exposed.

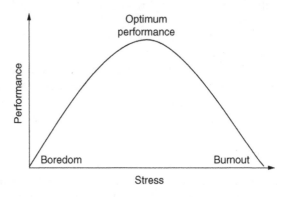

Adapted human performance curve

Stress isn't the same for everyone

Stress can be caused by a variety of stressors, including work situations (e.g. time pressure, fear of redundancy, overwork, bullying, and lack of tools and equipment) or personal experience such as home life or marriage breakdown. No two people react in the same way or to the same degree to a particular stressor. Some people seem to roll with the punches while others crumble at the slightest obstacle.

Earlier we introduced GAS and the idea that adaptation is required to respond to a stressor and that this can be expanded to consider factors relating to the individual – e.g. strength both physically and psychologically, perception and degree of control.

Various psychologists have researched the types and traits of personality or disposition. In Table 22.1 we consider six personality types, their preferred stress state and their vulnerability to the negative effects of excessive stress.

You might recognize some of the personality types in yourself or your work colleagues, although research concludes that most

Table 22.1 Disposition and vulnerability to stress

Type	Definition	Preferred stress level	Vulnerability to stress
Ambitious	Strong desire for success or achievement	High	High
Calm	Tranquil, placid and does not easily become disturbed, agitated or excited	Moderate/Low	Low
Conscientious	Meticulous and takes great care over everything	Low/Moderate	Moderate (high during change)
Non-assertive	Difficulty in standing up for themselves	Moderate/Low	Moderate
Lively	Full of vigour, experiences mental and emotional vigour	High	Low (high if pressure from self)
Anxious	Worried and tense, concerned about possible misfortune	Low	High

people combine traits of more than one personality type so this information should only be used as a guide for individuals. Good managers realize that people are far more complex than any single model can show and will use this information to build an overall picture of an individual and won't jump to conclusions about who fits into which precise category.

Age, gender and a number of other factors influence an individual's vulnerability to stress. The four important factors of control, predictability, expectation and support provide an initial understanding of what controls might be appropriate to combat stress, and we will consider these further later.

Control

If you have the ability to influence events (control the stressor) and meet the specific challenge it is easier to handle stress. This may be a result of your position/level of authority, experience and freedom within an organization. Older people with secure finances may feel they ultimately can walk away or not have to put up with the pressure. This in itself allows them to cope better.

Predictability

An individual is likely to feel greater stress if they are unable to predict the behaviour or occurrence of a stressor. For example, bullying is notoriously unpredictable in terms of knowing what the bully will do next. Predictability is linked with familiarity, knowledge and preparation. An effective technique employed by hospitals to reduce patient stress is to provide an option for patients to familiarize themselves with the hospital surroundings and timetable of events prior to an operation or giving birth. Think about the value of fire drills in preparation for a real emergency situation.

Expectation

People have expectations of their own ability to cope, as well as societal pressures. For example, men have traditionally been seen as breadwinners and so men may be more vulnerable to stress relating to financial pressures. Women on the other hand have traditionally been seen as carers so may appear to be tasked with caring for sick or elderly relatives as well as the stressor of raising a family. These expectations may also be impacted by perception of whether things are, or are likely to start, getting better.

Support

People who feel they have support, including support from colleagues, managers, unions, friends, family or doctors, are less likely to be affected by stress. Those who take comfort from some form of spiritual support, faith or belief system might also find it easier to cope.

Assessment of stress

In order to identify the signs of stress in the workplace and determine the magnitude of its impact, a manager or organization can start by analysing, using existing performance measures such as sickness absence, accident rates, productivity and quality metrics (customer complaints, volume of rework, etc.).

Generally a high degree of stress in the workplace will have a detrimental impact on these measures.

You may also be able to pick up on individuals showing signs of stress such as increased medication, smoking or alcohol use, nail biting or grinding of teeth. People often lose their sense of humour, become touchy or you might sense a general 'negative air' or 'atmosphere' in the workplace. Personal appearance and levels of grooming or personal hygiene may also get worse.

In order to gain a complete picture it is necessary, and in some countries a legal requirement, to make a formal assessment of stress.

Before an assessment takes place it is important to prepare by securing senior management and wider organizational support and buy-in, explaining the potential benefits and that everyone should be involved in the process. This might be seen as a significant change in the organization and we deal with the issues associated with change management in Chapter 27.

The formal assessment process is broken down as follows.

1 **Identify potential stressors**
   Think about the potential causes of stress within the organization, using the information from this book but also think specifically about the type of organization you are in and draw on your own and others' experiences.

2 **Identify who is at risk**
   Gather data, such as any existing performance measures as described above. Get feedback through a survey or questionnaire. Various templates for benchmarking surveys or questionnaires exist and having read the remainder of this book you will no doubt be able to create something that suits your organization.

3 **Evaluate the risk**
   Having collected the data, what does it tell you? Do any existing controls or practices have an impact? Which areas do you need to focus on? It is important to focus on preventing stress but you should also consider mitigation when stress does arise. How is stress identified, escalated and managed?

4 **Create an action plan**
   Create and communicate an action plan showing what will
   be done, by whom and when. Make sure the actions are
   followed up and completed.
5 **Monitor and review**
   Periodically check to make sure actions are effective. Regularly
   review the sources of data, perhaps redoing the survey if you
   feel it is necessary. You should review at regular intervals but
   also be aware of any changes within the organization (e.g.
   downsizing, introducing new equipment or work patterns)
   that may prompt an additional review or the need for
   improved controls.

No signs doesn't mean no stress

Regardless of what you have already learnt, a critical thing
to remember is people are often good at hiding stress. This
may be through fear or embarrassment, or perhaps driven
by the culture of an organization. Alternatively it may be an
individual's desire not to let the team down or feeling they have
everything under control or they may simply be blocking it out.

So just because your organization and the individuals within
it may look stress-free doesn't necessarily mean that is actually
the case – more often than not the opposite is true, with a calm
façade hiding the turmoil beneath. Think of a swan gliding
gracefully across a lake: the calm vision isn't the true picture as
beneath the waters its feet are flapping away like crazy.

Causes and impacts of stress

While an organization and work itself can cause stress, not all
stress is work-related and individuals often bring their own
stress into the workplace.

In the late 1960s two researchers, Dr Thomas Holmes and
Dr Richard Rahe, identified a relationship between life events
and illness. Their results, commonly known as the Holmes-
Rahe stress scale, show the relative impact of life events in
life-changing units (LCU) (see Table 22.2).

Table 22.2 The Holmes-Rahe stress scale of life-changing units (LCU)

Life event	LCU	Life event	LCU
Death of a spouse	100	Change in responsibilities at work	29
Divorce	73	Child leaving home	29
Marital separation	65	Trouble with in-laws	29
Imprisonment	63	Outstanding personal achievement	28
Death of a close family member	63	Spouse starts or stops work	26
Personal injury or illness	53	Begin or end school	26
Marriage	50	Change in living conditions	25
Dismissal from work	47	Revision of personal habits	24
Marital reconciliation	45	Trouble with boss	23
Retirement	45	Change in working hours or conditions	20
Change in health of family member	44	Change in residence	20
Pregnancy	40	Change in schools	20
Sexual difficulties	39	Change in recreation	19
Gain a new family member	39	Change in social activities	18
Business readjustment	39	Minor mortgage or loan	17
Change in financial state	38	Change in sleeping habits	16
Death of a close friend	37	Change in number of family reunions	15
Change to different line of work	36	Change in eating habits	15
Change in frequency of arguments	35	Vacation	13
Major mortgage	32	Christmas	12
Foreclosure of mortgage or loan	30	Minor violation of law	11

The LCU scores in the table are based on averages from the study. Using the stress scale, a score of 300 or more places an individual at high risk of illness, a score of 150–299 at moderate risk, and less than 150 only at slight risk of illness.

Individual stressors from outside work may overlap with those at work, such as financial problems at home linking with reduced hours or pay and job uncertainty. Old style management that says 'leave your worries at the gate' is no longer acceptable or effective. Forward thinking employers see the benefit in providing a sympathetic response, some flexibility or additional support for individuals with personal stress.

In the workplace stressors can be categorized into several groups.

- job roles, responsibility and control, i.e. the actual requirements of a job role, level of ambiguity in what is expected, any conflict of interest and the degree of autonomy or control
- workload and work pressure, the characteristic of the task, the capacity of individuals, equipment and processes and both the amount and type of work being undertaken
- the work environment, including the physical environment, space, lighting, heating and ventilation
- behaviour, conflict and support (interpersonal factors). These are associated with relationships between staff and management but also the organizational environment, how well or otherwise the organization is managed and its culture. Also included is the approach to harassment and bullying and level of support available, how people are recognized and how poor performance and behaviours are managed along with specific individual concerns
- change management and how the organization handles changes, from installing new equipment to dealing with growth or downsizing including redundancies.

It is clear from this list that some stressors might be easy to change with minimal effort, while others are harder to address and some are impossible. Understanding these causes of stress by definition will inform the type of controls that may be effective, which we will look at from Chapter 24 onward.

Summary

In this chapter you have covered a lot of ground, so well done. You started by understanding the difference between stressors (the causes of stress) and the response (the effects of stress) and went on to learn about the fight or flight response, general adaptation syndrome and how in today's world we use an interactive model for stress, considering the individual as well as the surrounding environment.

You learnt the principle of assessing stress in the workplace and how stress isn't always bad and can, in small doses, help improve performance. You saw that stress isn't the same for everyone and factors such as personality, control, predictability, expectations and the level of support available all play a part in how an individual may respond. You also learnt that stress can exist even if there are no visible signs.

You covered the main categories of stress in the workplace, which we will revisit through the remaining chapters.

Finally you saw how events in our personal life can overlap with work and how these events can vary in intensity and the impact they have on health.

Fact-check (answers at the back)

1. Which of the following is not an appropriate description of stress?
   a) The natural biological response to a threat or danger ❏
   b) The series of reactions to a stressor: alarm, resistance or adaptation and potential exhaustion ❏
   c) The negative effects or response to excessive pressure or other types of demands ❏
   d) The way weak people respond in a crisis with panic and confusion ❏

2. Which of the following is a true statement about stress?
   a) The signs of stress can always be seen ❏
   b) Some stress can be positive ❏
   c) Everyone reacts the same way when faced with a life-changing event ❏
   d) Jolly people tend to be less stressed than miserable ones ❏

3. Which of the following personality types may be the most vulnerable to stress?
   a) Ambitious ❏
   b) Calm ❏
   c) Conscientious ❏
   d) Non-assertive ❏

4. What important factors might affect the vulnerability of an individual to stress?
   a) Expectation ❏
   b) Predictability ❏
   c) Level of control ❏
   d) All of the above ❏

5. In the interactive model, which of these factors does not have an effect?
   a) An individual's perception of a situation or event ❏
   b) Whether the threat is physical or psychological in nature ❏
   c) Experience, previous exposure or relevant training ❏
   d) Perceived or actual ability to meet demands ❏

6. What might happen to sickness absence, accidents and customer complaints if a workforce is subject to stress?
   a) They are likely to remain unchanged ❏
   b) They are likely to decrease ❏
   c) They are likely to increase ❏
   d) Measuring these kind of things is irrelevant and a waste of money ❏

7. When assessing stress in the workplace what is the first thing you should do?
   a) Put together an action plan ❏
   b) Assess who might be at risk ❏
   c) Gain support and buy-in from senior managers ❏
   d) Send out a questionnaire ❏

8. When might you revisit your assessment of stress in the workplace?
a) Regularly or if the organization is about to or is going through change ❏
b) When human resources ask for a good news story for the company website ❏
c) If the survey results are bad ❏
d) Just before your performance review so you can show your boss how effective you've been ❏

9. Using the Holmes-Rahe stress scale, which of these events has the greatest impact in terms of life-changing units (LCU)?
a) Change in sleeping habits ❏
b) Pregnancy ❏
c) Change in line of work ❏
d) Marriage ❏

10. What might an organization do to support people with stress relating to their personal life?
a) Be sympathetic, show flexibility and provide support ❏
b) Give them a good talking to so they get a sense of perspective and move on ❏
c) Reduce their overtime or cut their hours so they have time to deal with personal matters ❏
d) All of the above ❏

CHAPTER 23

Understanding stress – some basic psychological and physiological aspects

In the previous chapter you learnt what stress is, the different models of stress and how in threatening situations the body reacts. Now we will look in more detail at the way the body responds to stress.

We will consider physical and psychological symptoms and the autonomic nervous system's effect on the body as part of the natural stress response. Then we will learn about some of the medical conditions that may be found in the workforce and diagnosed as a result of personal issues or experiences at work. These conditions include anxiety, depression, phobias and post-traumatic stress disorder. Finally we will see how stress can negatively affect an organization.

The aim of the chapter is not to make you a medical expert but to provide a basic understanding of some of the signs and symptoms of stress and how these link to biological processes in the body. You will be able to use this understanding to see warning signs in yourself and work colleagues and also be able to support those with diagnosed medical conditions in your organization.

Effects of stress

The effects of stress on the individual will vary from person to person but will broadly fall into two categories:

- **physiological effects** – the short-term and long-term effects on the body
- **psychological effects** – how people think, feel and behave (also termed cognitive, emotional and behavioural effects).

The following lists give some commons signs and symptoms of stress. The more you notice in yourself or others the closer you or they may be to a stress imbalance or burnout. Bear in mind that the signs and symptoms of stress can also be caused by other medical problems so wherever possible you should seek or encourage others to seek professional medical assistance.

Physiological signs and symptoms

Physiological signs and symptoms are short-term or long-term health effects, and can include the following:

- headaches
- nervous twitches
- memory problems
- mental ill health
- tiredness or sleeping problems
- frequent colds
- breathlessness
- chest pains, rapid heart beat
- high blood pressure and high cholesterol
- heart disease
- stroke
- feeling sick, nauseous or dizzy, fainting
- a craving for food or loss of appetite
- constipation or diarrhoea
- indigestion or heartburn
- diabetes
- gastric ulcers
- cramps or pins and needles
- arthritis

- sexual problems, lack of libido
- susceptibility to some types of cancer.

Psychological signs and symptoms

Psychological signs and symptoms involve how people may think, feel or behave, and include the following:

- anxiety
- fearing the future
- irritable, short temper or aggressive
- seeing only the negative
- frustration
- depressed, generally unhappy
- poor/irrational judgement
- inability to relax
- feeling overwhelmed
- feeling neglected, alone or uncared for
- breakdown in relationships
- job dissatisfaction
- restlessness, agitation, inability to concentrate or relax
- believing you are a failure, bad or ugly
- lack of interest in others
- loss of sense of humour
- avoiding making decisions or difficult situations
- denying there is a problem
- reliance on alcohol, cigarettes or drugs to relax
- nervous habits, nail biting, pacing.

The autonomic system

We've already learnt how the fight or flight response is linked to the body's autonomic system. In this system two sets of nerves are responsible for the automatic and unconscious regulation of the body's functions. The sympathetic system prepares the body to fight and the parasympathetic system is concerned with protection of the body with both systems acting in balance. For example, the sympathetic system causes rapid heart rate and breathing while slowing digestion, and the parasympathetic system in contrast reduces heart rate and breathing while increasing digestion. As you will see from the summary of autonomic responses in Table 23.1, it is the body's natural response that causes many of the basic signs and symptoms of stress.

Table 23.1 Effects of the autonomic system

Body part/ organ	Effect of parasympathetic system	Effect of sympathetic system
Brain	Reduced neural activity	Increased neural activity, quick decision-making
Heart	Decreased heart rate and output	Increased heart rate and output
Lungs	Breathing slowed	Airways increased, breathing rapid
Liver	Storage of glucose and fat	Breakdown of glucose and fat for energy
Spleen	Retains red blood cells	Contracts and empties red blood cells into the circulation
Digestion	Increased	Decreased
Kidney	Urine production	Reduced urine production
Eyes	Closed, pupils small	Open, pupils dilated
Mouth	Saliva produced	Saliva reduced, dry mouth
Ears	Hearing less acute	Hearing more acute
Skin	Dry, hair flaccid/normal	Sweating, hairs erect
Muscles	Relaxed	Tense
Blood	Normal ability to clot	Increased ability to clot

In addition to these general symptoms, certain chronic conditions may arise, with those listed below being the most common although other disorders exist. Specific advice for individuals will be available as a result of formal diagnosis. Whether you see symptoms of these disorders in yourself or others, professional help should be encouraged.

Depression

Depression is a state of low mood, associated with an aversion to activity and feelings of sadness, worry, restlessness and guilt. Depression may also be related to the presence of factors such as:

- family or personal history of depression
- life-changing events such as the death of a child or spouse
- drug or alcohol misuse
- chronic pain or illness.

A depressed mood is not necessarily a medical or psychiatric disorder in its own right but in some cases may arise as a side effect to some medical treatments or as a result of some infections or illnesses. Depression can also be the main symptom of some psychiatric disorders, including major depression (also called clinical depression), bipolar disorder (also called manic depression) and seasonal affective disorder where episodes of depression follow a seasonal cycle.

Anxiety

Anxiety is a feeling of unease, apprehension, worry and fear. Many people will feel anxiety at some point in their lives, particularly in response to a dangerous situation or disruptive life events as described in the previous chapter in the Holmes-Rahe stress scale. Anxiety is a perfectly natural response but can develop into a number of conditions.

Generalized anxiety disorder (GAD)

Generalized anxiety disorder arises from feeling anxious over a prolonged period of time rather than in response to a specific event. It can cause both physical and psychological symptoms as described above, and can have a significant impact on daily life. Treatments are available, including a variety of therapies and medication.

Panic disorder

Panic disorder is diagnosed when sufferers experience panic attacks on a regular basis. A panic attack is an overwhelming fear or apprehension and may be accompanied by physical symptoms such as nausea, sweating and palpitations (irregular heart beat). Sufferers may experience as few as one or two panic attacks per month while others may experience them at a frequency of several per week.

Attacks can occur at any time and without warning but may also be related to a particular situation or location. Although intense and frightening, attacks do not cause any physical harm. Treatment is usually by psychological therapies and or medication.

Phobias

Phobias are a fear response that is out of proportion to the risk posed by a particular object, animal or situation. People can gain an irrational fear of almost anything: heights, enclosed spaces, flying, spiders, snakes, clowns or the number 13. The level of anxiety may vary between sufferers, ranging from mild anxiety to a severe panic attack. Sufferers will often go out of their way to avoid all contact with the source of their anxiety, meaning it can have a significant disruptive effect on people's lives.

Those with simple phobias, such as fear of snakes, may be treated by gradual exposure to the animal, object or place, and over time, in incremental steps, sufferers can become desensitized. This can be done using self-help techniques or through professional help. Those with more complex phobias such as agoraphobia (fear of situations where escape might be difficult or help may not be available in an emergency), where an individual may be scared of public transport or may not even be able to leave their house, can be treated over a much longer period of time. Treatment will normally involve therapies such as counselling, psychotherapy or cognitive behavioural therapy (CBT).

Post-traumatic stress disorder (PTSD)

PTSD is an anxiety disorder triggered by a specific frightening or distressing event, including:

- wars, military combat
- terrorism attacks or being held hostage
- natural disasters such as floods or earthquakes
- witnessing violent deaths or serious crimes.

PTSD can develop immediately after the trigger event or become apparent weeks, months or even years later. Sufferers relive the event through flashbacks and nightmares and may experience feelings of guilt and isolation and become irritable and have trouble sleeping.

Treatment depends on the severity of symptoms and how soon they occur after the trigger event. Trauma-focused CBT as well as medication and other psychological treatments may be used.

As you might expect, certain types of work may expose people to greater risk of PTSD: those in the emergency services, armed forces or those who work with the potential threat of physical violence such as prison workers, some civil service positions (e.g. welfare and benefits workers) or even teachers of young adults. In addition to the work people undertake in your organization you should consider their working history as certain industries tend to attract those from a particular background as a second career – e.g. those with military service may be recruited by security or defence firms. In such situations you may consider additional training for staff to be aware of symptoms, and proactively consider support provisions.

Obsessive compulsive disorder (OCD)

OCD is an anxiety disorder characterized by ritualistic behaviours designed to fend off the cause of apprehension, fear or worry. Symptoms include excessive hand washing, cleaning or repeated checking. Some sufferers have a preoccupation with sexual, violent or religious thoughts and others exhibit an aversion to a particular number.

OCD is sometimes linked to high intelligence and sufferers often exhibit other personality disorders. It can be treated by a variety of behavioural therapies and medication. In extreme cases surgical options may be considered.

Other biological considerations

A circadian rhythm is any biological process that follows a 24-hour cycle and can be found across the natural world in plants, animals and fungi. Fundamentally, circadian rhythms are hard-wired into our bodies; however, they can be adjusted to the local environment by external causes. In humans the rhythm is most evident in sleeping and feeding patterns but can also be seen in regulation of core body temperature, brainwave activity, hormone production and cell regeneration.

Circadian rhythms are important when it comes to work patterns, particularly shift working or people who travel extensively crossing multiple time zones – e.g. airline pilots and crew. Inability to following usual sleeping patterns can lead to fatigue, disorientation or insomnia.

To mitigate the impact of shift work it is important to avoid rapid shift changes and permanent night shifts. Minimizing the number of consecutive nights worked and offsetting working time with clear days away from work will all help. Individuals can also improve their ability to sleep during the day by avoiding alcohol, heavy foods and exercise prior to sleep.

In addition to circadian rhythms the body may also be affected by other temporal cycles such as seasonal changes including reduced daylight hours. In the workplace there may be practical things you can do to accommodate these variations, such as varying lighting types and intensity.

Understand the signs of your own stress

We often see things in others, while failing to recognize the very same things in ourselves. As an individual it is important to consider what stressors trigger a specific reaction in you and what symptoms the response generates, whether they be physical changes or shifts in our feelings, thoughts or behaviour.

By reflecting and taking time to appreciate our own level of stress we can see early warning signs and ensure that we take appropriate action so that symptoms do not become serious and we manage the situation.

We will consider simple steps that everyone can take to reduce stress and improve their general wellbeing in Chapter 28.

Effects of stress on an organization

In addition to the effect on individuals, stress, irrespective of the cause (either generated by the workplace or brought in by an individual from their personal life) can have a significant impact on an organization. The effects of stress on an organization can include:

- employee loyalty and commitment to work
- employee recruitment and retention
- employee performance and productivity
- accident rates, sickness absence and customer complaints
- customer satisfaction
- reputation, brand and image.

In some situations, where an organization is the cause of stress, employers may also face legal responsibilities and failure to manage stress may result in regulatory action or litigation resulting in prosecution and or compensation claims.

Like individuals, organizations also vary in their vulnerability to stress, with certain occupations or organizations more prone by the nature of the work done. These might include the emergency services; teaching; work that involves a high degree of uncertainty or interaction with public or societal groups who themselves may be under stress, so employees end up on the receiving end of others' fight or flight responses; shift or night workers, where their diurnal rhythms are impacted; those who perform safety critical roles where errors may have catastrophic consequences, such as air traffic controllers.

Remember that if you decide to take action to manage stress, you must prepare individuals and organizations, as you do not want your efforts to backfire and cause additional pressure/demands on others. You will also need to be conscious that not all management techniques are appropriate for all organizations.

Summary

In this chapter you have learnt some of the psychological and physiological symptoms of stress as well as the link between these symptoms and the autonomic system's effect on a variety of organs and parts of the body.

You saw some of the common medical conditions associated with stress, and how circadian rhythms and seasonal cycles can impact the body and what steps may be taken to manage them. You should understand the importance of self-awareness in terms of what triggers stress for you personally so you can manage your own stress levels.

Finally you saw how stress in the workplace can negatively impact an organization through reduced employee loyalty, commitment to work, performance and productivity, increased accidents and sickness absence rates, low customer satisfaction and damage to an organization's reputation and brand. Organizations should also be aware of any specific regulatory requirement associated with the management of stress to avoid potential prosecutions or compensation claims.

Fact-check (answers at the back)

1. Which of the symptoms below is not a potential physical sign of stress?
   a) Headaches ❑
   b) Indigestion or heartburn ❑
   c) High blood pressure ❑
   d) Believing you are a failure, bad or ugly ❑

2. Which of these psychological signs of stress might you pick up on in the workplace?
   a) People avoiding making decisions ❑
   b) Staff making poor or irrational judgements ❑
   c) Work colleagues denying a problem exists ❑
   d) All of the above ❑

3. With regard to the autonomic system, which of the following is not part of the sympathetic nervous system response?
   a) Decreased digestion ❑
   b) Decreased clotting ability of blood ❑
   c) Increased breathing rate ❑
   d) Increased heart rate ❑

4. Similarly, which of these is not a true statement relating to the parasympathetic response?
   a) Pupils are dilated ❑
   b) Hearing is less acute ❑
   c) Skin is dry, hair normal/flaccid ❑
   d) Muscles are relaxed ❑

5. Which of the following is unlikely to be a significant factor relating to depression?
   a) Family or personal history of depression ❑
   b) Life-changing events such as the death of a child or spouse ❑
   c) Moderate consumption of alcohol ❑
   d) Chronic pain or illness ❑

6. Which of the following is not an event likely to trigger post-traumatic episodes?
   a) War ❑
   b) Natural disaster ❑
   c) Witnessing a fatal car accident ❑
   d) PowerPoint failure during an important presentation ❑

7. Which of the following is not a characteristic of obsessive compulsive disorder?
   a) Excessive hand washing ❑
   b) Keeping lists as a reminder of tasks to complete ❑
   c) Regular checking or cleaning ❑
   d) Preoccupation with violent or religious thoughts ❑

8. Which of the following temporal events is not recognized as influencing biological cycles?
   a) New Year celebrations ❑
   b) Changing of the seasons ❑
   c) Crossing multiple time zones ❑
   d) 24-hour cycle of day and night ❑

9. Why is it important to identify your own triggers, symptoms and levels of stress?
a) To be an example to others of how to cope ❏
b) To set challenging targets for yourself ❏
c) To see warning signs and take action to ensure that symptoms do not become serious ❏
d) To know when to book your holiday ❏

10. Which of these may be negatively impacted by stress in the workplace?
a) Employee loyalty, commitment to work, productivity ❏
b) Accidents and sickness absence rates ❏
c) Brand and reputation ❏
d) All of the above ❏

CHAPTER 24

Job roles, responsibility and level of control

The old adage that prevention is better than cure holds true for managing stress at work. Now we have learnt what stress is and some of its effects, we can start to look at ideas, methods and practical examples of how to prevent stress in the workplace.

In this chapter we will look at how lack of clarity around job roles, the failure to communicate or have an agreed understanding of what individuals are expected to do and the boundaries of their responsibility can lead to confusion, worry and stress. We will also consider how conflicting expectations can lead to frustration and errors.

We will learn how engaging with employees, allowing them freedom to determine how they work and the opportunity to get involved in decision-making processes can increase motivation and productivity, create a sense of power and ownership and reduce anxiety and stress.

The Dalai Lama once said:

> *If a problem is fixable, if a situation is such that you can do something about it, then there is no need to worry. If it's not fixable, then there is no help in worrying. There is no benefit in worrying whatsoever.*

Role clarity

Role clarity is about communicating clear expectations of what is to be done or achieved and the boundaries of responsibility. This is essential to reducing stress in the workplace.

Without understanding exactly what is expected of you, it is easy to be blamed for something you have done but that management felt you didn't have the authority to do, seemingly being punished for taking the initiative when things go wrong. Alternatively, you may also be blamed if you didn't complete an activity that management thought you should have done – e.g. being challenged as to why you didn't foresee a problem and take the initiative to solve it. Working in these circumstances you seem to be damned if you do something and damned if you don't.

Often you will also find that where there is an absence of role clarity there can be a considerable lag between a problem and its discovery. For example, a contractual or equipment specification change may be made and only discovered by management many months later when a dispute arises or the equipment has been installed and is found to be inappropriate. Inevitably an investigation more akin to a witch-hunt will ensue and all involved will try and point the finger elsewhere.

I am reminded of a simple story that illustrates the point on role clarity very well.

You have heard the story about Anybody, Nobody, Somebody, and Everybody?

An important job had to be done and Everybody was sure that Somebody would do it. Anybody could have done it, but Nobody did it. Somebody got angry about that because it was Everybody's job. Everybody thought that Anybody could do it, but Nobody realized that Everybody wouldn't do it. It ended up that Everybody blamed Somebody when Nobody did what Anybody could have done.

Language can also be a significant issue in role clarity; it is all too easy to write job descriptions or make statements that can be interpreted in more than one way. So it is important to avoid ambiguity and things that can be interpreted or taken out of context.

In Chapter 28 we will look at time management and the importance of prioritization. You can see that without role clarity and a true understanding of who is expecting you to do what, it is hard to assign priorities and allocate time appropriately.

All roles in an organization need to have a formal job description explaining what the role is for, what is expected, boundaries of responsibility and also cover any required knowledge or training. This should be agreed by both parties. Most people get a job description when they start a new job or join a new organization but over time you get asked to take on new responsibilities and the workplace may change, and bits of what you did may transfer to others or disappear because procedures or the technology has changed. A formal job description should never be used as a barrier to taking on or changing your duties but it should be reviewed regularly to make sure it stays current and meaningful.

Role conflict

When we talk about conflict we usually think about disagreements between two parties and this may occur in the workplace. Here we are thinking about conflict within an individual's role. There is a potential for stress when two parts or elements of a job are seemingly incompatible. If you are a parent of small children this is something you have to wrestle with on a daily basis. On the one hand you need to encourage your children to be honest and open and confident that they can confide in you, on the other there is a need to provide discipline when you find out something naughty has been done, thus discouraging the open and honest behaviour you are seeking to instil.

Work examples may include potential conflict between productivity over safety, or company loyalty over care for subordinates. Think of a medical doctor: they have to balance care for the individual patient with getting a certain volume of appointments completed in each day.

The most obvious solution is to deconflict a particular role, by designing jobs and allocating conflicting responsibilities to different people. While this may be practical in some organizations, particularly where the potential of role conflict can have catastrophic effects, such as safety critical roles in the nuclear or aviation industries, for many, role conflict has to remain part of the job and work becomes a balancing act to manage these conflicts.

In addition to role conflict inside the workplace, there may also be conflict from outside. The most common is the balance between work and home life. Parents have responsibilities to their family, perhaps there may be a sick or elderly relative at home or some workers may have more than one job.

Where role conflict can't be avoided and regardless of the source, these factors need to be considered and dealt with in an open and sensitive manner. I am a believer that bad news is in fact good news when delivered early. Knowing about a problem sooner rather than later allows you to deal with it before it gets out of hand. It is therefore important to provide a mechanism where people can express concern or validate their decision-making. One method is through the implementing of a **just culture** (see Chapter 26) where it becomes the organization's normal practice, within defined boundaries, to raise concerns and problems without the fear of punishments or reprisal and all employees have a clear authority to STOP, particularly if a problem relates to safety, quality or spiralling costs.

Being able to stop or raise issues without the fear of punishment or retribution prevents employees masking genuine mistakes or covering up problems.

Motivation

An understanding of motivation is important for any manager to get the most out of their team. It also has a direct link to stress in the workplace. If you feel undervalued, overlooked or stuck in a dead-end job, you are likely to look negatively on things and become susceptible to stress, particularly if you feel powerless to change your situation.

In 1943, Abraham Maslow presented his paper 'A Theory of Human Motivation' in which he described stages of growth through a 'hierarchy of needs'. This hierarchy of needs is often depicted as a pyramid with basic or physiological needs (air, food, water, shelter, etc.) at the base and self-actualization (the state of achieving your true potential) at the top.

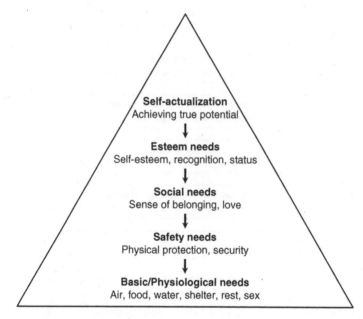

Maslow's hierarchy of needs

Maslow's model has been adapted and updated a number of times and a revised model from the 1990s is shown below.

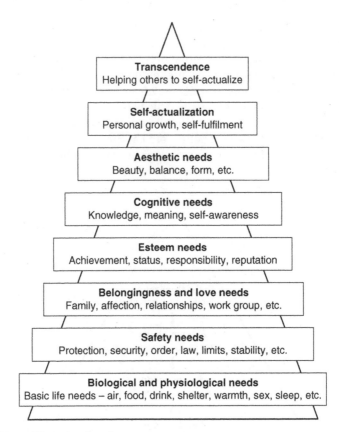

Adapted hierarchy of needs

Frederick Herzberg proposed the Motivation-Hygiene Theory, also known as the Two Factor Theory, of job satisfaction in the late 1950s following extensive research, where he investigated the factors that lead to employee satisfaction and dissatisfaction (see Table 24.1).

He discovered that certain factors were expected to be met in order to avoid dissatisfaction. These hygiene factors need to be present and well managed essentially to maintain a neutral level of satisfaction and have to be addressed before considering the factors that result in positive satisfaction. The factors having a positive effect are described by Herzberg as 'motivators'.

Table 24.1 Herzberg's Two Factor Theory

Motivators	Hygiene factors
Challenge	Salary and other benefits
Responsibility	Working conditions
Promotion	Safety arrangements
Interesting or stimulating work	Security
Recognition	Quality of supervision
Achievement	Interpersonal relationships
	Status

Herzberg also proposed the idea of job enrichment to improve satisfaction. This involves empowering employees to take greater control of their work through less supervision, freedom to select methods and approach to work.

One surprise from Herzberg's work might be that money (i.e. pay and benefits) is a hygiene factor rather than a motivator. Herzberg himself acknowledged that there was some degree of disagreement over this point but stated, 'viewed within the context of the sequences of events, salary as a factor belongs more in the group that defines the job situation and is primarily a dissatisfier'.

As a manager, it is often easy to try and retain staff by simply paying them more, but this actually has little impact in the long-term, despite what the individuals themselves may say. As with other hygiene factors though, the expectation is that pay is at least in line with the market to avoid dissatisfaction. If this requirement is met, effective managers need to seek to provide true motivators in the work environment.

Level of control

From the work of Maslow and Herzberg, we see that we have certain basic needs and other more complex motivational needs. Lack of, or failure to meet, either of these can lead to stress. Staff should be able to influence decisions and understand the reasons why, when factors are more rigid and less negotiable.

Lack of control can affect morale and self-worth and create frustration, whereas giving people greater freedom and a sense of self-determination over their place of work can encourage them to develop new skills, to undertake more challenging work, use their skills to be innovative and become more productive.

Job enrichment can be achieved by reducing supervision or allowing greater autonomy to employees to decide how they work. This approach should be supported by clear responsibilities and accountability and aligns well with an objectives-based approach to working.

It must be recognized though that some jobs (e.g. those of a repetitive nature) are less adaptable and so alternative methods need to be found to motivate employees. Here, increasing the responsibilities of staff to cover a wider remit will help to provide challenge. Alternatively, job rotation can provide variety which is beneficial both to individuals in terms of job satisfaction and the organization in terms of preventing mistakes. When engaged in repetitive and monotonous tasks employees can become complacent, distracted or blinkered to what is happening, essentially 'switching to auto pilot', which can lead to errors or accidents affecting safety, quality and productivity. Creating a sense of team and allowing for job rotation can ensure people remain focused and mutually supportive with collective responsibility for a series of tasks.

As an example, think of a manufacturing line with several stages, each requiring an operator with a specific skill. By training all the staff on the line to perform all tasks (multi-skilling), collectively the team can own the output from the line and freely rotate between positions to provide working variety. Multi-skilling may require an investment in training but this is usually outweighed by the benefits in motivation and productivity. Multi-skilling also means less reliance on individuals and a greater ability to accommodate leave, absences, etc.

In a previous role I was responsible for ride operations at a theme park. The larger rides would need a number of staff to operate, some managing queues, others batching, loading and unloading guests from the ride, looking after bags and an operator to start, stop and monitor the ride. Many of the positions required repetitive actions and had a safety dimension. Multi-skilling and job rotation proved very effective in ensuring safety was maintained but also by providing variety for employees they remained motivated and as a consequence interacted better with guests, improving the quality of their day out.

Objective output-based working

Objective output-based working means providing less prescription to employees and supports an increased level of autonomy and control. Mutually agreeing a specific work outcome and allowing the employee freedom to determine how to achieve the objective in a specific timeframe addresses many of the motivation factors identified by Herzberg.

A common acronym for effective objective setting is SMART:

- **S**pecific
- **M**easurable
- **A**chievable
- **R**elevant
- **T**imely or **T**ime bound

SMART work objectives provide clarity by defining **S**pecifically what needs to be accomplished, the reasons why, who is involved and any specific requirements, boundaries or constraints. The **M**easures of success define how much or how many and a clear end point, i.e. how you know when you have achieved the objective. They must be **A**chievable, which means providing stretch and challenge to an individual or team but not so extreme as to be unrealistic. Objectives must have a **R**elevance to an individual or team and the organization as a whole, otherwise it is hard to understand the context and value of what is to be done. A clear **T**ime constraint provides a guide as to the level of urgency and the prioritization of tasks.

Regarding the relevance of objectives, this is one area that is often overlooked as obvious, but failure to adequately think through the consequences of an objective can force actions and behaviours that may be counterproductive. An example is objectives for an organization's sales force. While it is obvious the sales team should sell more, if volume is the only measure of success, it will drive sales at any cost, reducing profit margins or even selling at a loss. Also the sales team may sell more than can be delivered, leaving customers disappointed or a workforce burnt out trying to deliver more than they can produce. So relevance needs to be assessed in a broader context.

Employee engagement and consultation

In many situations there are statutory requirements to consult with employees on a variety of matters. Irrespective of external requirements it makes good sense for managers to engage and consult with their staff, ensuring that everyone has a voice in influencing their work practices and environment. The ability to influence decision-making provides a feeling of power rather than powerlessness; as we have learnt, being powerless to impact your situation or surroundings plays a key part in levels of anxiety or stress.

Organizations might wish to create some form of employee forum or consultation group, or utilize existing bodies such as trade unions for this purpose. There are several challenges that need to be addressed for such a group to be effective. The group needs to be truly reflective of the workforce, a balance of management and employees, and adequately representative of different departments, functions and workgroups. Usually representatives should be elected, demonstrating they have the support of their peers, and serve for a defined period of time ensuring they can step down or periodically refresh representation if ineffective.

Representatives need to have time to consult with their peers to be effective, and need to be sufficiently robust to represent views, even if they have personal feelings to the contrary. It is important to keep individual, internal or external politics out of discussions and decision-making. The most important element is to ensure that the group actually has power and that feelings and comments from employees are acted upon, and where this is not possible the reasons why are clearly explained.

Engagement groups should be able to influence both hygiene factors and motivators in the workplace. For example, they may comment on safety and operational procedures, breaks and work patterns, levels of supervision and how pay and benefits are awarded in relation to performance as well as working with management to ensure work is challenging and people receive appropriate recognition.

In Chapter 27 we will look more closely at change management. When an organization is planning significant change, whether downsizing, expanding, implementing new work practices or machinery, employee engagement and buy-in is critical for success. Therefore, the engagement and consultation structures an organization uses day to day can become a powerful vehicle to ensure a successful change.

Manager's action

An effective manager should try to minimize conflict, improve clarity and empower employees. Sometimes you may not be supported by the organization as a whole, but you can set an example within your area of responsibility. You should regularly ask yourself some questions:

- Do you discuss working practices and arrangements with employees, and act on their feedback?
- Do you discuss employees' objectives, progress against objectives and aspirations for the future?
- Do you encourage training and development and provide opportunity for progression?
- Do employees raise issues and concerns early and help identify causes and solutions?
- Do you thank and recognize individuals and teams for their efforts?

Of the above I have found nothing motivates employees more than recognition that they have done well. So say 'thank you'

often and sincerely. Two simple words can reduce tension and flood the body of both manager and employee with feel-good chemicals. You will reinforce positive behaviour and build a bank of goodwill which you may need to draw on in the future. So whoever and for whatever reason, say thank you – you will find people are happy and more open, you can follow up with questions about what they have achieved, what they have learnt and what you can do to help in the future.

Summary

In this chapter you have leant how to reduce worry and anxiety for your workforce by setting clear expectations and responsibilities for individual job roles. You saw how to reduce role conflict and ambiguity and how to provide appropriate support to staff where conflict can't be avoided, using open and honest dialogue without fear of punishment or reprisal as part of a just culture.

You have examined the works of Maslow and Herzberg, and how these theories support the idea of allowing employees to have greater freedom and control concerning their work and work environment, and learnt how to set SMART output-based objectives to improve motivation.

Consideration was given to multi-skilling and job rotation to provide variety and reduce errors and to create a sense of team or collective ownership for a series of activities or tasks. Finally you covered some principles of employee engagement and consultation and considered some simple questions you should ask yourself as a manager to ensure you get the most out of your team.

Fact-check (answers at the back)

1. Why are clear responsibilities important?
   a) To ensure you know who to blame when things go wrong ❑
   b) To provide clarity so everyone knows what's expected of them and can manage their priorities accordingly ❑
   c) To ensure you know you are not paying someone too much ❑
   d) To give Human Resources the correct paperwork ❑

2. If an employee raises a concern regarding role conflict, you should...
   a) Tell your boss immediately to avoid being blamed ❑
   b) Get the employee to swap roles with a work colleague ❑
   c) Give the employee a pay rise and ask them to live with it ❑
   d) Discuss the issues and try to identify potential solutions with the employee's involvement ❑

3. In the hierarchy of needs, which needs should be satisfied first?
   a) Esteem ❑
   b) Social ❑
   c) Safety ❑
   d) Physiological ❑

4. In Herzberg's two factor theory which of the following is not a hygiene factor?
   a) Salary ❑
   b) Achievement ❑
   c) Working conditions ❑
   d) Quality of supervision ❑

5. Which of the following is not a motivator?
   a) Challenge ❑
   b) Interpersonal relationships ❑
   c) Responsibility ❑
   d) Interesting work ❑

6. Which of the following is not an element of SMART objectives?
   a) Specific ❑
   b) Measureable ❑
   c) Robust ❑
   d) Time-bound ❑

7. Why might setting a volume-only sales target for the sales team become counterproductive?
   a) It might drive behaviour that was unintentional, reducing margin or exceeding production capacity ❑
   b) Human Resources says everyone has to have a safety objective as well ❑
   c) We may have to pay the sales team extra commission if they meet the target ❑
   d) It wouldn't be counter-productive, increasing sales is a good thing ❑

8. Why might job rotation improve motivation?
   a) Employees get a greater variety of work and a sense of shared ownership ❑
   b) Employees get to spend more time training than working ❑
   c) Employees get to pick a job that pays more ❑
   d) Employees get to move around so no one knows who's responsible anymore ❑

9. What important factor should be considered in establishing an employee forum?

a) Make sure none of the trouble makers get elected as representatives ❏

b) Make sure you make decisions before the meeting so you can tell everyone what's happening ❏

c) Make sure all departments and functions are represented, including managers and employees ❏

d) Make sure representatives are kept busy to avoid them chatting to other staff ❏

10. What can I do as a manager to improve the motivation of my team?

a) Discuss concerns and issues ❏

b) Encourage training and development ❏

c) Say thank you ❏

d) All of the above ❏

CHAPTER 25

Workload, work pressure and work environment

It is easy to see ourselves as overworked. Sometimes this is genuinely true, other times it is down to personal negative perceptions or our own expectation of what good performance looks like, rather than being driven by management or others in the workplace. It is also easy to confuse activity for productivity. We may spend all our time travelling from site to site, in meetings or writing reports but never seem to get anything of value done.

In Chapter 28 we will consider time management and prioritization, an important skill for managing workload and pressure, in more detail. Now we will focus on how, as a manager, you can build on knowledge from the previous chapter to motivate employees without setting unrealistic targets to improve workload and pressure and will learn to distinguish between activity and productivity.

We will see how you can use Pareto analysis to identify the most significant factors in order to prioritize improvement activity and will consider some lean principles, tools and techniques to help increase productivity and reduce workplace stress by removing waste, eliminating bottlenecks and smoothing work demands.

Finally we will look at how elements of workplace design and the work environment can create or contribute to work pressures and stress and we will investigate how these elements can be effectively managed.

Workload and work pressure

In the absence of clear communication of expectations, people will make assumptions based on behaviour. As a manager you may think it appropriate to always be the first one into work and the last one to leave at the end of the day. This might be required or a self-imposed demand. Either way your behaviour will set an expectation among your team. Others will pick up and mirror your practice making an assumption that because you do it it must be important and therefore if you're going to get on, that is what is expected.

This innocent action now creates an atmosphere where, potentially, people fear to ask for time off or to leave early to attend their children's school theatre production, a dental appointment, etc. Staff may switch to auto pilot where they perceive it is more important to be seen sat at the desk, irrespective of what they are doing. Pressure mounts, resentment sets in and before long the entire office is stressed out.

This example is real, if perhaps a little extreme, and something I encountered first-hand, when a bold secretary came to see me to vent the frustrations of my team. My response was one of shock: of course I don't expect people to be there the same hours as me or miss the Christmas play. Today I make a point of varying my start and finish times so I am not always first in or last out, take an interest in what others are doing out of work and make a point of leaving early occasionally, and the impact is quite stark.

As well as driving psychological expectation, as a manager you also set physical expectations. These might be production or other performance targets, contracted working hours or shift patterns. We learnt in the previous chapter that challenge is an important part of motivation and setting SMART output-based objectives can provide employees with greater control over their working day. This work freedom also helps reduce work pressure as individuals have the power to influence how they work.

When setting SMART objectives other factors you should consider include:

- Are demands appropriate in relation to agreed timetables/hours of work?
- Is the individual physically capable of meeting the demands?
- Are equipment or processes capable of meeting the demands?
- Are skills and abilities matched to demands – does an individual have the appropriate competencies and training?
- Have any concerns been addressed and how will issues be raised?

Productivity and process improvement

In addition to a particular manager's approach, workload and work pressure are often associated with poor processes and productivity. This might be that work isn't divided equally among staff, creating a bottleneck for certain tasks or individuals, which in turn creates a feeling of overwork, pressure and stress. Alternatively, operational procedures or authorization processes might be unnecessarily complex or have been written without the involvement of those actually performing a task. The slogan *work smarter not harder* is often bandied around by managers but few actually act on this intention. How many times have you or work colleagues said 'This job would be so much easier if we just...'

In the next couple of sections we will learn some basic tools and techniques for improving processes and increasing productivity, thereby avoiding excessive workload and pressure.

Pareto analysis

Sometimes it is hard to know where to start. A useful tool for both managing your time and tackling problems is Pareto analysis. The idea is that 80% of tasks can be completed in 20% of the time and this has clear implications for time management. We can apply the same rule to work demands and productivity, assuming that 80% of productive activity can be completed with 20% of the tasks and the remaining 20% productivity taking 80% of the time or covering 80% of tasks.

Essentially Pareto analysis lets you determine where you will get your biggest impact for the time and money spent on improvement – 'the best bang for your buck!'

Sometimes you need to consider how you analyse your data. Consider the example below, a real situation I dealt with, in which you can see how powerful Pareto analysis can be.

A company runs a set of fast food restaurants in a particular town. Each of the six restaurants occasionally runs out of certain product lines of food. This causes customers to complain, and staff to become pressured as they think they might be blamed by management and will also have to deal with angry customers. They decide to solve the problem and collect data on which restaurants have the biggest problem and what the cause of the problems are, and graph their results.

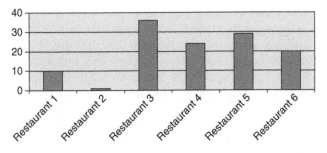

Number of product lines run out by restaurant

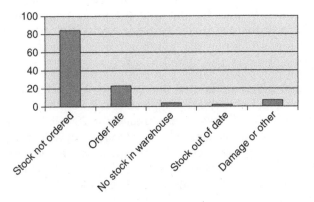

Causes of product lines running out

By simply looking at the number of events in the first graph they might choose to focus on restaurant 3 and deal with over 30 events. However, if they consider the causes across all restaurants they see that the single biggest problem is stock not being ordered. This means they can focus on over 80 events across all the restaurants, getting more from their effort. In the real-life situation, this was investigated and a simple reminder system implemented by the central warehouse. Each day they would ring round each restaurant at the end of the day to check orders had been placed in the electronic system. Problem solved, customers were happy, stressful situations for staff were removed.

Five lean principles

Terms such as Lean, Kaizen, Six sigma or Process improvement can sometimes get bandied around as management buzz words. They have been around for a number of years and all seek to improve productivity. While my personal feeling is that all of these practices can add value, you can take it too far and forget the social and people elements of work which in themselves contribute to productivity. However, the pragmatic application of some of the principles and tools can significantly improve workload and pressure and a summary is provided below.

1. Identify what adds value

Value-added activity changes something for the first time to meet a customer requirement, while non-added activity takes time and resources but does not change anything and/or does not help meet customer requirements. Here we are using the term customer to mean an external or end customer as well as an internal customer such as the next task in a production line, another department or facility.

It sounds obvious but think about your working day and how much of your time is spent on non-value added tasks such as waiting, rework, etc. It stands to reason that if you can reduce non-value added activity you will free up time to focus on other work demands and knowing that you are actually doing work that adds value can motivate you and the team.

It is important to note that some non-value activity may be essential to complete a process, but just because it is essential doesn't mean to say it has to be value-added. Don't take things for granted and don't be afraid to ask 'Why do we do this?'

In a previous job I used to spend at least two full days each month creating a very detailed operations report with dozens of graphs, dashboards and action plans. This was very demotivating and frustrating as I knew no one in head office really took any notice or rarely went beyond the summary front cover. I was wasting my time but someone long ago had decided we needed the report, so it had to be done. One month I decided to put my theory to the test and simply updated the front page and left the remainder of the report exactly as the previous month. No comments came back. When I explained what I had done to head office, the requirement for the monthly report was reduced to one page for all seven of our facilities, freeing myself and my opposite numbers at other sites to focus on other activity.

2. Eliminate waste

There are generally seven types of recognizable waste:

- defects or mistakes
- over-production
- transportation
- waiting or unnecessary approvals
- inventory or excessive stock
- motion
- over-processing.

The challenge is to reduce these in favour of value-added activity. Some examples that apply to stress management include motion and the reduction of physical labour, perhaps relying on mechanical aids rather than manpower, or perhaps unnecessary or burdensome procedures or approvals processes, that create frustration and pressure when work is 'stuck in the system'.

3. Make value flow at the pull of the customer

All too often our work rate or workflow is dictated by activities that occur prior to an activity reaching us, rather than our responding to the request of an internal or external customer. This essentially drives work rate that will find the weakest link and create a bottleneck.

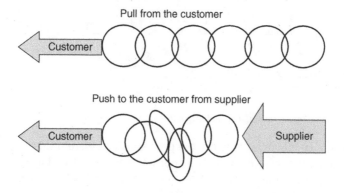

To deal with bottlenecks the temptation is to just add more resource or equipment. However, you might discover that with some simple analysis you can smooth demand across the existing resource, sharing the workload and reducing pressure on individuals.

The following real example relates to the operation of a roller coaster in a theme park that was regularly failing to meet its guest throughput target (the number of people going on the ride each hour). This affected queue times and customer satisfaction, as well as the stress of staff from pressure of failing to meet the target and potentially dealing with unhappy customers who had to queue for a long time.

The ride could theoretically be dispatched every 20 seconds (this is sometimes called takt, the available working time divided by the customer demand). To achieve this takt time of 20 seconds a number of activities or process steps had to be completed simultaneously: guest batching, bag collection, loading, ride dispatch, etc. When measured, each of these steps could be completed in the allocated time, as seen in the diagram below.

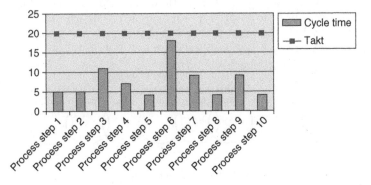

Process steps – ride loading and dispatch

Then we looked at how the ten process steps were divided among the five ride staff, the operator and four attendants, and from the load chart below, you can easily see that the bottleneck was the second attendant.

As you might imagine the second attendant position was one that no one wanted to do as they would always be seen as letting the team down – no matter what they did they were always holding the ride up. Rather than add more resource, we were able to allocate one process step each to attendants

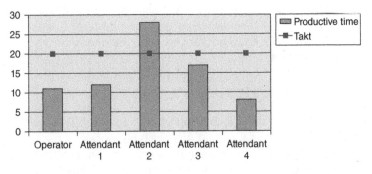

Ride staff load chart

1 and 4 from the second attendant as they were underutilized (also potentially demotivated as they spent time hanging around waiting for the second attendant).

So in the end everyone in the team was used efficiently and could work within the takt time and avoid the bottleneck, as seen in the final chart below, making both staff and customers happy.

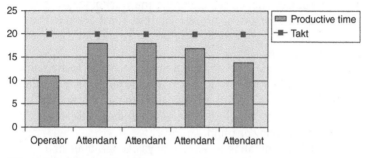

Ride staff load chart – after change

4. Involve and empower employees

When we look at change management in the next chapter we will see how employee engagement is critical to successful change. We also learnt in Chapter 24 how challenge and engagement can improve motivation and create a sense of team, a buzz and energy to make things happen.

5. Continuously improve

Once improvements have been made, revisit them regularly to make sure changes are effective. Customer needs, technology, staffing and the interaction between different processes all change over time and create additional opportunities to improve the way you work to smooth demand, reduce pressure and engage and motivate the workforce.

Workplace design and work environment

We've already looked at Maslow and Herzberg and learnt that basic biological needs and other hygiene factors need to be managed to avoid dissatisfaction. The work environment includes both the physical and psychological surroundings in the workplace. Therefore, designing the workplace, whether the layout of a factory or production line, right down to the way you organize your desk can play an important role in managing stress.

Ergonomics, sometimes called human factors, is the study of how humans interact with their work environment or other parts of a system. It plays an important role in workplace design to ensure that unnecessary demands or stress aren't placed on the body or mind.

Ergonomic evaluation looking at physical demands of a workplace is particularly important when jobs involve significant physical effort, sitting or standing for long periods as well as close-up or detailed work.

Ergonomics can also take into account psychological aspects. Think about the design of computer software and the frustration created if it is not 'user-friendly', the continual repetition of tasks that may lead to mistakes or poor warning signs and signals. For example, a warning light that flashes green is counterintuitive, as we usually associate red lights with danger or abnormal situations.

When considering ergonomics, the need to design workplaces so that elements can be tailored or adapted to suit the individual should be considered. This can cover everything from adjustable seating and workbench height to environmental factors such as heating, lighting, etc. After all, everyone is slightly different when it comes to their height, size, physical capability and personal preference as to what is comfortable.

The training of staff is also important so that they understand and utilize correct work methods. These might include lifting techniques, posture for standing or seating to reduce the impact of work on the body, or instructions on the use of systems and equipment.

In general, workstations or areas should be designed to:

● ensure the right tools and equipment are available
● allow for easy access of most frequently used items/tools
● avoid repetitive motions
● avoid bending, stretching, reaching and stooping
● avoid the need for transporting product by hand (use shoots, rollers, conveyors, etc.)
● be easily adapted, adjusted or modified to accommodate individual needs
● allow access for maintenance tasks and repair.

Processes tend to operate better when activities are arranged sequentially. Depending on available space this can be achieved using lines, circles or U-shaped designs. Some reorganization of the workplace can be done easily and cheaply – try using scale plans and moving furniture and equipment about to see how it might work before physically moving anything. Remember to engage with everyone who uses the workspace or area to get everyone's input and views. Clearly, if more significant change is required and at significant cost it is always advisable to get some professional support in the design process.

Most organizations take care of the basics of life through provision of shelter, toilet facilities, water and space to store, prepare and eat food, although in some cases provision of these essentials can be a challenge (think about those working in remote outdoor areas such as pipeline engineers, surveyors, forestry workers, etc.)

Other considerations should include:

● **lighting** – the use of daylight verses artificial light, intensity, suitability for the type of work, local bench or task lighting for detailed close-up work, changing level for night work or seasonal variations
● **heating or cooling** – variation dependent on the physical nature of work activities, ambient temperature of work environment and individual preferences

- **ventilation** – volume of ventilation to provide regular changes of air. This may be impacted by use or presence of chemicals, dust, vapours or even bad odours
- **noise and vibrations** – control of loud or excessive noise but also consider low level background noise such as equipment humming or office chatter (piped music can be both a blessing and a curse)
- **personal space** – sufficient to move about, stretch and complete work activity
- **maintenance** – consider the impact of poorly maintained or outdated tools and equipment

Playrooms and power naps

Some progressive workplaces can take design of the work environment to the extreme, making it more like home than the workplace. Playrooms encourage staff to take time out to relax from their usual work activity, play video games when things get too much and they need a release, or have a power nap. Evidence suggests that this can boost productivity, particularly in the afternoons.

Softer work surroundings such as lounge-like meeting rooms can provide a relaxed environment particularly appropriate for creative industries where innovation and problem-solving are a key part of day to day work. The relaxed environment makes it easier to think and brainstorm ideas.

This type of approach is not for everyone and is particularly popular with industries such as internet-based or software companies, marketing organizations or organizations attracting highly skilled younger workforces with a different perspective on work.

Summary

In this chapter you have learnt how management behaviour can set expectations among the workforce that can contribute to work pressure and stress; communication and clarity are required to manage these expectations.

You considered the difference between activity and productivity and how the use of some simple tools can help identify bottlenecks and smooth workload. You learnt how using Pareto analysis can help you determine which areas are a priority for improvement and you covered the five principles of lean thinking.

You saw how workplace design can reduce stress by considering the order of tasks, ergonomics, and some simple rules to ensure ease of use and reduction of physical effort. You learnt how environmental factors such as lighting, heating and noise also play a part and considered the need to design for individual adjustments.

Finally, you saw how some organizations take workplace design to the extreme, creating playrooms to stimulate creativity and innovation.

Fact-check (answers at the back)

1. As a manager, how might always being the first in and last out of the office negatively impact staff?
   a) It might drive expectation that staff should do the same and avoid leaving early or being seen as not spending enough time at work creating pressure or stress ❏
   b) Staff will resent you being good at your job ❏
   c) The office cleaners will not be able to clean your office ❏
   d) No negative impact; employees should follow their manager's example ❏

2. Which of the following is not a correct statement about Pareto analysis?
   a) It suggests 80% of tasks can be completed in 20% of the time ❏
   b) It suggests 80% of productivity can come from 20% of the tasks ❏
   c) If everyone worked at 100% efficiency you could reduce your workforce by 80% ❏
   d) Data may need to be viewed more than one way to see the biggest issue ❏

3. Which of the following are important lean principles?
   a) Identify what adds value ❏
   b) Eliminate waste ❏
   c) Continuously improve ❏
   d) All of the above ❏

4. Of the items listed below, which one would not be considered as waste?
   a) Waiting or unnecessary approvals ❏
   b) Maintenance activity ❏
   c) Transportation ❏
   d) Defects or mistakes ❏

5. Which negative impact might result from operating at a pace dictated by an internal or external supplier?
   a) Bosses will see who isn't pulling their weight ❏
   b) Bottlenecks may occur that create work pressure for certain individuals or tasks ❏
   c) Internal suppliers will be able to reduce their work rate ❏
   d) None of the above ❏

6. Why might continuous improvement be of value?
   a) To ensure everyone is always busy ❏
   b) To ensure that a new manager has an opportunity to put their stamp on the workplace ❏
   c) To ensure those not adapting to better ways of working are performance managed ❏
   d) To ensure changes are still effective and changes in customer need, process or technology are considered ❏

7. Why might effective workplace design reduce workplace stress?
   a) Changing the workplace is always seen as a positive thing ❏
   b) Good design can reduce the demands placed on the body and mind ❏
   c) Having chairs that adjust means people can work longer hours at the computer ❏
   d) Good design can impress customers when they visit the organization ❏

8. Which of the following is an appropriate definition of ergonomics?
   a) The study of human biology ❏
   b) The study of how humans interact with their environment ❏
   c) The study of human temporal behaviour patterns ❏
   d) The study of business finances ❏

9. Which of these is not a valid consideration when assessing lighting levels in the workplace?
   a) The amount of daylight coming from windows and skylights ❏
   b) The ability to control/switch lighting on and off to suit individuals needs ❏
   c) The level of detailed or close-up work undertaken ❏
   d) Ensuring that lighting levels are the same across an entire office, building or site ❏

10. What might be the benefits of designing a more relaxed working environment, including installation of softer meeting areas or playrooms, into the workplace?
   a) More effective use of rest breaks to improve productivity or to encourage creative thinking and innovation ❏
   b) Employees will spend less time working and will therefore be happier ❏
   c) It will make use of redundant office space ❏
   d) None of the above ❏

CHAPTER 26

Behaviours, conflict and support

So far we have looked at a variety of topics. While each chapter stands alone you will hopefully by now have started to see how all the elements overlap to form an effective programme that will help you manage stress in the workplace.

In this chapter we will look at how behaviours play a vital role in supporting the more procedural or physical elements of managing stress. We will look at submissive, assertive and aggressive behaviours as well as considering some classic psychological experiments that demonstrate the role authority can play in changing behaviours for both better and worse.

We will consider how management can set behavioural expectations and manage them like other performance objectives. Building on existing knowledge we will look at empowerment in more detail and consider a just culture model. Then we will examine types of internal conflict, workplace bullying and harassment as well as appropriate actions and methods of providing support.

Behaviour

Much research has been documented regarding submissive, assertive and aggressive behaviour and character traits. Table 26.1 summarizes some of the attributes relating to these behaviours.

As you might imagine, those who behave in a more submissive way may be at greater risk of bullying or harassment and may therefore benefit from assertiveness training. Likewise those exhibiting more aggressive tendencies would also benefit from coaching to consider the impact of their behaviour. As we saw in Chapter 22, we need to consider what we have learnt in context and avoid making judgements about individuals based on one set of observations.

In addition to personality traits such as submission, assertion and aggression, level of authority can have a significant impact on the behaviour of those with and those subject to authority. The following two experiments show just how easily behaviours can be influenced and modified in response to authority.

Table 26.1 Attributes of submissive, assertive and aggressive behaviour

Attribute	Submissive	Assertive	Aggressive
Perceived value of other	High	High	Low
Perceived value of self	Low	High	High
Approach	Submits or defends, others first, concedes easily	Respects others, both equal, negotiation	Attacks others, self first, stands firm
Speech and language	Apologetic, hesitant and avoids the real issue	Clear, concise, honest, open and positive	Threatening, accusatory, demanding, interrupts
Other visible cues	Head down, no eye contact, fidgeting	Eye contact on same level, open, balanced and relaxed	Staring, standing over or above others, hands on hips, waving and pointing

Milgram experiment

Stanley Milgram, a psychologist at Yale University conducted a study in the 1960s in response to war trials following World War Two. The study sought to examine obedience, a common defence in the trials with the accused maintaining they simply followed orders from their superiors. Milgram wanted to see how far people would go in obeying orders if it involved harming another human.

The experiment involved two volunteers (who thought they were participating in a learning study), one taking the role of a learner and the other a teacher. Finally, there was an experimenter, played by an actor and dressed in a white coat, representing a figure of authority.

The learner was strapped to a chair with electrodes, behind a screen and asked to memorize pairs of words. The teacher then tested the learner by reading one half of the pair of words and asking the learner to recall the other paired word. The teacher was told to administer an electric shock each time a mistake was made, and the level of shock increased each time, starting at 15 volts (a slight shock) and progressing to 450 volts (a severe, potentially fatal shock). No shocks were actually given but a sound recording was linked to the shock switches so the teacher heard what he thought was the learner being shocked each time.

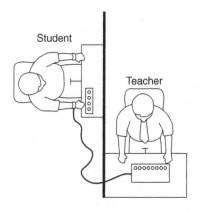
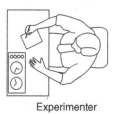

Student

Teacher

Experimenter

Layout of the Milgram experiment
© Barking Dog Art

When the teacher refused to administer a shock and turned to the experimenter for guidance, he was given a standard series of instructions:

1 Please continue
2 The experiment requires you to continue
3 It is absolutely essential that you continue
4 You have no other choice but to continue

The experiment was repeated numerous times and all the participants continued to 300 volts, and 65% of participants continued to the highest level of 450 volts. The experiment showed that people are likely to follow instructions given by an authority figure, even to the extent of killing an innocent human being. Society ingrains our obedience to authority from a young age, obeying parents, teachers, police officers and others in authority.

The Milgram experiment has been repeated in many countries since and although the percentage of teachers prepared to administer the maximum shock does vary, the overall findings remain consistent. The experiment has been criticized for its approach and methodology, even of psychological abuse to the participants.

Stanford Prison or Zimbardo's experiment

This experiment was a study conducted by Phillip Zimbardo in the basement of the Stanford psychology building in 1971, where he had created a mock-up of a prison. He aimed to study the psychological effect of being a prisoner or prison guard.

Twenty-four male students were selected and assigned roles as guards and prisoners in what was supposed to be a two-week study. Guards were dressed appropriately and given wooden batons, while the prisoners were subjected to standard processing including fingerprinting and mug shots, and were then assigned numbers which were displayed instead of names on their prison uniforms. Prisoners had to remain in their cells overnight but guards could leave when they had completed their shifts.

In a short period of time the participants had adapted to their roles to such an extent the guards started to enforce authoritarian measures and even subjected some of the prisoners to psychological torture. Prisoners accepted abuse passively from the guards and even harassed those other prisoners who tried to prevent it. Two prisoners left the experiment and the entire study was abandoned after only six days. In his finding Zimbardo concluded that the situation rather than the individuals' personalities caused the participants to behave as they had done – comparable with Milgram's result.

We have seen from the results of both Milgram and Zimbardo that behaviour is heavily influenced by authority and situation. It is therefore important that organizations set clear expectations for behaviour and actively manage the behaviours of the workforce. We started to consider this in the previous chapter concerning the management behaviour of being first in and last out of the office each day, creating expectation and work pressure among their staff.

Just culture

Some organizations drive a culture of fear and blame, by seeming to react negatively when things go wrong, making examples of people when a mistake is made, irrespective of whether there was a malicious intent or not. Fear of speaking out, stopping work or being seen to have made a mistake drives behaviours of covering things up, concealing the truth and lying. This inevitably means the issues will escalate and get worse until they become so significant they are no longer concealable. In fact, fear and blame cultures have been shown as significant factors in many serious industrial disasters, with multiple opportunities to have prevented fatal consequences if someone had only spoken up.

A just culture is one that recognizes normal human fallibility (we all make mistakes) and seeks to install mutual trust between an organization and its employees. So when something goes wrong the focus is on learning and prevention of recurrence rather than blame and punishment. However, a just culture does not mean no blame, rather a proportionate response. Where deliberate or wilful acts cause damage, harm or loss, individuals can expect to be appropriately managed.

A just culture requires a significant level of organizational maturity and for management to take it seriously, ensuring that those who do admit to mistakes or errors receive positive recognition and even reward for speaking up. When it comes to conflict and bullying, a just culture makes it easier for victims to raise concerns knowing they will be heard and creates an environment where others witnessing poor behaviour can speak out on behalf of the victim.

Managing conflict and bullying

Conflict in an organization may arise for a whole host of reasons: disagreements about operational requirements, change, simple misunderstandings and deliberate acts with malicious intent. In order to manage conflict or poor behaviours, organizations should set clear expectations so that everyone is aware of what is acceptable and what is not. Having considered what an organization believes to be acceptable and unacceptable, this should be communicated to all staff. It should be made clear what constitutes bullying or harassment along with the consequences of engaging in such behaviour. Managers should lead by example and promote positive behaviours in others to avoid conflict and ensure fairness.

Physical violence, sexual advances, verbal abuse or derogatory comments relating to gender, age, race, religion, sexuality or disability might be obvious behaviours that should be managed. However, other more subtle forms of bullying may occur – e.g. failing to pass on information relevant for work, discriminating between individuals when allocating work tasks, or providing reward and recognition may also be considered forms of bullying.

Certain occupations, such as the emergency services, security guards or those handling complaints, are also susceptible to conflict and bullying from external sources such as customers or members of the public. Their needs should also be considered and appropriate behavioural standards communicated through signage, etc. to clarify that certain behaviours will not be tolerated.

Once expectations have been set, it is important to ensure unacceptable behaviours are reported and resolved. The type of resolution will be dependent on the severity of the unacceptable behaviour. In circumstances where there is simply disagreement or misunderstanding this can be cleared up with discussion, a sharing of views and potentially an agreement to disagree. Perhaps where comments have inadvertently caused offence or in response to an isolated malicious incident, more robust communication of the required standards may be required or some form of formal mediation between parties. More serious issues might be managed through a formal disciplinary process, including independent investigation of the facts and action, ranging from formal verbal or written warnings up to and including summary dismissal. In extreme cases, where a criminal offence may have been committed such as physical assault, it will be necessary to involve the police or other law enforcement agencies.

Employee welfare services

In addition to clear expectations and processes to manage unacceptable behaviours, organizations should consider what support services may be offered to employees. As we have learnt, good managers provide flexibility and support to those suffering from stress, regardless of the cause, whether it is work-related or not. We have already considered how those occupations with susceptibility to disorders such as PTSD should be assessed for the need for additional workforce support.

In addition to internal support for employees, many organizations provide access to external advice and support services. These usually involve some form of hotline or contact number so that employees can discuss matters in confidence and with someone independent from the organization or employer. They can then receive direct advice or be directed to other service providers for support. Services typically include counselling, health and wellbeing, legal and financial services.

Communicating clearly what support is available and how to access these services is essential, as is the need for maintaining complete confidentiality.

Managing behavioural performance

Behaviours can have as much impact on the success of an organization as any other factor. It is therefore essential that behaviours are managed in the same way as other deliverables or results. Managers should provide regular, objective feedback on both what individuals are delivering and their behaviours. Managers should also not be afraid to use disciplinary action including dismissal for poor behavioural performance. Even where an individual is seen as indispensable because of their results (e.g. the leading sales person with twice as many orders as the next best), if this person's behaviours are incompatible with those expected by the organization then removing this person is not only the right thing to do but inevitably the whole organization breathes a sigh of relief. and it It becomes apparent that others can step up and fill the gap – or more often realize that although the leading sales person historically got the credit their behaviours masked the work others were already doing, so the loss is minimal overall.

The performance matrix has been used in two organizations where I have worked and has proved effective in both, particularly when linked to pay and bonus awards. Rating employees by their results and behaviours allows for meaningful discussion and prompts action if issues exist in either area.

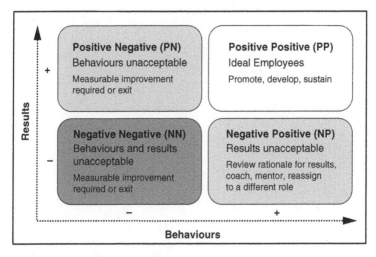

Performance matrix for results and behaviours

Summary

In this chapter you have learnt the importance of behaviours and how these can be effectively managed. You saw how both the Milgram and the Stanford Prison experiments showed that authority can have a significant effect on behaviour, that driving a fear and blame culture can cause issues to be covered up and grow into significant problems. You considered how a just culture might aid in identifying and addressing problems early, allowing for management intervention and proportionate response.

You learnt how conflict, bullying and harassment can take many forms, some more obvious than others, and that certain people or occupations are more likely to suffer from the behaviours of others. You considered some key principles in managing unacceptable behaviours and supporting employees and gained an understanding of the pivotal role managers have in leading by example.

Finally you saw that behavioural expectation should apply equally to all and can be performance managed in the same way as other more tangible results.

Fact-check (answers at the back)

1. Which of the following is not one of the three behaviours/character traits discussed at the start of this chapter?
   a) Assertive ❏
   b) Submissive ❏
   c) Subversive ❏
   d) Aggressive ❏

2. Which of these are attributes of those with assertive behaviours?
   a) Respects others, high value of self and others, clear, concise and honest ❏
   b) Attacks others, high value of self, low value of others, demanding and accusatory ❏
   c) Concedes easily, low value of self, high value of others, hesitant and apologetic ❏
   d) None of the above ❏

3. What form of support might be appropriate for someone with submissive behaviours?
   a) Assertiveness training ❏
   b) Coaching to consider the impact of their behaviour ❏
   c) Self-defence classes ❏
   d) Formal disciplinary action ❏

4. What do both the Milgram and Stanford Prison experiments show us?
   a) Students are easily manipulated ❏
   b) Those in authority do what needs to be done to get results ❏
   c) Authority and situation can significantly influence behaviour ❏
   d) All of the above ❏

5. What are some of the key elements in developing a just culture?
   a) Discipline and punishment ❏
   b) Mutual trust, acceptance of human fallibility ❏
   c) No blame for anything ❏
   d) Encouraging staff to tell management about their work colleagues ❏

6. Which of the following may be considered bullying?
   a) Physical abuse ❏
   b) Withholding important work information, unfair allocation of work activities ❏
   c) Malicious comments concerning gender, race, sexual orientation and religion ❏
   d) All of the above ❏

7. Which of the following is not a means to deal with conflict in the workplace?
   a) Coaching or mediation ❏
   b) Formal disciplinary, verbal or written warnings, dismissal ❏
   c) Transferring victims to an alternative department ❏
   d) Notifying local law enforcement agencies where appropriate ❏

8. Which of the following is not an important consideration for employee support services?
a) Assessment of the most appropriate services considering the workforce needs ❑
b) Communication of what services are available ❑
c) Publicity for those who have used services ❑
d) Clear means of access to support services ❑

9. What management action might be taken for those exhibiting poor behaviours but excellent business results?
a) Formal performance management, leading to exit if no improvement ❑
b) Promotion ❑
c) Assign to a different role or department ❑
d) None of the above ❑

10. What management action would not be appropriate for someone who shows good behaviours but poor business results?
a) Understand reasons for poor results ❑
b) Promotion ❑
c) Consider reassignment to a different role more suited to skills ❑
d) Coaching or mentoring ❑

CHAPTER 27

Change management

Change is a fundamental part of modern life and the pace of that change seems to continually increase. In the workplace change can happen at the organizational level through downsizing, mergers or acquisitions, privatization, contractualization or demographic change. Change may also happen at the job level with new equipment, changes to shift patterns or in reaction to short-term demands.

Change management is worthy of a book in its own right and indeed many hundreds if not thousands already exist – not to mention countless millions of internet articles and other reference materials.

In this chapter we will be focusing on the people side of change and how an understanding of people's reactions to change can lead to greater buy-in and reduced stress for management and workforce alike. We will learn how organizations and their employees have unwritten psychological contracts with each other and why people resist change. We will look at some of the many models for change, understand how engagement with stakeholders can ensure understanding of why change is needed, and how considering the views and opinions of those affected by change can deliver a better solution that staff have already invested in, making the change process easier to implement and more likely to be sustained in the long term.

Resistance to change

Ask yourself why we resist change. Perhaps it is because of a fear of the unknown, security in the way we know, others may be resisting so people follow the pack, or some aren't convinced the change will work and don't see where the personal benefit is for them. Perhaps too much else is going on or people think it will pass like other changes that have appeared.

All these feelings are completely normal and understandable, but are often overlooked as managers simply try to force through predetermined solutions to timescales seemingly plucked from thin air. When it comes to change, it has been said that a majority of managers spend 10% of their energy selling the problem and 90% selling the solution. However, if the problem isn't properly understood then the solution won't be either.

The psychological contract

The psychological contract is an informal, unwritten arrangement built over time between an organization or employer and its employees. It represents inferred or implied obligations based on experience and future expectation. The concept of the psychological contract is especially relevant to organizational

Table 27.1 Change in workers' psychological contract

Old contract	New contract
Stability	Change
Predictability	Uncertainty
Permanence	Temporariness
Standard work patterns	Flexible work
Valuing loyalty	Valuing performance and skills
Paternalism	Self reliance
Job security	Employment security
Linear career progression	Multiple careers
One-time learning	Lifelong learning

change, in particular the move for outsourcing jobs from public to private sector, and helps us understand and plan to accommodate the reactions of the workforce.

Jamais Cascio, a writer and ethical futurist, began designing future scenarios in the 1990s. He believes that business trends drive change in order to adapt to market conditions, globalization and demands for technology to maintain competitiveness. He also suggests that change causes a shift in the psychological contract that binds workers to an organization.

Change as a transition

We can help our understanding of how change affects people by considering a few of the many models for change. Kurt Lewin proposed just such a model in 1947, and although the world has changed much since then, arguably most other models are derived from the basics of his theory of three stages of change:

1 **unfreezing** – getting an organization and its people ready for change, motivating and making decisions
2 **change or transition** – implementing a new way, people are unfrozen and move towards the new approach
3 **freezing** – establishing stability in the new way

In the mid-1990s significant progress was made in change management, primarily in response to the frustrations of large organizations who continually failed to deliver sustainable change. Most of this work focused very much on the people side of change, rather than the top down methods historically used. William Bridges developed an alternative three-phase model to describe the transition.

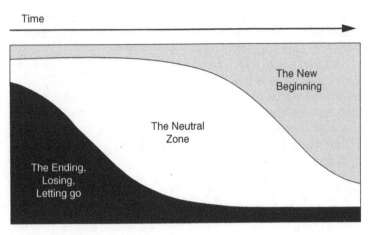

Time

The New Beginning

The Neutral Zone

The Ending, Losing, Letting go

Three phases of transition

1 The first phase is an **ending**, where people are letting go. It is important to agree and sell the change, understand the impact and help people to come to terms with the loss.
2 The second phase is the **neutral zone**, where the new way isn't fully implemented and some are still working to the old way. In this phase realignment and re-enforcement are required to show progress and deal with resistance.
3 Finally there's the **new beginning**, where the change is beginning to work, energy needs to be harnessed to keep momentum going and successes need to be visibly rewarded.

Kotter's eight-step change model

In 1995 John Kotter, a professor at Harvard Business School, introduced an eight-step approach for leading change.

Step 1 – Create urgency

For change to be effective a majority of people must want it – it is important to create a sense of urgency through logical discussions on the need for and the detail of the change.

People will start to talk about the change and, like a snowball rolling down a hill, the sense of urgency will build and grow.

Step 2 – Form a powerful coalition

In any organization there are usually one or two key players to whom everyone looks for leadership. They might not be the most senior hierarchically, but obtaining their visible support can make the difference between success and failure.

Step 3 – Create a vision for change

People need to see what you are trying to achieve. While there may be various ideas and solutions floating around in the early days, it is important to link these into a single vision that is straightforward, easy to understand and remember.

Step 4 – Communicate the vision

The vision needs to be communicated frequently and become embedded into everything that is done. It is often easy for messages to get swamped or overshadowed in large organizations and so be relentless. Remember it is not just about what is said, people are far more likely to be influenced by what is done and others' behaviour.

Step 5 – Remove obstacles

Empower people to make the change and continually monitor for barriers, whether they are systems, processes or people. Recognize and reward those who are making progress and manage those who aren't, and help them understand the need and process for change.

Step 6 – Create short-term wins

Create short-term targets and milestones and celebrate these successes. Success motivates people and encourages others to adopt the change. Incremental successes will also make it harder for those resisting the change as they will not be able to point to a lack of progress as justification that the change isn't working.

Step 7 – Build on the change

Real change takes time and continual re-enforcement. Declaring the job is finished too early may mean people revert back to old ways rather than continuing with new ways.

Step 8 – Anchor the change into the organization's culture

Make the change stick for good. Continue to integrate the change activity into the everyday life of the organization. Link it to reward and continually communicate ongoing successes.

Change and the personal transition

Looking back at the early models for change, we saw that individuals and whole organizations go through a variety of phases. Following research into service organizations, John Fisher's work in the noughties (early 2000s) has resulted in a very helpful model of how individuals deal with change, the process of transition curve. Although consistent in its elements, the journey will be unique for each individual – some may adapt quickly, others may never fully adapt or accept change. As you read on, consider change you have witnessed or experienced and you will no doubt be able to correlate Fisher's findings with your own experience.

Anxiety

We learnt about anxiety and the feeling of unease or apprehension in Chapter 23. In the transition process people may be unsure or feel a lack of control or visibility of a change.

Happiness

In this phase employees might feel relief that someone is doing something, satisfaction that change is coming and that things will be different from before, perhaps with feelings of anticipation and excitement. There is a risk that expectations will be raised as assumptions are made concerning what will happen and the impact. Some will think about opportunity for progression, promotion, etc. Others may think that an exit route is coming – 'they're bound to make me redundant' – and already start to spend their severance package. Thorough engagement at this stage will minimize impact.

Denial

Here people carry on regardless, 'put their head in the sand' refusing to accept that the change is happening, sticking to the old ways and ignoring anything that contradicts their view of the world.

Fear

This is a realization that things will be different in the future and everyone will need to act differently.

Threat

It dawns that the change is going to have a fundamental impact. Old choices will no longer stand. Staff may be unsure how to act in the future. Old ways are gone but new ways aren't established yet.

Anger

Anger may exist in the early stages of the transition. At first others might be blamed for forcing a change that wasn't wanted. Employees might also start to reflect on their own actions and think they should have kept control or known better. This anger at oneself can lead to guilt and depression.

Guilt

This is a realization that previous behaviours were inappropriate and that they may have had a negative impact. Being part of the problem causes a sense of guilt and sometimes shame.

Disillusionment

Disillusionment may set in if staff realize there is a fundamental difference between the individual and the organization. They become increasingly withdrawn and almost switch off, becoming dissatisfied. Recovery is possible but if the difference is too great exiting may be the only solution.

Depression

Awareness that old behaviours, actions and beliefs are no longer compatible with what employees are now expected to do or be. There may be confusion or lack of motivation as what was done and past behaviours are viewed in a negative way.

Hostility

Here, some might continue to try to make things work that have already proved a failure and others have moved on from, but they maintain the belief that it will somehow come good if they continue to plug away and ignore the new way of working.

Gradual acceptance

People start to see some of the early wins and successes of the change and start to see how they will fit into the new order. They are starting to make sense of change and acknowledge that they on the right track. There is light at the end of the tunnel.

Moving forward

Things are getting more positive and are starting to feel comfortable. Everyone is becoming more effective and understands the new environment.

Behaviours during change

We have seen above how change has distinct phases and that people go through a personal transition at a pace specific to the individual. It is important to note that while people may be at various points along the transition their behaviours may be modified by other factors – e.g. it is possible to be actively supportive of change even though you are suffering anxiety about what exactly might happen.

In the engagement and satisfaction model you will see how people may respond to a particular change in terms of their level of satisfaction and level of engagement. This model enables us to consider an appropriate management strategy for certain behaviours. Being in any one zone is perfectly normal and all are manageable; people will change their behaviours over time or in relation to different change activities.

Both axes in the engagement and satisfaction model are continuous so you will get extreme behaviours in each group. However, at the centre you tend to find those who are indifferent, those who may be easily swayed in any direction. If they see the change is happening and successful they are likely to join in, so show them the plan and keep them informed of progress. Don't be afraid to explain the dangers of 'sitting on the fence' and failing to commit one way or the other.

In the top right hand quadrant, Zone 1, you will find those who are satisfied with the change and engaged in the change process. These people can be enthusiastic and energetic and want to spread the word. Tactics for managing

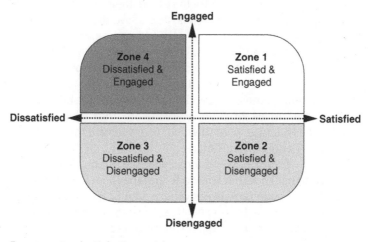

Engagement and satisfaction model

413

this group include using them to win over others and giving them plenty of support and authority to help progress the change. Make sure they are recognized, rewarded and kept motivated.

At the opposite end of the scale you have those in Zone 3. They are dissatisfied with the change and disengaged or passive in their response, failing to get involved. They may be cynical and may play a political game, agreeing in public but creating problems, spreading rumours behind closed doors. In order to manage people in this zone it is crucial to understand why they are unsupportive and tackle them on their objections. Don't dismiss their input as they may well have seen the change from a different perspective and come up with issues that you hadn't previously been aware of. Show them the change can and is working and seek their involvement.

In the bottom right are 'the saboteurs' – those who are dissatisfied with the change and are actively engaged in their opposition, potentially trying to derail the process. Sometimes their actions may be overt, other times more subtle, such as slowing up decision-making. You will need to show you understand their concerns but be able to put your case as to why you think differently. Try persuasion to bring them round to your way of thinking and try to resolve their concerns. Avoid stooping to their level and tactics, rise above them. Ultimately you may have to confront them – the change is here and if they can't engage and help make it work then perhaps they don't have a role to play in the organization. This conversation is tough but often bears fruit. If they know you are serious they may change their view and if not, it may be best for both parties if they move on. Often everyone breathes a big sigh of relief when the issue is dealt with. The important thing is to have robust adult conversation.

Finally, in Zone 4, you find those who see things as inevitable. They are satisfied but unwilling to engage fully. This group needs lots of engagement: ask them a lot of questions, gauge their views and use their expertise. Recognize and reward them but don't take their support for granted.

Timing of change

It is important to briefly mention the timing of change – get it right and you may make things easier, get it wrong and it could be a whole lot worse.

Arguably there is never a good time to change and you can always find reasons why not to do something today when you can put it off till tomorrow. However, this shouldn't stop you giving proper consideration to objections and or alternate time scales. You will need to consider other change activity: announcing that you are going to make redundancies, implementing a new computer system and relocating your manufacturing plant 50 miles up the road all at the same time, might be seen as over-adventurous and detrimental to your organization. Perhaps the computer system and relocation overlap and it makes sense to deliver them at the same time, but redundancies, particularly if these relate to efficient savings from the other projects, might be better postponed.

When working in theme parks I had to undertake a major reorganization of staff, including a significant outsource of facilities management activity. I considered long and hard the timing; we could wait till the winter maintenance period when the park was closed but risk not being ready for the start of the following season, or get it over and done with while the park was open and risk impacting customers now.

After speaking with key employee representatives, we went for the peak summer season, and the restructure went without a hitch. By listening to key staff I learnt that most were expecting something anyway and that they wanted it over and done with, and that on the whole most people were so energized dealing with the day to day excitement of the park during the summer that the reorganization was not their priority. Waiting for winter would mean uncertainty for longer and the change would happen when people were already low after the season had finished, their focus switched to menial tasks of cleaning, painting, etc. and they would probably be miserable due to the bad weather and short daylight hours.

Gauging the right time is more of an art than a science and nobody gets it right all the time. Remember to listen to others, and even if you don't agree make sure people understand your reasoning.

Examples of change

In my career I have witnessed and been involved with both good and bad examples of change. Good examples include the process improvement work in the theme park reorganization I have mentioned already, while the following case study serves as a lesson in what not to do.

I was working for a US aerospace company based in London, with a sister facility in Frankfurt, Germany. One Friday a senior executive flew into Frankfurt, called a staff meeting and through a translator basically said, 'We're closing you down with immediate effect, don't come to work on Monday and the London office will manage everything including the disposal of the building'.

Clearly this came as a shock, to the German workforce but also to my team in London as we had no prior knowledge either. The senior executive flew straight back home and left us to pick up the pieces. He had failed to understand some of the basic legal rights of the workforce as well as any understanding of the implications for all concerned. While legal challenges progressed and transitional plans devised, the German workforce continued to operate the facility for a number of weeks, openly hostile to the team from London.

Law, culture, language and customer loyalty had all been misunderstood. In the end the facility was closed, many customers were lost or moved to a new company set up by former German employees and the final cost came in at an order of magnitude more than planned, which essentially much negated the business case for the closure. Interestingly, no criticism was ever made of the executive, only of those working in Germany and London!

Summary

In this chapter you have learnt some of the reasons why we resist change, that individuals behave differently and that this variety of reactions is perfectly normal, to be expected and can be managed.

You saw a variety of models for change: Bridges' three-phase transition, Kotter's eight-step change model and Fisher's process of transition curve, each of which provides clues as to how change can be implemented effectively. You considered engagement and satisfaction to characterize types of reaction and behaviours to change and some of the management techniques appropriate for each group.

Finally, you saw how the timing of change is critical and many factors need to be considered at the planning stage to make sure bad timing doesn't create additional management issues.

Remember change management is not an exact science, but considering the principles covered in this chapter will make the process more bearable for all concerned.

Fact-check (answers at the back)

1. Why might people resist change?
   a) Fear of the unknown or lack of security ❏
   b) Comfortable with the status quo ❏
   c) Too busy to care ❏
   d) All of the above ❏

2. Which of these is not a true statement about managing change?
   a) A variety of behaviours and reactions to change is perfectly natural ❏
   b) Those negative about change simply don't understand it ❏
   c) People may change their reaction and behaviours through the change ❏
   d) All types of behaviours are manageable ❏

3. With regard to Cascio's work, which of the following is part of the 'old psychological contract'?
   a) Predictability ❏
   b) Change ❏
   c) Employment security ❏
   d) Lifelong learning ❏

4. Which of the following is not one of the three phases of transition proposed by Bridges?
   a) Unfreezing ❏
   b) The neutral zone ❏
   c) The beginning ❏
   d) The loss or ending ❏

5. Thinking of Kotter's eight-stage change model, which of the following is a true statement about forming a coalition?
   a) Coalitions must always be with the most senior people ❏
   b) Coalitions will only work if you offer concessions to the other party ❏
   c) Visible support from key people can make the difference between success and failure ❏
   d) All of the above ❏

6. Why are Steps 7 and 8 of Kotter's model so important?
   a) Failure to reinforce or embed change may result in people reverting back to old ways ❏
   b) The true benefits of the change may not be realized ❏
   c) New people to the organization simply adopt new ways as part of everyday working ❏
   d) All of the above ❏

7. Which is not a true statement about Fisher's personal transition model?
   a) The more senior a person is the quicker they transition ❏
   b) Each individual takes a unique journey through the transition ❏
   c) Some people may miss stages of the transition; others may never accept change ❏
   d) Some people may feel guilt over the way they have previously acted ❏

8. Which of the following is a classification of reactions/behaviour to change?
a) Zone 4: Dissatisfied and disengaged ❏
b) Zone 3: Disorganized and empowered ❏
c) Zone 1: Satisfied and disengaged ❏
d) Zone 2: Satisfied and endangered ❏

9. What management tactic should not be used for those who are dissatisfied but engaged?
a) Have robust adult conversations ❏
b) Avoid adopting their tactics ❏
c) Try persuasion to bring them round to your view ❏
d) Give them a role to lead the change ❏

10. Which of these is not an important consideration when planning the timing of a change initiative?
a) The presence of other change initiatives ❏
b) Customer demands ❏
c) Being seen to make a quick impact in a new job ❏
d) Proximity to holiday times or cultural festivals ❏

CHAPTER 28

Personal responsibility and actions

No matter who you are or what you do, life can be stressful. So far we have learnt about stress, its symptoms and what organizations can do to reduce and manage stress. At an individual level it is important to understand the specific triggers or activities that cause you stress and, using the information we covered in Chapter 23, be able to recognize the signs of your response to stress and finally to understand what control strategies are effective for you.

In this chapter we look at some simple steps you can make to take responsibility for managing your own stress levels regardless of the type of organization you work for and the attitude of that organization towards effectively managing stress.

Much of what is discussed in this chapter may seem very simple and to some extent just common sense: manage your time, get regular exercise, and watch your diet and how much you drink or smoke. As is often the case, the simple things can be some of the hardest to do; they get overlooked by other more exciting options or it simply takes too long to embed them into our behaviours. So read on, and congratulations if you already do some or all of these things but be open to trying something new.

Make it a habit

Small changes in lifestyle and the choices you make can have a big impact, and quite often these changes are incredibly simple, such as take more exercise, eat more healthily, drink less alcohol. But we often struggle to maintain our discipline and soon revert to old ways of behaving. We've looked into behavioural change and although actions appear straightforward you need to make a positive effort to embed them in your daily life so that they become habitual. I took up running a few years ago and the first few weeks were really tough – making the conscious effort to get up early, stretch, warm up and run, warm down, all before hitting the shower and starting my normal daily routine took real will power. After a few weeks, with positive support from my wife and focusing on the positive benefits of losing weight and having more energy during the day, it became easier to the point where the daily run was as much a part of the routine as the shower, no longer requiring thought or effort. The same will be true for any of the suggestions in this chapter.

Be positive

At some low point in your life someone will no doubt have said to you 'Don't worry, there's always someone worse off than yourself'. On hearing this, a usual response is that people don't understand what you're going through or it may even spark a stronger response, as although probably true (statistically it is highly unlikely that you happen to be the human being who genuinely has got the worst possible life) it doesn't actually help.

That said, you might want to consider this quote from Marcus Aurelius, Roman Emperor A.D. 161–80:

> *If you are distressed by anything external, the pain is not due to the thing itself, but to your estimate of it; and this you have the power to revoke at any moment.*

When stressed we often can fall into negative feelings or 'mind traps' that can lead to self-criticism and become self-perpetuating to the point where you eventually believe that your negative perception of yourself is in fact reality. By being aware of these thoughts, when they arise you can help yourself break the negative spiral. Common negative thoughts include the following.

Seeing extremes

The thought that 'one mistake' will result in total failure. Everyone makes mistakes and on the whole most are easily recovered. Unless you have been wilfully negligent most organizations have a formal policy of helping you improve and at least a verbal and formal written warning before it comes to the boss letting you go.

Over-generalization

If you find yourself saying 'this always happens', just pause to consider the real evidence. When emotions run high it is all too easy to shoot from the hip and ignore the facts. Think of the average married couple – at some point over a 40-year partnership one or other party will forget a birthday, anniversary or dinner date. Inevitably the focus is always on the one time you forgot rather than the 99 times you remembered and had a great time.

Rejecting the positive

You receive a compliment with a small note for improvement on the end – e.g. your boss says, 'That was a great project, delivered on time and on budget and the team really appreciated your leadership, well done. Next time I'd appreciate a bit more communication to me of potential risks to the programme.' All you hear is that the boss didn't think you communicated with them enough.

Learn to listen, acknowledge the good done and accept positive praise. If you manage others there's a lesson here, for you. Keep praise separate from criticism as people tend to focus on the latter.

Jumping to conclusions

You respond to information by making assumptions based on your perception of yourself. For example, you hear a rumour that the department is going to be reorganized and some people will be made redundant, so you instantly think this will be you. Just consider the evidence and you might actually see how a critical skill or knowledge makes you far more indispensable than your colleagues.

Time management

Rather like change management there is a plethora of programmes and self-help books to help you better manage your time. Most are based around the need to:

- create an appropriate work environment
- set priorities
- perform tasks or activities against the set priorities
- minimize the time spent on non-priorities.

We touched on some organizational elements of time management in Chapter 25 when we looked at workload, work pressure and the work environment (e.g. value and non-value added activity, Pareto analysis and workflow analysis) but you can apply some simple rules to make your personal time management more effective.

Prioritize

Prioritization is key to time management. I use a very straightforward questioning system based on the 4Ds: Do it, Defer it, Delegate it or Drop it.

Does this activity need to be done by me and does it need to be done now? If the answer is yes to both questions it has to go in the **Do it** pile. Sometimes you have to really challenge yourself: do you have some unique knowledge, skill, experience or authority that means it has to be you?

Think about the time pressure and who this is being driven by. You might be being chased for a piece of work but you know that it is going to sit on someone else's desk for two weeks because someone else is on vacation or the next approvals committee isn't for a fortnight. If it has to be done by me, but the time pressure isn't critical then the work goes into the **Defer it** pile. I will do it, just not now. Clearly, as time moves on 'defer it' items eventually make their way into the 'do it' category.

If someone else can do it, either now or later, then **Delegate it.** You will need to provide some guidance on the level of urgency as the person you delegate to may need to prioritize your requests with others from different sources. Make sure they understand their accountability and leave them to get on with it. Be prepared to let them make the decision to delegate it further but hold them to account for any deadline agreed.

Finally, if is not important for you to do and no one is going to be chasing anytime soon simply **Drop it.** A word of caution – make sure the originator of a task or activity knows that you have dropped it. You don't want it to come back and bite you in six months' time because they made an assumption it was still on your radar.

Effective meetings

When it comes to time management, I have found the best way to free up more time is to have effective meetings. I used to spend a significant proportion of my time in meetings – meetings that seemed to have no purpose, or that felt like repeats of other meetings I'd already attended, and ones I'd leave not knowing whether or not a decision had actually been made.

Poor meetings can create uncertainty, blur responsibility and accountability and lead to confusion, particularly for those who weren't there. It is also worth remembering that they cost money. Next time you are in a meeting, consider the hourly rate of everyone round the table, add it together and see what it is costing per hour – you are likely to be shocked.

Every meeting should have a chairperson to take control, and all attendees should follow some simple rules.

Responsibilities of the meeting chairperson
- Start on time
- Make sure all phones and unnecessary IT equipment are off
- Have a time-bound agenda – no agenda, no meeting
- Confirm the purpose/objective of the meeting
- Check attendees can make a contribution
- Control the discussion and keep to time
- Summarize actions
- Conclude with a discussion on what went well, opportunity for improvement and what needs to be covered next time
- Record the outcome, log and circulate minutes/records of actions
- Finish on time.

Simple rules for all attendees
- Be on time
- Be prepared (read reports/papers circulated in advance and have any questions ready)
- Know the agenda
- Contribute effectively (if you can't contribute, don't attend)
- Help solve problems
- Be respectful of others' opinions
- Keep to the point (don't get side-tracked by discussions that aren't on the agenda)
- Make notes
- Follow up actions.

Like any other form of behaviours, these rules for meetings need to be adopted and linked to performance reviews.

Say no

Everyone is an adult and in order to prioritize and limit the workload you have to learn to say no. Think back to the common mind gaps: how often do you say to yourself, 'I can't say no or I will get into trouble'? If you say yes to tasks or activities most managers or colleagues assume you have given it conscious thought and have decided you can accommodate the request.

People in authority often don't see stress, particularly if people are good at hiding the signs. They may think you are very capable and because you keep saying yes keep giving you more to do. Say no, and when you have said no once you will find that people understand and will respond by saying 'Ok, no problem, I'll get John to do it instead' or they might give you additional information and provide assistance in determining what the priorities are. Try saying no but following up with 'but I can if you help me by taking on a task for me or by helping me to prioritize your request against all my other demands'.

Working from home

A regular time management action I take is to avoid commuting. Over the past decade I have changed jobs a number of times and have commuted for anything up to two hours to get to the office. Time in the car, on a bus or train can be helpful and allow for thinking time or act as a break between work and home life but on the whole, in the absence of a need for face to face contact, it can be a waste of time and money just commuting 'to be in the office'. Even if you don't have the space to work from home you might consider other local places to work from – e.g. the local library, or nearby offices of a subsidiary organization. These days the technology exists to work from home – the challenge here is discipline, and you might find it helpful to consider the pitfalls of working from home that can make it counterproductive.

First, make sure the technology works. Remotely connecting to work systems can be fraught with problems if you don't have the right equipment and technical support. Second, make the work environment right. Home can be very distracting – home comforts such as the lounge to relax in with your tea or coffee, raiding the fridge and 'five-minute' breaks to watch TV, walk the dog, etc. can all become a drain on your productive time. Working from home can also work the other way with constant access to work encroaching on your family or home life.

Create a clear work place and stick to clear work times, avoiding distraction and the blurring of the work–life boundary. If necessary you might want to create an artificial commute, say a short walk round the block just to mentally separate your time in the home office from time with the family.

Personal health and wellbeing

In addition to positive thinking and better time management, general wellbeing and personal health have an important part to play in both combating stress and mitigating the psychological and physiological effects. Certain illnesses, health problems and even our genes may predispose us to particular stress responses so taking care of our mind and body is essential for successful management of stress, but also as part of a happy, long and fulfilled life.

Activity and exercise

Life is getting more sedentary: we are collectively spending longer in cars, sat at desks or in front of the TV or a variety of other electronic devices. Studies have shown that those with higher levels of activity in their lives live longer than those less active and have a better quality of life, improving heart and lung functions and bone health while reducing blood pressure and the risk of a variety of health conditions. Physical activity includes time spent on leisure activities such as walking/ hiking, swimming, dancing, games and sports; transport activities like walking and cycling; and daily tasks such as physical paid work, household chores and community activity.

Activity is split into aerobic exercise (that which increases heart and breathing rates and involves low to moderate intensity over longer periods) and anaerobic exercise which helps build muscle with short periods of high-intensity activity.

The World Health Organization (WHO) has issued guidance on appropriate levels of physical activity for three age ranges: 5–17 years, 18–64 years and 64+:

- Children aged 5–17 should complete at least 60 minutes of moderate- to vigorous-intensity activity daily.
- Adults aged 18–64, should complete at least 150 minutes of moderate-intensity aerobic physical activity throughout the week or do at least 75 minutes of vigorous-intensity aerobic activity throughout the week or an equivalent combination.
- Aerobic activity should be performed in bouts of at least 10 minutes' duration.

- For additional health benefits, adults should increase their moderate-intensity aerobic physical activity to 300 minutes per week, or engage in 150 minutes of vigorous-intensity aerobic physical activity per week, or an equivalent combination.
- Muscle-strengthening activities should be done involving major muscle groups on two or more days a week.
- In addition older adults, with poor mobility, should perform activity to enhance balance and prevent falls on three or more days per week. When older adults can't do the recommended amounts of physical activity due to health conditions, they should be as physically active as their abilities and conditions allow.

When we talk about exercise we might think about signing up to a gym or contemplate investing in lots of training equipment or a personal trainer. While these are fine, you can start simply and for free. Likewise we may complain we just don't have the time but again you can start to make a real impact with some minor changes to your routine. Try taking the stairs rather than the lift, go for a walk in the park or round the block instead of spending lunch time sitting in the staff room or at your desk, and get off the bus a stop early and walk into work.

In addition to the physical benefits, taking up a physical hobby or sport that can be done with others or in a social group or club can improve mental wellbeing and create a vital social network of friends and support.

Diet

A healthy diet consists of the right mix of foods and the right amount. For the average person, a balanced diet consists of 33% fruit and vegetables, 33% carbohydrates from bread, pasta, rice, etc., 15% milk and dairy products, 12% protein (meat and fish) and 7% fats and sugars. Salt intake should also be limited as this has an effect on blood pressure.

In terms of amount this is best represented by the energy supplied by the food in calories. Recommended levels for calorie intake are 2,500 for men and 2,000 for women, although these are averages and the energy needs of individuals will vary dependent on age, lifestyle and size. Larger people and those with physically demanding work or leisure activities will require more calories and a more tailored diet.

Alcohol

Alcohol is a drug and it affects the body in a variety of ways. Over time and with prolonged exposure, like other drugs it can become addictive. As with certain foods that pose a health risk, it is a case of everything in moderation.

Certain professions, usually those putting particular stresses on staff through high expectation or pressure to perform, are seen as drinking professions – e.g. journalism, legal professions and corporate/investment banking – and there is often significant peer pressure for work colleagues to drink, particularly after work.

Individual governments and health agencies provide guidance on the level of alcohol consumption deemed 'safe' for both men and women. There are a variety of values, which reflect the level of uncertainty from research regarding what levels may have an adverse effect on health. Likewise local agencies will set alcohol limits for driving and other activities which are legally enforced so it is always advisable to check local data sources, particularly if travelling or working overseas.

Relaxation

Relaxation is a very personal thing, whether snuggling in an armchair with a good book, a long hot bath, lying in the sun on a summer's day, having a massage, aromatherapy or any one of a variety of formal meditation and/or breathing techniques.

Care should always be taken to make sure you take a break from work. Holiday entitlement is there for a reason. Even if you don't go away and stay at home, the break gives you time to unwind. Make sure you take an 'unplugged' break – the temptation to access work in the evening or while on holiday is made all the easier by the plethora of electronic devices that give us instant access to e-mails, work networks, etc. Try to avoid this when away from work; if it is essential you maintain contact with the office when on holiday, allocate specific times to work so you can focus the remainder of your time on you, your family and friends.

Summary

You should now know that in order to cope with stress in your own life you need to:

- recognize the existence and the signs of your response to stress
- understand the specific triggers or activities that cause you stress
- understand what control strategies are effective for you.

In this chapter you have considered how you can place demands on yourself through negative feelings and 'mind traps', how you might reduce work pressures and demands through better prioritization by deciding to Do it, Defer it, Delegate it or Drop it as well as looking to reduce commuting by working from home and to make the most out of meetings.

Finally you learnt about the importance of your personal health and wellbeing, considering the importance of regular exercise, a balanced diet and reducing alcohol intake as well as the need to understand the best way for you to unwind and relax.

Fact-check (answers at the back)

1. Which of the following is a mind trap that can cause you to create demands on yourself?
   a) Seeing extremes ❏
   b) Over-generalizations ❏
   c) Jumping to conclusions ❏
   d) All of the above ❏

2. Which of the following statements about 'saying no' is likely to be true?
   a) Your boss will fire you ❏
   b) You'll never be asked to undertake a new challenge again ❏
   c) People will understand, will ask someone else or help you prioritize their requests ❏
   d) Your work colleagues will think you are not pulling your weight and shun you ❏

3. Which of these is not one of the 4Ds for better prioritization?
   a) Do it ❏
   b) Delegate it ❏
   c) Deny it ❏
   d) Drop it ❏

4. Why might ineffective meetings contribute to stress?
   a) They use up time that could be spent on other priority tasks ❏
   b) They may create confusion or lack of clarity of who is doing what ❏
   c) You might feel uncomfortable/ embarrassed if invited to contribute to a discussion not relevant to you and where you have no knowledge of the subject ❏
   d) All of the above ❏

5. Which of the following is not good practice for the chairperson of a meeting?
   a) Start on time ❏
   b) Confirm the purpose or objectives for the meeting ❏
   c) Let the meeting overrun if the discussion is lively ❏
   d) Summarize actions ❏

6. Why might working from home have a negative impact on your stress levels?
   a) You can avoid unnecessary time spent commuting ❏
   b) You might blur the boundary between home and work and end up working in the evenings and at weekends ❏
   c) You can focus on work without the continual interruptions you get in the office ❏
   d) You are still contactable throughout the day, should someone need to speak with you ❏

7. Which of the following is the recommended level of exercise for an adult?

a) At least 150 minutes of moderate-intensity aerobic physical activity or at least 75 minutes of vigorous-intensity activity throughout the week or an equivalent combination ❑

b) At least 60 minutes of moderate- to vigorous-intensity activity daily ❑

c) At least 90 minutes of moderate-intensity aerobic physical activity or at least 60 minutes of vigorous-intensity activity throughout the week or an equivalent combination ❑

d) No more than 120 minutes of vigorous-intensity aerobic activity throughout the week ❑

8. Which of the following is a true statement about diet?

a) You can eat as much fat and sugar as you like providing you do more exercise to compensate ❑

b) Your ideal calorie intake will depend on age, size and lifestyle ❑

c) A balanced diet should contain at least 33% protein from meat and fish ❑

d) An average calorie intake for a woman is 2,500 per day ❑

9. Which of the following is not an important consideration concerning the intake of alcohol?

a) Local legal blood alcohol limits for driving and other activities ❑

b) The special offers on during happy hour at your local bar ❑

c) Whether you are taking prescription medication ❑

d) Peer pressure from work colleagues ❑

10. What is the best way to relax?

a) Taking a foreign holiday ❑
b) A long hot bath ❑
c) Having your in-laws to stay for the weekend ❑
d) Find out what works for you ❑

7 × 7

1 Seven key ideas

- Stress isn't always bad and isn't the same for everyone; its signs and symptoms are often hidden.
- Lack of clarity on job role, responsibilities and objectives drive a significant proportion of work-related stress.
- Pareto analysis (also known as the 80–20 rule) can be applied to many events, i.e. roughly 80% of the effects come from 20% of the causes. Put another way, 80% of tasks can be completed in 20% of the time, or 20% activity creates 80% of the value.
- The work environment (light, temperature, noise, ergonomics, etc.) can have a significant effect on behaviour and productivity.
- People's motivation is determined by how well their needs are met, from basic survival needs (food, water, safety, etc.) to social, cognitive and esteem needs (knowledge, belonging, self-actualization, etc.).
- The timing and communication of change is more important than what the actual change is.
- Our minds tend to distort and generalize information to fit our own view of the world, meaning we can fall into 'mind traps' that reinforce a particular belief or behaviour creating a downward spiral we feel is beyond our control.

2 Seven best resources

- http://lean.org The Lean Enterprise Institute strives to answer the simple question of every manager, 'What can I do on Monday morning to make a difference in my organization?'
- http://mind.org.uk Mind, the mental health charity, provides information and support for a variety of mental illnesses.

- http://www.hse.gov.uk/stress/index.htm The Health and Safety Executive, the UK's government regulator for health and safety, provides free information and tools to manage stress at work.
- Mo Shapiro, *NLP In A Week* (John Murray Learning, 2016). The acceptance and use of NLP in organizational management is increasing and this book (among others) provides a good introduction.
- Stephen Covey, *The 7 Habits of Highly Effective People* (Simon & Schuster, 2004). A highly influential management guide.
- http://www.businessballs.com/ Website offering free and fun career help, business training and organizational development.
- http://en.wikipedia.org/wiki/If Rudyard Kipling's poem 'If' offers some helpful advice on life!

3 Seven inspiring people

- Frederick Herzberg (1923–2000) for his early work on motivation and job enrichment.
- John Fisher for his model of personal change – The Personal Transition Curve.
- Richard Bandler and John Grinder for their founding work in Neuro-linguistic Programming.
- James Reason for his work on managing human error and organizational safety culture.
- John Kotter for his work and publication on change management.
- William Edwards Deming (1900–93) for his 'System of Profound Knowledge' and leading the way for others in the field of lean thinking and process improvement.
- Elisabeth Kübler-Ross (1926–2004) for her pioneering studies and her theory of the five stages of grief.

4 Seven great quotes

- 'God give us the grace to accept with serenity the things that cannot be changed, the courage to change the things that should be changed, and the wisdom to distinguish the one from the other.' Reinhold Niebuhr (1892–1971), American theologian
- 'Life is not a matter of having good cards, but of playing a poor hand well.' Robert Louis Stevenson (1850–94) Scottish novelist and travel writer
- 'Many companies have long contended that stress in the home causes productivity loss in the market place ... and it does. But research now reveals that stress on the job causes stress at home. In other words, they feed off each other.' Hilary Hinton 'Zig' Ziglar (1926–2012) American author, salesman and motivational speaker
- 'To achieve great things, two things are needed: a plan and not quite enough time.' Leonard Bernstein (1918–90) American composer and author
- 'The mind can go either direction under stress – toward positive or toward negative: on or off. Think of it as a spectrum whose extremes are unconsciousness at the negative end and hyperconsciousness at the positive end. The way the mind will lean under stress is strongly influenced by training.' From *Dune*, Frank Herbert (1920–86) American science-fiction writer
- 'Stress is caused by being here but wanting to be there.' Eckhart Tolle, spiritual teacher and author
- 'Stressed spelled backwards is desserts.' Loretta Laroche, motivational speaker, author, humorist

5 Seven things to avoid

- Judging people based on their behaviour: we are all human, subject to mistakes and are heavily influenced by our environment.
- Ambiguity in roles, responsibilities and objectives.

- Command and control, unless there's a real emergency; people respond better when allowed to determine their own approach to deliver an objective.
- Your personal stressors, or at least plan your coping mechanisms in advance.
- The 'mind traps' of seeing extremes, focusing on the negative and overgeneralization.
- Creating conflicting demands and conflicts of interest (e.g. productivity and safety), or at least provide a means to escalate concerns when they arise. Ensure everyone understands what is expected of them and where boundaries lie.
- Change for the sake of it. Make sure there are clear benefits to any change and that the costs of the change both financially and emotionally have been properly assessed.

6 Seven things to do today

- Say 'no'. Most people will simply accept you are busy and go elsewhere. Even if they don't, the consequences will never be as bad as you think.
- Engage and take time to understand staff problems and concerns. Everyone is an adult and everyone is human and besides you might learn something to your advantage.
- Say 'Thank You.' Nothing motivates employees more than recognition that they have done well. Two simple words can reduce tension and flood the body with feel-good chemicals. You'll reinforce positive behaviour and build a bank of good will which you may need to draw on in the future.
- Prioritize and help others prioritize. Use the four Ds:
  * Do it – it has to be you and it has to be now.
  * Defer it – it has to be you but you can do it later.
  * Delegate it – it can be someone else (make sure they know if it needs to be now or later).
  * Drop it – no one needs to do it any time soon.

- Allow individuals control over their work. Set clear objectives and allow individuals and teams to determine how they are delivered. Consider multi-skilling to allow for job rotation and balance the work load.
- Set clear expectations for behaviours and manage them in line with other performance measures. Do not tolerate bullying or harassment, make sure employees are aware of what this means within the organization and the consequences of such behaviour, how they can raise or report concerns, access help and support services.
- Make time for yourself to relax and do the things you enjoy. Keep fit, eat well and get some sleep.

7 Seven trends for tomorrow

- The pace of organizational change will continue to increase – embrace it. Appreciate that others will go through their own journey. Create urgency, get buy-in and create alliances, communicate continuously, celebrate short-term success, reinforce positive behaviours and embed the change.
- The boundaries between work and home life will eventually blur and overlap. Always be clear on what you are doing, for whom and why. Amongst it all make time just for you.
- Technology will continue to provide new ways to share and access information. Information is only of value when you do something with it.
- Time is becoming a scarce commodity. You will need to learn the skills of influence and persuasion to get others to allow you to use it.
- You will be challenged to spend an increasing amount of time in meetings. Meeting are for decisions not discussions.
- Technology, fashions and trends will be superseded quicker and quicker; if you try and keep up with them all, you will lose both your time and money. Be selective on when you become an early adopter and in other areas get comfort

from periods of continuity and stability. A great lifestyle isn't the same thing as a great life.

- The world will continue to find 'others' to blame for mistakes, failures and anything negative. By taking responsibility for yourself, your behaviour and actions and feelings, you can never be a victim.

References

Arnsten, A. F. (1997). Catecholamine regulation of the prefrontal cortex. *Journal of Psychopharmacology, 11*(2), 151–62.

Arnsten, A. F. (1998). Catecholamine modulation of prefrontal cortical cognitive function. *Trends in Cognitive Sciences, 2*(11), 436–47.

Arnsten, A. F., and Li, B. M. (2005). Neurobiology of executive functions: catecholamine influences on prefrontal cortical functions. *Biological Psychiatry, 57*(11), 1377–84.

Asch, S. E. (1951). Effects of group pressure upon the modification and distortion of judgments. *Groups, Leadership, and Men.* 222–36.

Bandura, A. (1999). Moral disengagement in the perpetration of inhumanities. *Personality and Social Psychology Review, 3*(3), 193–209.

Baumeister, R. F., Bratslavsky, E., Finkenauer, C., and Vohs, K. D. (2001). Bad is stronger than good. *Review of General Psychology, 5*(4), 323.

Brown, K. W., and Ryan, R. M. (2003). The benefits of being present: mindfulness and its role in psychological well-being. *Journal of Personality and Social Psychology, 84*(4), 822.

Brown, K. W., Ryan, R. M., and Creswell, J. D. (2007). Mindfulness: Theoretical foundations and evidence for its salutary effects. *Psychological Inquiry, 18*(4), 211–37.

Carlson, D. S., Kacmar, K. M., and Wadsworth, L. L. (2002). The impact of moral intensity dimensions on ethical decision making: Assessing the relevance of orientation. *Journal of Managerial Issues*, 15–30.

Chiesa, A., Serretti, A., and Jakobsen, J. C. (2013). Mindfulness: Top-down or bottom-up emotion regulation strategy? *Clinical Psychology Review, 33*(1), 82–96.

Chugh, D., Bazerman, M. H., and Banaji, M. R. (2005). Bounded ethicality as a psychological barrier to recognizing conflicts of interest. *Conflicts of Interest: Challenges and solutions in business, law, medicine, and public policy*, 74–95.

Corbetta, M., and Shulman, G. L. (2002). Control of goal-directed and stimulus-driven attention in the brain. *Nature Reviews Neuroscience, 3*(3), 201–15.

Creswell, J. D., Way, B. M., Eisenberger, N. I., and Lieberman, M. D. (2007). Neural correlates of dispositional mindfulness during affect labeling. *Psychosomatic Medicine, 69*(6), 560–65.

Dane, E. (2008). Examining experience and its role in dynamic versus static decision-making effectiveness among professionals. In *Academy of Management Proceedings*.

Eisenberger, N. I., Lieberman, M. D., and Williams, K. D. (2003). Does rejection hurt? An fMRI study of social exclusion. *Science, 302*(5643), 290–92.

Epley, N., and Caruso, E. M. (2004). Egocentric ethics. *Social Justice Research, 17*(2), 171–87.

Goleman, D. (1996). Emotional Intelligence: why it can matter more than IQ. *Passion, Paradox and Professionalism, 23.*

Hallowell, E. M. (2005). Overloaded circuits: Why smart people underperform. *Harvard Business Review, 83*(1), 54–62.

Herndon, F. (2008). Testing mindfulness with perceptual and cognitive factors: External vs. internal encoding, and the cognitive failures questionnaire. *Personality and Individual Differences, 44*(1), 32–41.

Hölzel, B. K., Lazar, S. W., Gard, T., Schuman-Olivier, Z., Vago, D. R., and Ott, U. (2011). How does mindfulness meditation work? Proposing mechanisms of action from a conceptual and neural perspective. *Perspectives on Psychological Science, 6*(6), 537–59.

Hoyk, R., and Hersey, P. (2010). *The Ethical Executive: Becoming aware of the root causes of unethical behavior: 45 psychological traps that every one of us falls prey to.* Redwood City, CA: Stanford University Press.

Jones, T. M. (1991). Ethical decision making by individuals in organizations: An issue-contingent model. *Academy of Management Review, 16*(2), 366–95.

Kabat-Zinn, J. (1994). *Where Ever You Go There You Are.* London: Piatkus.

Killingsworth, M. A., and Gilbert, D. T. (2010). A wandering mind is an unhappy mind. *Science, 330*(6006), 932–32.

Lieberman, M. D., and Eisenberger, N. I. (2008). The pains and pleasures of social life: a social cognitive neuroscience approach. *NeuroLeadership Journal, 1,* 1–9.

Milgram, S. (1963). Behavioral study of obedience. *The Journal of Abnormal and Social Psychology, 67*(4), 371.

Neisser, U., and Becklen, R. (1975). Selective looking: Attending to visually specified events. *Cognitive Psychology, 7*(4), 480–94.

Ochsner, K. (2008). Staying cool under pressure: insights from social cognitive neuroscience and their implications for self and society. *NeuroLeadership Journal, 1.*

Pashler, H. J., and Johnston, J. C. (1998). Attentional limitations in dual-task performance. *Attention,* 155–89.

Rest, J. R. (1986). *Moral Development: Advances in research and theory.* Santa Barabara, CA: Praeger.

Rock, D. (2008). SCARF: A brain-based model for collaborating with and influencing others. *NeuroLeadership Journal, 1*(1), 44–52.

Ruedy, N. E., and Schweitzer, M. E. (2010). In the moment: The effect of mindfulness on ethical decision making. *Journal of Business Ethics, 95*(1), 73–87.

Schneider, S. C., Oppegaard, K., Zollo, M., and Huy, Q. (2005). Socially responsible behaviour: Developing virtue in organizations. *Organization Studies.*

Shapiro, K. L., Raymond, J. E., and Arnell, K. M. (1994). Attention to visual pattern information produces the attentional blink in rapid serial visual presentation. *Journal of Experimental Psychology: Human perception and performance, 20*(2), 357.

Shapiro, S. L., Carlson, L. E., Astin, J. A., and Freedman, B. (2006). Mechanisms of mindfulness. *Journal of Clinical Psychology, 62*(3), 373–86.

Smith, E. E., and Kosslyn, S. M. (2013). *Cognitive Psychology: Pearson New International Edition: Mind and Brain.* Pearson.

Teasdale, J. D. (1999). Metacognition, mindfulness and the modification of mood disorders. *Clinical Psychology and Psychotherapy, 6*(2), 146–55.

Tenbrunsel, A. E., and Messick, D. M. (2004). Ethical fading: The role of self-deception in unethical behavior. *Social Justice Research*, *17*(2), 223–36.

Tencati, A. (2007). Understanding and responding to societal demands on corporate responsibility (RESPONSE): Final Report.

Wager, T. D., and Smith, E. E. (2003). Neuroimaging studies of working memory. *Cognitive, Affective, & Behavioral Neuroscience*, *3*(4), 255–74.

Wolff, S. B. (2005). *Emotional Competence Inventory (ECI) Technical Manual*. The Hay Group. Retrieved 31 January 2010.

Zimbardo, P. G. (1973). On the ethics of intervention in human psychological research: With special reference to the Stanford prison experiment. *Cognition*, *2*(2), 243–56.

Zollo, M., Casanova, L., Crilly, D., Hockerts, K., Neergaard, P., Schneider, S., and Tencati, A. (2007). Understanding and responding to societal demands on corporate responsibility (RESPONSE): Final Report.

Answers

Part 1: Your Managing Yourself Masterclass

Chapter 1: 1b; 2c; 3a; 4d; 5d; 6c; 7b; 8c; 9d; 10a

Chapter 2: 1a; 2d; 3c; 4b; 5a; 6d; 7b; 8c; 9c; 10b

Chapter 3: 1b; 2d; 3b; 4c; 6c; 7a; 8d; 9a; 10b

Chapter 4: 1c; 2b; 3a; 4d; 5a; 6b; 7b; 8d; 9b; 10c

Chapter 5: 1c; 2d; 3c; 4b; 5a; 6d; 7b; 8c; 9b; 10d

Chapter 6: 1d; 2a; 3c; 4b; 5b; 6c; 7a; 8d; 9a; 10d

Chapter 7: 1b; 2b; 3d; 4b; 5c; 6b; 7a; 8c; 9d; 10b

Part 2: Your Time Management Masterclass

Chapter 8: 1a; 2c; 3b; 4c; 5a; 6d; 7b; 8c; 9c; 10a

Chapter 9: 1b; 2a; 3c; 4a; 5d; 6b; 7d; 8a; 9c; 10d

Chapter 10: 1a; 2b; 3b; 4c; 5d; 6c; 7c; 8a; 9b; 10a

Chapter 11: 1b; 2a; 3a; 4c; 5d; 6c; 7b; 8a; 9b; 10d

Chapter 12: 1c; 2c; 3a; 4c; 5d; 6b; 7b; 8c; 9d; 10d

Chapter 13: 1b; 2c; 3a; 4c; 5d; 6a; 7b; 8c; 9c; 10d

Chapter 14: 1a, 2c; 3c; 4b; 5d; 6d; 7c; 8c; 9a; 10c

Part 3: Your Speed Reading Masterclass

Chapter 15: 1d; 2d; 3d; 4a; 5b; 6d; 7c; 8c; 9d; 10d

Chapter 16: 1d; 2c; 3b; 4d; 5a; 6d; 7d; 8c; 9a; 10d

Chapter 17: 1d; 2d; 3b; 4b; 5d; 6d; 7a, b, c, d; 8c; 9d; 10d

Chapter 18: 1b; 2b; 3c; 4d; 5d; 6c; 7a; 8b; 9a, b, c, d; 10d

Chapter 19: 1d; 2 a, b, c, d; 3 a, b, c, d; 4d; 5 a, b, c, d; 6c; 7d; 8 a, b, c, d; 9 a, b, c, d; 10d

Chapter 20: 1a; 2a; 3d; 4c; 5d; 6c; 7b; 8d; 9d; 10b

Chapter 21: 1a; 2d; 3a, b, c, d; 4d; 5a, 6b; 7a; 8a; 9b; 10a, b, c, d

Part 4: Your Managing Stress At Work Masterclass

Chapter 22: 1d; 2b; 3a; 4d; 5b; 6c; 7c; 8a; 9d; 10a

Chapter 23: 1d; 2d; 3b; 4a; 5c; 6d; 7b; 8a; 9c; 10d

Chapter 24: 1b; 2d; 3d; 4b; 5b; 6c; 7a; 8a; 9c; 10d

Chapter 25: 1a; 2c; 3d; 4b; 5b; 6d; 7b; 8b; 9d; 10a

Chapter 26: 1c; 2a; 3a; 4c; 5b; 6d; 7c; 8c; 9a; 10b

Chapter 27: 1d; 2b; 3a; 4a; 5c; 6d; 7a; 8a; 9d; 10c

Chapter 28: 1d; 2c; 3c; 4d; 5c; 6b; 7a; 8b; 9b; 10d